The
MouseDriver™
Chronicles

THE MOUSEDRIVER™ CHRONICLES

The True-Life Adventures of Two First-Time Entrepreneurs

JOHN LUSK

AND

KYLE HARRISON

PERSEUS
PUBLISHING

Many of the designations used by manufacturers and sellers to distinguish their products are claimed as trademarks. Where those designations appear in this book and Perseus Publishing was aware of a trademark claim, the designations have been printed in initial capital letters.

Copyright © 2002 by John Lusk and Kyle Harrison

ISBN: 0-7382-0573-7

CIP card is available.

Perseus Publishing is a member of the Perseus Books Group
Find us on the World Wide Web at
http://www.perseuspublishing.com

Text design by Jeff Williams
Set in 11-point New Caledonia by Perseus Publishing Services

Perseus Publishing books are available at special discounts for bulk purchases in the U.S. by corporations, institutions, and other organizations. For more information, please contact the Special Markets Department at the Perseus Books Group, 11 Cambridge Center, Cambridge, MA 02142, or call (617) 252–5298.

First printing, December, 2001
1 2 3 4 5 6 7 8 9 10——04 03 02 01

This book is dedicated to all those who have sacrificed the need to follow in order to pursue their dreams and passions.

This book is a true narrative based on the lives of the authors. To protect trade secrets (two of them), business relationships (three), and some long-standing friendships (again, about two), the names of some companies and characters have been changed. Also, some events in this book are composites of several actual events. Otherwise, everything is mostly true.

CONTENTS

ACKNOWLEDGMENTS

Our thanks go to Alison Marquiss and Ethan Anderson for their essential roles in writing this book. Also, we want to express our appreciation of Linda Mead, Jacqueline Murphy, David Goehring and Arlinda Shtuni for believing in the story; Dr. Rick McKinney, John C. Lusk, Kevin Harrison, Tarané Sayler, John Brown, Maria Murnane, and all of our *MouseDriver Insider* subscribers for the inspiration and help they provided; and The Coffee Roastery, Starbucks and The Grove for providing affordable office space during our time of need.

Most of all, our deepest gratitude goes to our parents, Randy and Cathy Lusk and Ron and Marsha Harrison, for encouraging and supporting us as we went our own way.

PROLOGUE

Spring 1999 was a strange time for us. On one hand, my room-mate Kyle Harrison and I were living a cliché as starving graduate students. On the other hand, we were weeks away from finishing our MBAs, and the world seemed to be at our feet. Old economy companies and investment banks beckoned us to start climbing the good climb to middle management. Dot-coms with cool and silly names dangled flashy titles, mountains of stock options, and fairly sizable hills of cash to come change the world. We each had job offers anyone would be grateful for, the kind your mother would smack you for turning down, if she didn't faint dead away first.

So here's what we did. We skipped all the jobs, borrowed money from friends and family, loaded up on credit card debt, and started a company that manufactures and sells a computer mouse that looks exactly like the head of a golf driver. Also, we waited a while before we told our mothers.

I'm John Lusk, and this is the story of and how and why my business partner Kyle Harrison and I passed on spring '99's sure things to go off the beaten path. To boldly pit our skills against the wide-open unknown (if, by the wide-open unknown, you mean the market for a computer mouse cleverly designed to look like a golf club head). To become entrepreneurs.

We wanted to run our own business. Why should you care? The odds are good that you haven't heard of our company (Platinum Concepts, Inc.) or the mouse we manufacture (we call it MouseDriver). We don't know the secret to business success. And much as we'd like it to, we've come to accept the fact that no matter how well it does, MouseDriver won't change the world.

Well, you might care if you're interested in what a start-up business really looks like. We began with one simple product idea, not an earth-shaking breakthrough technology. We didn't have a venture capitalist throwing money at us. We didn't have years and years of expertise in our field of business. We just borrowed a little money, planned a lot, took a deep breath, and went to work.

In short, we didn't do anything you couldn't do. That's the point.

There's only one thing Kyle and I did that most entrepreneurs don't do: we kept an ongoing record of what was happening with our company. We started a diary during the first summer of our venture, making entries roughly every other day, just as an exercise in collecting our thoughts and blowing off steam. We wrote about the realities of everyday life as entrepreneurs—the screwups and masterstrokes, the boredom, excitement, dumb luck, humor, and mood swings that come from creating a product and a business out of an idea sketched out on the back of a coaster in a Texas bar.

At first we wrote only for ourselves, but within months we started converting our diary entries into short newsletters, called the *MouseDriver Insider*, which we sent sporadically to a small online mailing list of family, former classmates, and friends. To our surprise, the *Insider* took off. Entrepreneurs we'd never met jumped on our mailing list, and business professors wrote to tell us they'd added the *Insider* to their students' reading lists (we'd like to take this opportunity to apologize to those students).

This book grew out of the *Insider,* which grew out of our desire to tell the truth about starting a business. We invite you to laugh with us and at us, second-guess our decisions, and puzzle over our mistakes. And we hope this account of our experience helps you think about your own, whether it inspires you to pull your own idea for your own company out from under a pile of papers thrown in the bottom drawer of the file cabinet you never open in your basement, or simply to rest easier at night, knowing that no matter what else, at least you had the good sense not to quit your day job.

TAKING THE LEAP

I remember sitting somewhere near the last row of Wes Hutchinson's marketing class, wondering what the hell I was going to do. I had just sleepwalked through a presentation for my version of an I-phone, a cell phone with three key features.

(1) It could access the World Wide Web for e-mail, stock quotes, sports scores, etc.

(2) It looked and worked almost exactly like three other I-phones already on the market.

and

(3) It was never, ever going to be built, by me or anyone else.

It wasn't original, it wasn't exciting, but I knew I had enough to pass, so I was relaxed pitching the I-phone. Too relaxed. Sometime between Professor Hutchinson barking out "Next up, John Lusk," and my last PowerPoint slide, my big problem crept back into my head and stayed there as I wrapped up and shuffled back to my seat.

I was three months away from leaving Philadelphia with an MBA from the University of Pennsylvania's Wharton School of Business and in immediate danger of getting a job.

I didn't want a job. I'd had one for four years at Ernst &
Young, working on big projects for big companies like American Airlines and BellSouth Telecommunications. I liked the
job, I cared about it. The job was nice, but in the end I left it for
Wharton.

I'd come to Philadelphia with a good idea of what I wanted
to do. I'd studied entrepreneurship and marketing, the overly
syllabled names for the art and/or science of creating companies
that make and/or sell products and/or services, with a specific
goal in mind. I wanted to start and run my own business.

Sitting in the back of Professor Hutchinson's class with three
months left in school, watching imaginary marketing show-and-
tells, my problem boiled down to two words: What business?

Definitely not the I-phone. No way, and that was my best
shot at the moment, for all the digging I'd done. And I'd done a
lot of digging. I'd worked during school at the Wharton Small
Business Development Center and seen dozens of start-up
ideas, and nothing had seemed right for me. I'd worked off-
campus with the Pennsylvania Private Investor Group, reviewing dozens more start-up plans for a bunch of angel investors.
Still nothing. I didn't have an answer. And without an answer
for what business, it was on to the next question in line: What
the hell was I going to do?

If I didn't have a business to start, I'd have to get a job. Thinking about jobs was giving me a headache. I'd already researched
a few with venture capitalists (VCs) and some technology start-
ups. At least with those guys, I'd be working alongside entrepreneurs, while still earning a living with a . . . job.

But I just couldn't get over the idea of being so near to what I
wanted and yet so far. Regardless of what job I took, I wouldn't
ultimately be responsible for the success of the company. Even
on the VC front, where I figured I could find work analyzing

seed-level and early-stage companies, the possible fringe benefits of learning the ins and outs of lots of start-ups (before picking one to sign on with) weren't enough. I just couldn't see
myself looking the poor, tired, hungry creator of any start-up
business in the eye and saying, "Hey, with all my corporate experience and my Wharton MBA, I can tell you that you should
be doing X and Y and Z as an entrepreneur."

For me, the bottom line was I wanted to feel the pain of
starting a company. I wanted to pay my dues, and I wanted to
pay them now. Yes, I wanted to go into debt, have my ego
crushed, and experience firsthand the thrill of working like a
dog for months on end without a paycheck in sight. I wanted a
battle, I wanted a chance to win a war.

I most definitely didn't want a job.

So I wallowed through my near-term future for the millionth
time. Meanwhile, my roommate Kyle Harrison was getting totally crushed in front of Hutchinson's class. I had no doubt he
was headed for a failing grade. Neither did any of our classmates. It was fun to watch.

Kyle was choking his way through a pitch for something he
called MouseDriver, a novelty computer mouse that looked like
the head of a golf driver. Nothing was going right for him up
there. Presentations in Professor Hutchinson's class had to be
in a set format, with spreadsheet data to support claims, all
arranged just so. Something had gone badly wrong in Kyle's
spreadsheets—the numbers didn't work, the spreadsheets were
in disarray, and he couldn't recover on the fly. It was a toss-up
whether I'd give him a hard time or a pat on the back on the
way home. Either way, he was going to have to redo the assign-
ment to pass.

The funny thing was, unlike my bogus I-phone, MouseDriver
was a real product, one that just might work. From rooming

with Kyle, I knew that he and a former work colleague named
Ed McClung had come up with the idea for MouseDriver
while sitting in The Ginger Man restaurant in Dallas in 1995.
The two of them worked for Andersen Consulting at the time,
and had been killing a few minutes before meeting clients
when they idly began to wonder if there might be anything better than T-shirts, paperweights, pens, and baseball caps to give
clients as promotional items. They'd started sketching their first
designs on the back of a coaster at the restaurant bar.

Ed gave Kyle most of the credit for the idea, and Kyle had
kept working on designs and plans for MouseDriver as a hobby,
even securing a design patent for it. When he'd left Andersen
for Wharton, it had been for many of the same reasons I'd
come to Philadelphia—he'd wanted to learn about entrepreneurship. And though he'd run through a number of start-up
ideas in the classes he'd taken and the small on-campus group
of entrepreneurial brainstormers he'd joined, Kyle kept returning to MouseDriver. He saw MouseDriver as a good product
for starting a modestly profitable company, and he liked its simplicity. He saw it as something that, someday soon, he might
make and people might want to buy.

So here we were, in Professor Hutchinson's marketing class.
I'd pitched the I-phone, a knockoff product idea I'd pulled out
of my ass. Kyle proposed MouseDriver, an original product he
really believed in. Therefore, I pass with flying colors, and Kyle
goes back to the drawing board.

Even though Kyle had bombed completely, there wasn't any
shame in it. Marketing and entrepreneurship classes are valuable, but it's hard to tell what it means to get good or bad grades
in them. However many timed-tested methods, case studies,
theories, and war stories they throw into the air, ultimately these
courses are about new products, new plans for old products,

the future, and the unknown. And every business school student knows the story of Fred Smith, who took his C-minus Harvard Business School marketing paper home to Memphis, Tennessee, and turned it into a start-up called Federal Express.

I watched Kyle slink back to his seat and thought about his post-graduation options. He was staring down the barrel at job offers from Dell and a handful of dot-coms. It was 1999, and those kinds of companies were hot. I, on the other hand, wasn't exactly hot for them.

As Kyle's offers had rolled in, my feelings about dot-coms were mixed. When we'd started business school in 1997, the idea of e-commerce on the World Wide Web was just around the corner from being big, still more of a private discovery than a mass revelation. I'd thought I'd caught the Internet wave a bit ahead of everyone. After all, I had an undergraduate MIS (management information sciences) degree from Southern Methodist University, and my years with Ernst & Young were spent in IT (information technology) consulting. It seems laughable now, but I had even been a little territorial about the Internet.

The truth hurts: I had thought of the "New Economy" as my sandbox. When, within months, every single one of my Wharton classmates had contracted dot-com fever, it felt as if they'd all jumped in my play area and wrecked my sand fort. I just wanted to take my shovel and pail and grumpily go home.

Besides, at this point, as exciting as the possibilities were in the dot-com world, joining an already existing start-up didn't seem like the same thing as hammering out something of my own in the real world. A lot of my classmates would disagree, but that's how I saw it.

Kyle saw it my way. He was pleased with his job offers, but a lot more enthusiastic about starting his own business. Now, nearing the end of his last semester at Wharton, he'd narrowed his choices down to two entrepreneurial plans.

One was an Internet start-up concept called PayMyBills.com, which had been dreamed up by John "J.T." Tedesco, a Wharton student Kyle had met in his entrepreneurial brainstorming group. J.T. was a great guy, and Kyle had spent a lot of time fleshing out PayMyBills.com with him and Jeff Grass, who had helped J.T. develop the idea.

Kyle's other idea for a start-up, despite the Hutchinson Marketing Bellyflop of '99, was MouseDriver. Kyle and J.T. had worked together on that one too. Both ideas had promise. Both needed funding. With graduation looming, it was time for Kyle and J.T. to choose between projects.

PayMyBills.com was an Internet start-up idea at a time when the sky was the limit for online businesses. It was a Web world in 1999; Amazon.com's founder and CEO Jeff Bezos peered out from the cover of *Time* magazine as its Man of the Year. New metaphors and acronyms came flying in from all directions, and it was hip to know what they meant. B2C, B2B, portals, content aggregators, infomediaries, digerati, lol. It was the corporate equivalent of the early days of rock 'n' roll, when companies could vault from garage obscurity to worldwide success on the strength of one hit. Dot-coms rocketed to the top with software based on a single idea or customer-focused insight, and in that light PayMyBills.com looked like it had as good a chance as any to take a ride, maybe better than most. It addressed a consumer need: To consolidate and automate the presentation and payment of household bills. It had the potential to take advantage of all the revenue streams available to the most promising start-ups—sign-ups, subscriptions, banner ads, product tie-ins—and room for value-added alliances with other hot Web services.

PayMyBills.com was J.T.'s baby, and it held the potential for changing everyday life and generating millions (maybe even hundreds of millions) of dollars in revenues. MouseDriver was Kyle's baby, and it was, well, a clever-looking computer mouse. It wasn't going to change the world. Before it could change the fate of even a few gift shops, MouseDriver needed money, manufacturing, and marketing. Even then, it would never have the potential of PayMyBills.com.

Kyle had a lot on his mind. He had to turn down job offers. He had to pick between two start-up dreams, and try to talk J.T. into agreeing with his choice. And if he wanted to pass marketing, he had to completely redo his presentation for Professor Hutchinson.

Then again, while I dreamed of starting my own company, my roommate was already working on two.

Class was over. Kyle and I packed up our presentation notes and headed home together with separate worries, walking down Locust Street.

*   *   *

A few weeks later, I was staring down at the empty snack packet directly in front of me on a United nonstop out of San Francisco, returning to Philly as a partially changed man, one that wanted a few more honey-roasted peanuts.

I'd had a round of interviews with a handful of Bay Area VC firms and dot-com start-ups, and I'd learned a few things. On one hand, the five-day trip had reinforced my beliefs: I was interested in what the VCs and dot-commers had to say, but I wasn't ready to join them. I still wanted to start something of my own.

On the other hand, walking around San Francisco and talking with some of the players slugging it out in the New Economy was a real thrill. It was energizing to see people starting companies all over the place. I got it in my head how great it would be to move to San Francisco, just to be in an environment where it seemed like everyone was looking to do something new. Even though it was in an expensive area of the country, San Francisco looked like an ideal place for starting a company, establishing contacts, finding funding, and ferreting out entrepreneurial mentors to brainstorm with. And if I failed, well, so what? The entire Bay Area was booming. I'd land a job somewhere in the city or Palo Alto or San Jose and maybe dream up another venture and go from there.

I still hadn't figured out what business to sink my teeth into, but I was raring to go. I wanted to move to San Francisco.

Kyle, meanwhile, had made the most of his time in the weeks following his swan dive in Hutchinson's class. He'd redone his presentation to resuscitate his marketing grade. More important, he'd all but made up his mind to go with MouseDriver as the vehicle for his start-up.

A series of large and small financial events had turned Kyle in the direction of MouseDriver. The first came out of a conversation between Kyle and Mike Rinzler, another Wharton classmate. Kyle and J.T. had been speculating on how to manufacture at least a sample MouseDriver, when Mike offered to hook them up with a contact of his named Carmine. Carmine was the president of East Asia Action Express, a company out of Hong Kong that served as a sort of manufacturing agent, brokering deals between would-be entrepreneurs like Kyle and J.T. and Asian manufacturing companies. Carmine was American, a young guy right around our age, who had already spent ten years in Hong Kong.

Finding East Asia Action Express had been a terrific stroke of luck. One of the hardest things for any product entrepreneur to do is find a manufacturing solution, and this one had fallen right in Kyle's and J.T.'s laps. East Asia Action Express was an agent, and a reliable referral from a friend. Carmine would shop among manufacturers for the best possible deal for MouseDriver. The only catch was he was half a world away. Kyle and J.T. had searched briefly for a U.S. manufacturer, but when East Asia Action Express came in with an offer that was about one-quarter that of any domestic bids, it was off to Carmine. Carmine of Hong Kong.

Kyle and J.T. scraped together $1,000 of their own money, the low-low price at which Carmine agreed to produce a proto-type of MouseDriver. Their investment was small, but it impressed me. They didn't have much pocket money; $1,000 showed they were serious about MouseDriver.

When the prototype arrived in Philly, everyone was impressed. It was only a gray plastic model for a novelty mouse, and it was a strange-looking thing, twice the size Kyle and J.T. had hoped it would be. None of that mattered. What people saw was a student idea turning into something real. Classmates took time out from chasing down offers at investment banks, consulting firms, and dot-coms to ask about it. Professors perked up when they saw it—especially Len Lodish.

Len Lodish is an entrepreneurial marketing professor at Wharton. The limited-enrollment class he teaches is always one of the most sought-after; it usually ends up being bid up during the course auction process, so most students don't have a chance to attend. Kyle and I were among the fortunate few to get into one of his courses.

Professor Lodish is also a successful entrepreneur. When he'd first seen what Kyle and J.T. were doing with MouseDriver, he'd challenged them to follow through. When he saw the prototype, he locked onto the project. He wanted to know what the next steps were. Kyle and J.T. talked about building a manufacturing tool to produce MouseDrivers. Lodish asked if they knew what it would cost. Kyle had already talked to Carmine: East Asia Action Express could get it done for $20,000.

Len Lodish wrote Kyle and J.T. a check for $20,000. It was both an investment and a challenge; accepting the money meant going ahead with MouseDriver as a real product, the basis for a real start-up business.

Kyle and J.T. took the money, and MouseDriver was on its way.

I was floored. Absolutely floored. And yes, maybe a little envious. Kyle and J.T. had walked into Lodish's office with an oversized blob of dull gray plastic and walked out with a business. I set up a meeting with Professor Lodish myself, to talk about what he'd done for MouseDriver and lay out my own hopes for creating a start-up after graduation, just to hear what he had to say.

My meeting was less lucrative than the Kyle/J.T. session. Lodish didn't write any checks—I didn't have anything worth writing a check for. I didn't have an idea for my own company, but he challenged me just like he'd challenged Kyle and J.T. Everyone's going in the same direction, he said, and I knew what he meant. My classmates were engaged in a very understandable stampede toward banking, consulting, and dot-com companies. This is the time to try something different, he said. Run it out of your kitchen if you have to, but take a risk and start something of your own. Now is the time. If it doesn't work out, he said, you can always join the stampede.

He was preaching to the choir, but time was running out on the school year. I left Lodish's office, caught my plane, and walked and talked and buzzed with possibility in San Francisco.

I flew back into Philadelphia without a viable idea for a start-up in sight, not knowing that during my West Coast trip, everything had changed for MouseDriver.

J.T. had struck gold again. Within days after agreeing to accept Professor Lodish's investment capital to launch MouseDriver, J.T. had landed a $250,000 investment in PayMyBills.com. Idealab!, a start-up company incubator (a kind of alternative VC firm) out of Pasadena, California, had put up the money and, in doing so, had put Kyle and J.T. in a bind.

Idealab!'s investment was enough to pull J.T. out of the mix as far as MouseDriver was concerned. It wasn't the size of the investment so much as the fact that PayMyBills.com was J.T.'s creation, and the temptation to turn his own idea into a real dot-com was too good to pass up. He offered Kyle a job with PayMyBills.com, but Kyle turned it down because of his interest in seeing MouseDriver, his own creation, all the way through. They settled it with J.T. agreeing to invest in MouseDriver and then peeling off to start PayMyBills.com with idealab!. Kyle was left alone to start his own company.

I didn't know it at the time, but I was only twenty minutes away from having a mouse in my future.

I got back into town on a Monday, and ran into Kyle on the stairway of our brownstone apartment. We started talking about my trip and about how I wanted to start my own company. Kyle was just like me on that front, and we started going through all the reasons why we wanted to run our own businesses. It was all about how we wanted to bring our own ideas to fruition and execute a marketing strategy we made on our own. We wanted to have control, and we wanted to go through the entire experience of building something from next to nothing.

Kyle told me the news about J.T., idealab! and PayMyBills.com. And then it jumped into both our heads.

We said it at the same time, with different pronouns.

"I/You could do MouseDriver with you/me."

There was no debate, just the instant realization, followed by an avalanche of ideas and plans about moving to San Francisco and teaming up to try and create a start-up around MouseDriver.

That was it. All that fretting and speculation answered by a short conversation with my own roommate on our own stairway. It was as close as I've ever come to a eureka moment. In all of my interviews in San Francisco, I'd been toeing the line, playing it safe. Now we were crossing the line.

It felt exhilarating, and it felt right. School was almost over, and Kyle and I were ready to go. Of the 750 students in our class at Wharton, maybe 10 were starting companies right out of school. Two of them were talking on the stairs of their apartment, hatching their first plans together.

OUR PLAN FOR WORLD DOMINATION

Our last weeks at Wharton slipped by; we put on funny hats, shook the dean's hand, and graduated. During that time, Kyle and I scrambled around school, taking advantage of all the free resources (or finally using resources our mammoth tuitions had paid for, depending on how you looked at it). I recall a lot of printing, grabbing, copying, highlighting, sorting, and assembling. I annoyed everyone I ran across in campus libraries, asking for every reference volume I could think of, plowing through marketing databases, and hogging Lexis/Nexis stations. Kyle was wrapping up his involvement with J.T. and PayMy-Bills.com, and trying to get educated about the logistics and legal nuances of everything from incorporating to manufacturing to export/import. Sometimes we didn't know what we were doing, but we were doing it very fast.

Some of the things we did came in handy immediately. I got up to speed on QuickBooks (useful and boring PC accounting software). Kyle and I used it to run numbers and brainstorm.

We churned out strategy summaries, pro formas (detailed financial projections), and business and marketing plans, then tore all of them up to churn out better versions.

When the dust settled, Kyle and I knew we had a few things.

We had a product. We had MouseDriver, which was without a doubt the only PC mouse in the free world that looked like the head of a driver golf club.

We knew this because MouseDriver had won the prestigious U.S. Patent No. Des. 377,933 on February 11, 1997, good for fourteen years from that date, thanks to savvy Kyle. So if anybody dared to even think of manufacturing a PC mouse that looked like a golf club head, they'd have to mess with us first. At least until February of 2011.

After its journey from a Dallas restaurant through the U.S. Patent and Trademark Office and two years of brainstorming in Philly, what exactly was MouseDriver?

Technically speaking, MouseDriver was a patented plug-in PS/2-type mouse designed for IBM PCs.

In English, MouseDriver worked on IBM-style PCs like the ones made by Dell, Compaq, Gateway, Sony, Hewlett Packard, eMachines, and, um, IBM. Best of all, it required no software. Installation couldn't have been simpler: Turn off computer, plug in MouseDriver, turn on computer, use MouseDriver.

MouseDriver's technical limitations were as follows: It didn't work on Apple computers, and there wasn't a version for left-handed people. We had nothing against Mac enthusiasts or lefties, but we'd decided to focus on a single technical design, and that meant concentrating our efforts on the largest market we could think of: The vast, ever-multiplying army of right-handed PC users.

As for styling, MouseDriver was shaped and modified to look like the head of a golf club, specifically a state-of-the-art titanium driver. It was made of basically the same hard plastic material as a standard computer mouse. It worked like a typical mouse as well, with a long cord that plugged into a standard mouse slot on a PC, leading to a plastic housing device (the mouse itself). The mouse had two buttons on top and no scroll wheel. It had a standard rollerball underneath. Our mouse was a bit wider than average, but otherwise it was still lightweight, and it felt and moved in the hand like any other mouse.

MouseDriver was ergonomic, easy to install, and most important of all, it was undeniably the coolest mouse on the planet. By far.

We had a name. Platinum Concepts. Our winner emerged after a number of contenders fell by the wayside. Fun Factory had put up a serious fight, until Kyle smiled and said, "Hey, kids! Stay tuned for Fun Factory, followed by an all-new Teletubbies!" We moved on. Imagix seemed too much like a name for a software or biotech or pharmaceutical company. And Groovy Gadgets was, well, a little too groovy.

To us, Platinum Concepts conveyed a sense of stability. We thought it was important to give the impression that we'd been around a while, even when the truth was we were a two-person company just making our way into the marketplace. We considered fun names like Groovy Gadgets, but we were wary of sounding fly-by-night. We decided to go for the solid sound of Platinum Concepts, and let our sense of fun come out in the product name (MouseDriver) and our new tag line ("Bring Your Game to Work"). We had a bunch of other tag line ideas, but most of them were so bad that we vowed never to mention them again.

We had a business plan. We'd worked everything out, all the way to the end of December 2001, and we knew it all quarter by quarter.

Our pro formas were odd mixes of speculation and reality, just like anybody else's pro formas. We had income statements to show how our sales and expenses contributed to our earnings in any quarter. We had cash flow statements to keep track of what we'd spent and collected in any quarter, and how much money we had in the bank. And we'd laid out our balance sheet quarter by quarter, to cumulatively record everything we were about to do right and wrong.

We'd already taken action in some areas of our plan, and those actions had produced hard, reliable numbers. There were other areas we knew very little about, however. So we did what any red-blooded can-do all-American capitalist would do in our situation.

We guessed.

At least we knew about manufacturing. Kyle had been pleased with East Asia Action Express's work on delivering the MouseDriver prototype, and Carmine's $20,000 quote for producing the manufacturing tool was reasonable, so we decided to stay with our man in Hong Kong. After a couple of rounds of telephone negotiations, we also agreed to terms for our first order of real live MouseDrivers, 500 of them. East Asia Action Express would arrange for their manufacture in Taiwan, and make them available to us at a few dollars a pop, not including shipping.

Once we got over the excitement of committing to manufacture the first true MouseDrivers in the history of civilization, we plugged in the numbers we'd learned from East Asia Action Express.

The results were even more thrilling than the manufacturing news.

For 1999, our pro formas had us scheduled to sell 17,000 MouseDrivers. Which was chicken feed compared to 2000 and

2001, when we were looking at moving a combined total of something north of half a million units. In other words, a freaking ton of MouseDrivers.

Depending on what kinds of volumes we sold to which types of customers (wholesale, or direct to corporate or retail), our gross margins would fluctuate between an attractive 45% and a supermodelesque 70%.

If both our guesses on volume and gross margins panned out, even after all kinds of expenses (like the cost of the MouseDrivers, administrative costs, shipping, and debt retirement), Kyle and I would still each be millionaires by the end of 2001.

Millionaires in just over two years. It was right there in the numbers.

My first thought was, wow. Kyle admitted his first thought was rated NC-17 (but in a good way). Our second thoughts coincided. Platinum Concepts was looking at something in the neighborhood of $5 million to $10 million in retail revenues in 2001. That was tremendous, especially considering that our current mid-1999 retail revenues were right around zero. Perhaps we were projecting impossibly fast growth.

Then again, maybe we weren't. We were about to market a product that had never before existed. On one hand, that was an advantage—we could say MouseDriver was unique and truly mean it. On the other hand, when a completely new product hits the marketplace for the first time, nobody really knows what might happen. Consumer polls and focus groups are great for assessing small changes in existing products, but they can't estimate the market acceptance of original products.

Looking at comparable products doesn't usually help much either. Even if it did, what products would we compare MouseDriver to? There wasn't much in the way of public information on the sales of novelty mice. We could have dug up comparisons with vaguely similar gift items, PC accessories, golf gadgets, and corporate promotional items, but we might have ended up more confused than when we'd started.

We based our paper millions on the best tool left—estimating markets, an inherently crazy task. There were too many variables, even for a simple product like MouseDriver.

It went like this. We knew there were a certain number of golfers in the United States. And we knew there were a certain number of PC users who were interested in golf. We guessed that if MouseDriver appealed to both of those groups, we would get a certain percentage of each.

That was the rough basis for guessing the number of MouseDrivers we'd sell. We did a few more calculations, but that was the core of it.

The numbers could have been fantastically wrong or right on target. We could be right about the potential market, then go on to blow our chance by doing the wrong things with marketing, pricing, or distribution. There was no way of knowing until we tried.

We couldn't perfectly predict demand. That uncertainty didn't discourage us because there was one very encouraging thing we did know: Our gross margins gave us a lot of leeway.

We knew the power of this. We were confident that we could charge between $29.95 and $39.95 for MouseDriver, and we had developed test strategies that would pinpoint the optimal price. And if we were roughly right on price—and we had every reason to believe we were—then we knew we could be wrong about demand by a wide margin and Platinum Concepts would still be a viable business.

Why? Because our gross margins were strong. If we sold many fewer units than we'd anticipated, we might not reach millionaire status by 2001, but the company would still be okay because we'd make enough back on our investment with each sale. Our gross margins were strong because our product was simple and relatively inexpensive to manufacture. So long as we were even close to being right about what we could charge, and we were careful about not overinvesting in inventory, Platinum Concepts could survive reasonably wide swings in demand for MouseDrivers.

I thought that was a pretty good position for a new business to be in. When I pointed this out to Kyle, he agreed with me and stopped yelling at our pro formas.

We had a marketing plan. We had some good (and fairly obvious) guesses as to who might go for MouseDriver. First, corporate buyers, as in the promotional departments of big companies, who would put their logos on MouseDriver and give it to clients and employees, just like Kyle and Ed had envisioned back at The Ginger Man restaurant. Second, retail customers, that is, golf lovers with PCs and the women and men who loved them.

There were Zen questions about marketing we could have asked. Things along the lines of, if you were walking in the forest and thinking about MouseDriver, were you thinking about golf, or were you thinking about your computer? Who could say? We chose not to ask.

Instead, we put our trust (and marketing approach) in the pages of Geoffrey Moore's excellent book on marketing, *Crossing the Chasm.* (Yes, this is a shameless plug, but at least it's an unpaid one—it's a great book. Get it.) To summarize grossly, Moore advocated knocking the ball out of the park with a particular niche before moving on to another area of the marketplace. In practical terms, that meant building MouseDriver's strength and establishing our brand in one small corner of the market, then rolling out to larger segments and eventually the mass market, letting our reputation precede us each time.

To that end, we had the idea of hitting the corporate and retail markets at the same time, but focusing on the high end in both.

The high end in the corporate market meant the type of companies our business school classmates had chosen to work for. Our first corporate target would be financial services firms—investment banks, commercial banks, and insurance companies. We would position MouseDriver as a promotional item featuring their corporate logo, a fun, memorable gift for clients and employees. Once we'd learned to do things right in financial services, we would expand our marketing efforts to include consulting firms and pharmaceutical companies.

The high end in retail meant top-of-the-line specialty retailers like Brookstone and The Sharper Image, catalog kings like Hammacher Schlemmer, and specialty golf retailers like Edwin Watts. Once we'd built our high-end retail business, we'd look to roll out MouseDriver into the mass market, opening it up to department stores like Dillard's and consumer electronic stores like Circuit City.

In retail, we would position MouseDriver as an impulse purchase, probably a gift item. We wanted to be able to add that MouseDriver featured the logo and endorsement of the PGA (Professional Golf Association). All Kyle and I had to figure out was how to go about getting the rights to the PGA logo and earning a PGA endorsement. So we had our work cut out for us on that front.

The potential for crossover customers in the corporate and retail high ends was not lost on us. Financial services firms tend to be conservative in nature, and MouseDriver, being golf-related, had a somewhat conservative appeal. Financial services firms might buy MouseDriver for their conservative clients and employees, who (generally speaking) tended to have higher than average incomes and therefore a greater tendency to take an interest in golf. So by selling to corporations, we would also succeed at putting MouseDriver in the sights of the very consumer who might look it over in the cubicle and then go out and buy it for home use or as a gift at a retail outlet. Thus the circle of life was completed.

In both corporate and retail markets, we thought a high level of customer service would be the way to build our brand. We intended to achieve that standard by being hands-on, starting with selling MouseDriver personally.

We liked that idea on a couple of fronts. One, we thought it would differentiate us from vendors with a complete line of novelty gift products if we made our own sales pitch. Two, we thought our MBA backgrounds might give us a leg up on our competitors when trying to get Wall Street firms and insurance companies in Hartford to take our calls. Three, quite honestly, we thought it would be fun to call on stores and corporate clients, tell our story, and get direct feedback on our product.

To support our direct selling efforts, we budgeted for 4,000 rather expensive brochures (they ran well more than a dollar a pop) and 500 promotional kits, with product samples and company information (a few dollars per kit).

The brochures we intended to use quite liberally; the kits had a specific purpose.

We planned to mail some of the kits out to friends and family, Wharton classmates, and other assorted business contacts as a way to build up a network of product "evangelists," people who would give us feedback and talk up the product informally with others when they saw fit. We saw it as an inexpensive way to develop potential market leads and build enthusiasm for the product.

In addition, we planned to offer a handful of samples to a small group of retail outlets (maybe three to six MouseDrivers per store) and suggest different retail prices within our $29.95-$39.95 range at each. We thought this was the least expensive (and most realistic) way of nailing down what our retail pricing structure should be, once and for all. Once we knew, it would inform our corporate pricing.

We had grander marketing dreams for if and when we grew larger—ads in golf magazines topped the list. But we were a long way from that territory. We had to get our hands on some samples and brochures and start making calls.

We had the same goals. Kyle and I may have had some short-comings going into business together, but misunderstanding each other's personal and company goals wasn't one of them. We'd spent so much time talking as roommates and classmates, we knew what each other was about way before teaming up for Platinum Concepts.

Kyle and I wanted to run through the entire start-up experience with Platinum Concepts. We wanted to build it our own way, executing our own plans. This wasn't just a philosophy, it was a financial commitment: We had to hold on to the majority of our equity, which meant we weren't going to go hat in hand to VCs, merchant bankers, or private investors, the usual suspects to finance a company of our size. We would survive on a modest budget, take on small minority investments from friends and family, and borrow money where we could to keep as much control over company decisions as possible. To make it work, our pro formas showed zeros in the salary columns for the first six months of business.

Stomaching a half-year without a paycheck, let alone parting with the thousands we each initially sunk into the company, would have been impossible if not for our years as consultants.

We'd made decent money and lived anything but large (it's hard to find the time in a sixty-plus-hour workweek). I'd invested in a townhouse in Dallas and steadily built my securities portfolio, while Kyle kept putting it all in the stock market. Both strategies paid off. I sold the townhouse for a profit right after we graduated, and Kyle got in on the best years of the market. Still, both of our balance sheets were negative overall. Business school had left each of us with student loan debts of around $75,000, which we had to start paying back in six months—right when we expected to start paying ourselves.

Our financial commitment underlined how important it was to us that we maintain total control of Platinum Concepts. Without it, there wasn't much of a chance of getting a full entrepreneurial experience, and we'd probably have learned more (and certainly earned more, at least at first) joining the vast majority of our business school classmates who had opted for jobs in banking, consulting, or dot-coms.

We were also up-front with each other about our time horizons for the company. We both wanted to put in approximately two years on this venture, with the intention of selling the company at the end of that time. While a gigantic IPO would have been our wildest dream, we chose to focus on a much likelier scenario. We both saw Platinum Concepts as a single-product company and thought MouseDriver would enjoy an 18- to 24-month life span in the marketplace. Adding some time to get up and running—and leaving a little time left in MouseDriver's life span—meant selling the company (probably to a company looking to expand its product line) within two years.

There were other reasons why it hadn't been hard to arrive at a two-year commitment to Platinum Concepts. One was the simplicity of the company. We weren't launching a mission to Mars; we were introducing a fairly simple novelty item into the marketplace. To us, MouseDriver seemed like an attractive, manageable vehicle for an entrepreneurial experience, but we never saw it as a lifetime's worth of work. For richer or for poorer, we thought cashing out of Platinum Concepts would be an important final step in our start-up initiation and a springboard to other things, either in another start-up or the corporate world.

Another reason, to be honest, had to do with the pressure we were putting on ourselves. We were inspired by what Len Lodish had told us, and proud of ourselves for not following the Wharton herd as it rushed into corporate America. But that didn't mean we weren't still paying attention to the herd. I wouldn't say it gnawed at us, but I would say the kinds of opportunities our classmates were getting helped shape our time horizon. Two years seemed like enough of a commitment for something with an unknown outcome. If things didn't go well, we wanted to have an out.

We had financing. Compared to the average all-American start-up, our financing was fairly typical; compared to the average VC-financed tech start-up, our financing was microscopic. Microsoft spent more every week on soft drinks than what we started our company with.

We began with around $45,000, which broke down to $20,000 in cash we'd already received from Lodish and $25,000 of our (and J.T.'s) own. We had another $75,000 lined up from Ed McClung, my parents, my uncle, and my granddad to help fund our scheduled inventory investments, along with some outside borrowing. Boiled down, the finance picture looked like this:

Our investors: Kyle Harrison, John Lusk, John "J.T." Tedesco, Len Lodish, Ed McClung, and assorted Lusk family members.

Our lenders: My stockbroker (I could borrow against my modest portfolio), Visa, and MasterCard.

Our financing may have been relatively simple and modest, but that didn't mean there wasn't a lot to think about. Kyle and J.T. had put in $5,000 each to start and I'd jumped in with $15,000, substantial investments for people with our means. That was one matter. Borrowing against my portfolio and filling up our personal credit cards with corporate debt—which we were soon going to have to do when it came time to finance big inventory orders—was another thing altogether. We were far more excited than fearful about our venture, but when we thought about taking on that level of debt, we certainly understood the risk.

We also naturally understood what accepting investments from friends and family would mean: A good deal of the happiness/unhappiness of future social events and holiday get-togethers would ride on the fortunes of Platinum Concepts. It was an obvious motivation to succeed, or at least not lose the shirts of our friends and family members as well as our own. Fortunately, most of our investors represented patient money—we didn't have any cut-and-dried timetable for paying out a return to anybody. All of them were on board with our tentative plan to cash out of the company in approximately two years' time.

Our initial $120,000 would carry us only into the beginning of October, the beginning of our fiscal 4th-quarter 1999. At that point, we would need to have MouseDrivers on hand and start selling them. So our budget included a down payment on the purchase of 25,000 MouseDriver units, after a few test runs. Roughly $40,000 of our total budget was allotted to SG&A (selling, general, and administrative expenses—things like the cost of brochures, office supplies, and so on, but alas, no salaries).

All of which left us with roughly $30,000 to $40,000 in the bank at the beginning of October.

The remaining balance for our 25,000-unit order was a little over $50,000, and it would come due in the first quarter of 2000. So we had our work cut out for us.

We had people who wanted to help us. A small but valuable group of people had really opened up to us once we committed to starting Platinum Concepts. At the very beginning of our start-up adventure, Len Lodish and Ed McClung topped our list.

Len Lodish had taught and inspired us. He'd invested in our company, and now he was talking to us frequently and guiding us through our first days as a start-up. It was a real luxury having someone so knowledgeable about the ins and outs of being an entrepreneur take an active interest in first-timers like us. We took full advantage, keeping him informed of everything we were doing.

Ed, the co-inventor of MouseDriver, was incredibly helpful, swapping calls with us frequently, helping us tackle all sorts of problems as they arose. He became an investor in Platinum Concepts and served as an unofficial sounding board and a reliable resource for technical help on issues like setting up a Web site for the company.

We had really impressive job titles. I became Platinum Concept's cofounder and vice president of marketing. Kyle took the title of cofounder and president. Great titles. We saw the fun in them—there were only two of us, after all. But the titles meant something to us.

On a simple level, they reinforced how much responsibility we had to the company and ourselves. Kyle had invented MouseDriver with Ed McClung, but the two of us created Platinum Concepts equally. We were our own go-to guys, for better or worse.

And though we collaborated on almost everything, our titles helped us divide the workload, sometimes in subtle ways. There was a chicken-and-egg effect at work here: I felt my strengths were in marketing, and it was also my title, which reflected my strengths. The titles helped settle who should do what without wasting a lot of time discussing it beforehand. If it had to do with marketing, I considered myself the lead. If it had to do with product design and manufacturing, Kyle took the reins.

The titles also had a pragmatic side. We thought they would help us get our phone calls answered by suppliers and manufacturers and customers. Finally (and truthfully), they also served as entrepreneurial insurance in case things didn't work out with Platinum Concepts. They looked great on résumés and reflected the level of responsibility we'd assumed for and by ourselves.

In tough times, the titles encouraged us. In good times, they reinforced the excitement of what we were doing. In start-ups, sometimes seemingly small things help push you through one challenge and on toward the next. Like looking at your business card and seeing words like vice president, president, or co-founder under your name.

We had no firsthand knowledge of our industry. This was potentially the most troublesome weakness in our plan. Kyle and I had never worked anywhere near the territory we were entering as entrepreneurs. We were inexperienced, plain and simple. We even harbored mild doubts as to what industry we were in. Specialty gifts, golf accessories, corporate promotions, impulse purchases, general-purpose retail, mail order, specialty e-tailing—what was our playing field? Any of them? All of them? We had a lot of strong ideas on the subject, but deep down, we knew we weren't sure. It was something we knew we'd have to learn by doing.

We knew the most important gaps in our business and marketing plans were a direct result of our lack of experience. We didn't spend a lot of time working through distribution issues, in part because we still had much to learn about the differences between the real market for MouseDriver and the market as we imagined it. Our initial ideas for distribution focused on direct selling by Kyle and myself. We thought it would be fun to pitch our own product, and we thought our Wharton contacts might serve us well. But we also understood our distribution methods might change as we learned more about what needed to be done.

We had access to smart people with general retail expertise like Len Lodish, but there was no way around it—we needed industry-specific contacts as soon as we could find them. And we needed a mentor. Someone who could tell us about distribution, supply chains, pricing, margins, product life cycles, revenue seasons—the dos and don'ts of moving a product like ours through the marketplace. Otherwise, we would waste a lot of valuable time and money learning for ourselves what more experienced people could tell us in a few minutes' time. We would have to reinvent the wheel just to move our mice.

We had a big gray lump of plastic that cost $1,000. That was the cost of our prototype. A thousand bucks. Enough for a frighteningly large television, or a weeklong Mexican getaway for one, suntan lotion, ceviche, cervezas, Pepto Bismol, hotel, and airfare included.

It was too late for the fun stuff—Kyle and J.T. had invested in a prototype instead. It had been a hit on campus, but there was only one of them, and that wasn't enough to convince people to buy or invest in our product. We needed samples, maybe 300 to 500 of them. They had to be the right size and the right color, and they had to work. We needed MouseDrivers, real ones.

We'd put in our first order for 500 with Carmine, but we were already impatient. And already we were wondering if we should have ordered more right off the bat.

We had to get out of Philly. School was just about over, and the brick-baking heat and relentless high humidity that define summer in Philadelphia's Center City weren't too far off. We couldn't afford to wait around for them. We needed to blaze to San Francisco and get rolling.

Fine. No problem. Except we didn't yet have an office in San Francisco. Or a place to live. Or MouseDrivers in stock. We had all our plans, but everything real about running a business lay ahead of us. Immediately ahead.

GO WEST, YOUNG MEN

Kyle and I spent June at the Platinum Concepts research and development labs in Texas, preparing for a July 1 move to our world corporate headquarters in San Francisco. Research was located in Austin, in my old bedroom at my parents' house. Development was in Cypress, a small, pleasant town outside Houston where Kyle grew up, next to a couple of rodeos and a whole lot of nowhere.

Both places were scorching hot. Desperate to escape the feeling that I'd time-warped back to high school, I would often head over to Mozart's coffee shop on Lake Austin, renting a few hours at a table for the price of a large iced coffee. It was a three-minute drive; too short for my car's air-conditioning to have any effect, but long enough to feel beads of sweat forming on my forehead.

Kyle had a much sweeter deal in Cypress, rolling across the floors of his dad's freshly renovated, state-of-the-art home office in an overstuffed leather executive chair. Ron Harrison had just finished spending several months and a few thousand dollars redoing the office, adding the latest and greatest in home office online connections, printers, copiers, scanners, computers, staplers, you name it. It was his pride and joy. And just when it was ready to go, Kyle appeared and somehow convinced his dad of what a good idea it would be to let Kyle run Platinum Concepts out of the new space for a while. In Texas, we call this hornswoggling.

Working by ourselves in separate Texas cities, the reality of being completely on our own (aside from living with our parents, of course) was finally sinking in. No classmates, no colleagues, just us.

We'd gotten our first taste of being entrepreneurs at the end of May, when we'd hired Big and Little Jim's Movers to pick up all of our worldly belongings in Philadelphia and deliver them on July 1 to an address to be named later, somewhere in San Francisco. Every one of our friends was celebrating graduation by handing over the keys of their student apartments to corporate movers and signing delivery orders for New York, London, or Los Angeles. While their employers had planned and paid for every detail of their moves, it had been up to Kyle and me to phone around to find the cheapest deal possible to get us to San Francisco. Hello, Big and Little Jim.

Once the movers had come and gone, the clock was ticking on our time to find an apartment in San Francisco. I'd imagined what Big and Little Jim might do if they arrived in California with all our boxes and no delivery address, and it wasn't pretty. With no time to lose, Kyle and I had hopped in my car, dropped off the Locust Street keys, waved good-bye to Philadelphia, and hit the road for Texas.

It had been great to be on the road, fresh out of school at the beginning of summer. We'd indulged in a day of water skiing with a Wharton buddy in Charlotte (where Kyle had swept the awards for Best Overall Skier and Most Painful-Looking

Wipeout), but after that we'd buckled down and spent most of the rest of the billion-mile drive to Texas going over our plans for Platinum Concepts. We'd taken turns driving too fast down I-10, racing thunderstorms, dodging cops, and trying to type notes on the laptop we'd plugged into the cigarette lighter.

Five days after we'd left Philly, we'd reached Kyle's parents' home in Cypress, where a package from East Asia Action Express was waiting for us. In it we'd found a CNC (computer numerical control) sample of MouseDriver. Produced by a sophisticated type of machine tooling, the CNC sample was way better than MouseDriver's first physical model, our oversized gray prototype. It looked a lot more like the real thing, mainly because it was the right size. But it was orange ceramic, weighed about five pounds and had no moving parts. Still, with no real working MouseDriver yet in existence, we'd been excited to see something close.

But there were a few problems with the CNC sample. It didn't look quite like the MouseDriver we'd imagined. Some of the angles weren't right, especially in the lower right corner of the mouse, where it was too rounded and sloped. We'd sent a couple of driver clubs to use as design models to Hong Kong already, but their translation to mouse was going to take some fine-tuning. We'd agreed that Kyle would have to call Carmine and request some changes. But overall our sample MouseDriver was close to looking like a golf club head, and all of the things that bothered us about it definitely looked fixable.

Especially in Kyle's hands. I'd watched in disbelief as he cast his voodoo spell on his dad, then felt like a bigshot entrepreneur as we hunkered down in the finest home office in the greater Houston area. The next day, we'd completed our absolutely-positively-final-for-now marketing plan, shot it to Mr.

Harrison's lightning-fast, super-quiet laser printer, and I'd taken my marching orders on to Austin.

I would go full steam ahead with sales and marketing research, making calls from my parents' and reviewing results at Mozart's, while Kyle would grind his way through all the dirty work—the countless phone calls and forms that constituted legal, corporate infrastructure, and product development.

Kyle thrived in his father's home office. He blasted through a lot of legal and business structure headaches like incorporating and moving our assets from the limited liability company to the corporation. He finalized an equity ownership package and profit structure, bought our World Wide Web domain name, obtained product codes, and set up importing. He was also working on getting our 500 sample mice from Hong Kong.

I could hardly wait. Getting bona fide MouseDrivers to our evangelists and in front of retail and corporate promotions buyers was key to our marketing plan. Once we did, I knew they would sell themselves. And once we made sales, we would have contacts in place to build upon, and the only thing we'd be worrying about would be manufacturing enough mice to fill all of the orders.

But first, Kyle reminded me, we had to get the mouse right. The CNC sample had brought a few potential design problems to our attention, and Kyle's calls and e-mails to Hong Kong were uncovering a few more.

Kyle had started working with one of Carmine's engineers, a guy named Kenny, on the first problem we'd spotted—fixing MouseDriver's shape. Kenny was just as detail-oriented as Kyle, and they formed an instant alliance devoted to making MouseDriver perfect. With the time difference between Texas and Hong Kong, they were on the phone literally day and night. Kyle would talk to Kenny about an adjustment or tweaking, then go to bed. When he woke up, he would call Kenny back and check on the progress. It was an efficient way to do business, and it was nice to think that MouseDriver was getting round-the-clock attention.

Correcting MouseDriver's shape was one problem; finding the right color was another. To go forward, Kenny needed MouseDriver's PMS color. PMS as in Pantone Matching System, sort of a standardized catalog of colors for the printing industry.

We had figured that we wanted MouseDriver to be metallic gray, like the actual drivers we'd sent. That sounded simple, but neither of those drivers exactly matched a PMS color. What we'd imagined would be a simple choice turned into a gateway to hundreds of other decisions that could only be made once we'd learned the code of the printing industry, an industry we didn't want to be in. PMS (no jokes, please) was a major hassle. Because of it, we had to become instant experts on the differences between hundreds of shades of gray, as well as figure out corresponding options for texture and coating and all sorts of other incredibly tiny details designed to drive us out of our minds.

We didn't know the first thing about PMS, and we certainly didn't have a PMS book, apparently an essential. Kyle reached a graphic designer friend, Dave Ramsey, at work in Philadelphia, and he helped us out by matching PMS 425C to a Big Bertha from his boss's trunk. The four-character code was all we needed to tell Kenny to go ahead with the order.

But neither one of us had seen it for ourselves. Even as we came across decisions we'd never anticipated making, we still wanted them to be ours. In an inspiring display of diligence, Kyle drove all around Houston in 100-plus-degree heat, searching for a print shop with a PMS color book so that he could double-check Dave's suggestion. He finally found one and stood at the counter with the printer, flipping the pages to PMS 425C. The verdict: Too green.

Kyle stood at the store counter for a minute, staring at the open PMS book, knowing it was impossible to choose among the other likely contenders—PMS 426C, PMS 427C, PMS 428C, and so on—based only on the perfect MouseDriver vision he had in his head. He swore at himself for not carrying the ideal driver head with him at all times. Then the printer, who had watched the whole drama unfold, bailed him out.

The printer wordlessly handed the PMS book to Kyle and steered him out the front door and to the left. Looking up, Kyle saw golf club after golf club—right next door was a used golf equipment store. He walked around holding color samples up to clubs until an Orlimar driver matched with PMS 429C and solved everything.

The pattern was set: Before yielding to solutions, decisions brought problems. That rule was holding true for me in Austin as well. We'd decided we wanted to put the PGA logo on MouseDriver, so I was checking out the golf industry, trying to clear the way. My research revealed that a single company had an exclusive licensing agreement with the PGA for use of its logo on all computer peripherals.

That was weird. There was another company that made PC accessories that already had the rights to use the PGA logo. Even weirder, they were in Texas (Dallas). Maybe they even made specialty mice. In fact, they almost had to—their name was Team Mouse.

But not a mouse shaped like a driver head. I learned about Team Mouse's products (standard computer accessories, emblazoned with golf images and the PGA logo), then called Team Mouse's president, Steve Little, to discuss setting up a meeting.

Our businesses might complement each other, I explained, and suggested that we pursue some sort of partnership. He agreed. A few days later, Kyle hustled up to Austin with our huge gray plastic prototype and orange ceramic CNC sample and joined me for the three-hour trip to Dallas.

The good news: Steve Little liked our mice, especially our CNC mouse à l'orange, and wanted to work with us. The bad news: He thought we were already too late to hit retail stores for the holiday season. The buying period for retail was spring, he explained, and we'd missed it. Just like that, half of our 1999 sales strategy was gone.

We left Dallas dejected. I'd just begun my retail sales research, and now it was irrelevant. The retail sales we'd forecasted were now hinging on Father's Day 2000, six months further out than what we'd anticipated. We couldn't wait that long to get some momentum and become profitable. It was time to kick off our sales plan, and aim it exclusively at the remaining half of our sales strategy—the corporate promotions market.

All 500 units of our initial MouseDriver order—which we needed to get ASAP—would go toward penetrating that market. An informal agreement with Steve Little had gotten us the PGA logo artwork from Team Mouse, so that was a good place to start. We had already planned to ask Kenny to print the MouseDriver name in small type on the top edge of all of the mice; now we decided to have him add the PGA logo on 50 of them, right in the center. Over the next couple of days, we upped the PGA number to 100, then 200. We wanted to use these samples to show the corporate promotions market that MouseDriver was the place to promote a brand.

Our sales plan for the corporate promotions market basically consisted of the unsystematic approach of cold-calling corporations, mostly investment banks, and asking to speak to the person who bought promotional gifts. The typical conversation went something like this:

"Hi, this is John Lusk calling from Platinum Concepts. Could I please speak to the person who handles your promotional gift buying?"

"That would be so-and-so; just a moment."

It was rarely a direct connection, and I braced myself to suffer through a few seconds of ad drivel for the company or, worse, the Muzak versions of songs like "Stayin' Alive." The reward for my patience, far more often than not, was voice mail.

"Hi, this is so-and-so of such-and-such corporation, and I'm either on another call or away from my desk right now. Please leave me your name and number and I'll get right back to you."

"Hi, this is John Lusk, VP of marketing at Platinum Concepts. I'd like to talk to you about our product, which involves golf and computers, as a potential promotional item for your company. Please give me a call back at 512-867-5309 and let me know a good time to discuss this with you. Thanks."

I knew my messages were almost information-free and far from compelling. But I didn't want to say too much—well, anything—about MouseDriver. At least not until I was talking to a live person who I could count on being a potential purchaser. I wouldn't say I was paranoid, but the word "knockoff" scared the crap out of me.

When I did reach company reps, I kept hearing the same thing. As the "Oh, sorry, we get all of our corporate gifts through our distributor" responses piled up, making our way with direct corporate sales began to look less and less likely.

Undaunted, I took the next logical step and went after the distributors themselves. As I did, one name kept popping up over and over. It seemed like everyone I talked to mentioned ASI. Everywhere I turned, ASI.

I remembered that Steve Little, too, had referred to ASI a number of times on the day he'd turned our plans upside down at Team Mouse. We'd meant to ask him about it before we left, preferably without revealing too much of our ignorance. Maybe "Hey, by the way, what's the latest with ASI?" or "How's ASI been treating you?" But when we'd heard that we were too late for Christmas retail, we'd forgotten about ASI, and it would make us look lame if we asked now. But clearly ASI was big in this industry. ASI was a player. If we were going to make it, ASI was key.

I had no idea what the letters ASI stood for. ASI: A company, an association, what what what? Every morning, Kyle would kick off the first of several daily calls we made to each other by asking if I'd figured it out. After I'd followed with my daily answer of no, we'd blow at least a couple of minutes trying to crack each other up guessing what lay behind the letters ASI. Alcoholic Super Investors. Awesomely Sexy Iowans. Against Summer Interns (Monica Lewinsky was in the news). It started to get competitive.

I looked to the Internet for answers. But all ASI searches gave me were a million dead ends. It was all unpromising leads like the American Society of Indexers, Analytical Surveys, Inc., and Artemis Society International (that was Kyle's favorite—a private venture to establish a permanent, self-supporting community on the Moon). I myself had a soft spot for Arbeitsgemeinschaft Sozialwissenschaftlicher Institute and held out a little hope that it might be the German branch of what we were looking for.

Every time I talked with anyone on the phone who seemed familiar with ASI, I was on the alert for another potential piece of the puzzle. I kept trying to slip low-key questions into my discussions. Finally, I got tired of the pose and one day just grilled some poor woman who sold logoed pens to local Texas banks.

She spilled the beans, and the truth set us free. ASI stood for the Advertising Specialty Institute, the governing body of a $16 billion industry solely dedicated to serving companies and corporations by slapping logos on everything. Mugs, T-shirts, pens, golf balls, condoms, you name it. ASI was all about logos, and it was the largest subindustry within the $100 billion promotions industry. Manufacturers, suppliers, and distributors of logoable merchandise could join ASI for a onetime fee of $75. Membership entitled them to a wide range of trade information, along with initial credit from member suppliers.

"Everyone puts their ASI numbers in their ads and catalogs," she said. "It's very well respected."

I wasn't convinced. We had a novelty gift item, a quality product. Based on what I'd just heard, ASI included a lot of trashy trinkets, and no subsequent research changed my impression. MouseDriver's strength lay in its perception as a unique high-end product. The last thing we wanted was for it to be lost in the ASI shuffle of cheesy corporate giveaways.

In the first of a series of marathon Cypress-to-Austin calls, Kyle and I discussed the ASI image issue and weighed our options. In corporate promotions, we had multiple buyers telling us they went through ASI exclusively. In retail, we had Steve Little telling us we'd missed Christmas. Sure, he knew what he was doing, but he was just one guy, with just one company, dealing with just one industry. He could be wrong, couldn't he?

I hung up and made some quick calls to any retailers I could think of to check Christmas cut-offs. By the time I got through to a few, I'd heard dates from all over the calendar. I reported back to Kyle, who had checked manufacturing timelines. We decided to return our focus to retail, trying to get into a few "upstairs" retailers (high-end gift shops and department stores like Macy's) for the 1999 holiday season. At the same time, we would keep working on penetrating the corporate promotions market, trying to find a way around ASI. ASI itself might be an option for later in 2000, when we also planned to move MouseDriver into "downstairs" retailers (mass-market stores like Wal-Mart) after hitting upstairs retailers hard at the beginning of the year.

As a consumer, it's un-American not to complain about the commercialism of the holidays. Thanksgiving isn't Thanksgiving unless someone at the table moans about how Turkey Day has been reduced to a mere marker of the beginning of the Christmas shopping season. Now that Kyle and I were in the vendors' camp, spinning from our strategy turnarounds, we saw the other side of the holiday rush. Kyle ended our last call by saying, "The holiday season is just around the corner," and I agreed with him. It was June 17.

*   *   *

We were two weeks from (supposedly) being fully operational in San Francisco, and so much still had to happen. More than anything, we needed to find the worldwide headquarters of Platinum Concepts, Inc. We could now officially call ourselves an "Inc."—the legal incorporation had come through, making Platinum, not us, liable for anything that happened with MouseDriver. A corporation could be a beautiful thing. But this one desperately needed an apartment.

We were enthusiastic about San Francisco, even though we understood that, logistically speaking, the city was (and remains) one of the worst places to try and bootstrap a single-product company. Forget housing and office space prices—the costs for everything associated with doing business were higher in San Francisco. And since at this point we were basically virtual (with no employees and no warehouses), it made far more sense to stay in Texas.

Except we couldn't hedge our bets in Cypress and Austin. That was a very big part of the point of moving to San Francisco. Both of us figured that if no one, not even our moms, wanted to buy a MouseDriver, we'd at least already be in an area of the country where we could jump aboard a technology start-up in a heartbeat. That kind of backup plan wasn't as possible in Texas.

There were other bright sides to San Francisco, beyond the business aspects. The dot-com boom gave San Francisco something Texas couldn't offer—a great, non-college-dependent, thirty-something social scene. Sure, Kyle had a girlfriend, but I was definitely single. And with all the work we'd be doing, both of us were going to need to get out and let off some steam. Also, San Francisco boasted an incredible outdoors environment, great for all kinds of sports (including golf).

We were both eager to select an apartment, but Kyle's girlfriend was heading to Houston from Philly to hang out before making the drive west with him, so he had to stick around. The idea was that I would fly to SF, find an apartment, fly back, pick up my car, drive to SF, and be at the apartment on July 1 to meet the movers. A simple, straightforward plan.

That's not to say the plan didn't have pitfalls.

There was no flexibility in the dates. I had booked a round-trip flight out of Dallas (where I planned to visit friends before taking off and attend my friend Andrew Ashmore's wedding upon return) leaving on Friday, June 18 and returning on Thursday, June 24. This was a nonrefundable—and therefore nonchangeable—ticket. That gave me exactly one week to find an apartment.

After that, I had another week to move from Texas to California. If I wasn't back in San Francisco on July 1 to meet Big and Little Jim, bad things would happen. Things like our stuff traveling all the way back to Philadelphia to sit in storage. Driving from Dallas to San Francisco would take at least three days. So I absolutely had to leave Dallas no later than June 27.

But the worst part was the San Francisco apartment vacancy rate. On good days, it was hovering around 1%.

I got to San Francisco on plan and crashed on some Wharton friends' couch at their place in Cow Hollow. For seven days I was off the couch and out on the street by 8 A.M., scouring the area in search of the ever-elusive "For Rent" sign. I signed up for every one of the apartment search services. MetroRent, Apartments Unlimited, RentTech. (We were in the wrong business—these places were making a killing.) I called realtors and looked in the classifieds. I searched the Internet. I begged friends, acquaintances, and people walking out of nice buildings to check with their landlords for me.

I was due to leave on Thursday afternoon. On Tuesday, I started to wig out. By mistake, I managed to get in touch with a real estate agent who was listing a house in Pacific Heights. In my desperation I must have willed the house to be an apartment complex or something and noted the listed number. Anyway, this real estate agent listened to my sob story and was even intrigued that we were coming fresh from business school to start our own company. He had once started a company himself and must have felt sympathetic. So he put in a good word for me with one of his real estate buddies, and suddenly I was looking at not only a vacant apartment, but a sweet apartment in Cow Hollow.

I liked everything about the place. Except the twenty other freshly minted graduates, married couples, and dot-com millionaires looking alongside me. "Go away," I glowered at them.

I took a cursory look at the place (YES! YES! It had key features like rooms and doors and a street address), told the woman who was showing the apartment that this guy, the agent I'd spoken with, had sent me over and that I would take it. Terrific, she said. I just needed to fill out an application and give her a deposit. Then she would consider me along with the twenty other candidates.

That was my lesson for the day in San Francisco rental reality. The market was so tight that unscrupulous agents were taking bribes and bidding up rents, and scrupulous agents were carefully selecting ideal-profile, guaranteed trouble-free tenants. And it didn't take much imagination to guess that two guys from Texas with no history of renting in San Francisco weren't going to top anyone's list.

Then a miracle occurred. The agent connection came through, and Wednesday morning I heard from the woman saying that we got the apartment. She had only one caveat: We had put down on our rental application that we were making $85,000 a year, and she needed to see proof of income. I explained to her that we were starting a company and we didn't have income yet, but once we did, we would pay ourselves $85K (considerably less, by the way, than the average starting salary of a Wharton MBA).

She didn't buy it. Determined not to lose the apartment, I offered to pay three months' rent up front. No, she said, she needed to see proof of income. I offered to pay six months in advance. No dice. I couldn't believe this woman! How could she not want cash now as opposed to later? Was she somehow missing the obvious, or was she only pretending to, just to keep us from getting the apartment? Gambling a good chunk of our cash on hand that it was the former, I decided to find out with a final proposal. I offered to advance the entire first year's rent in cash.

Her response: "You just don't get it, do you? I have to know that you can pay on a monthly basis, otherwise the owner runs the risk of not having monthly income to cover all of the expenses." I was speechless—we were in the land of nonsense, where nothing I could say would make her understand. I was also running out of time. I asked her to tell the owner of the apartment what I had offered and get back to me.

On Thursday morning, about an hour before I had to leave to return to Dallas, the agent called to say that the owner had approved us. "I just need a check for first and last months' rent," she said.

So I left the insane market with that final insane call, plus an apartment.

When the time came for the drive back to the West Coast, I had someone to ride shotgun. My friend Andrew Ashmore and his almost-Mrs. Ashmore had called off their wedding at the last minute. Andrew had nothing to do for a week and was in the mood for a road trip, especially one that involved Las Vegas. The cool part was that this trip was much cheaper than the honeymoon he'd planned, so he picked up a lot of our expenses.

Andrew and I rolled into San Francisco late on June 30 and stayed at a friend's. I spent most of the next day looking out the window of Kyle's and my empty new apartment for signs of Big and Little Jim, who finally showed up around 3:30 P.M.

The place may have been a minor nightmare to find, but it also couldn't have been more optimal for starting a business. Close to Kinko's, close to the post office, and close to The Postal Chase, which was better than the post office for shipping stuff. Plenty of room for storage, plus some makeshift storage in the garage. And a block away from Union Street, which had tons of cool bars and restaurants.

The apartment itself was great—two big bedrooms, each with its own bath, a decent living room, and a kitchen with a dining area. Andrew and I thought the kitchen/dining area would be the best area to designate as the primary office space, since we didn't anticipate that Kyle and I would use it for anything else, not with dozens of restaurants and delis within a five-minute walk. I got the electricity and gas turned on, phones connected (here our lack of income got us a discount), desks set up, and information on high-speed Internet service providers so that we could hit the ground running when Kyle arrived.

Andrew helped me set up the apartment, including hanging a huge Texas flag on the wall. He left for Dallas at the end of what would have been his honeymoon.

Meanwhile, Kyle and his girlfriend were on a ten-day sightseeing trip of the Southwest and eastern California driving from Houston to San Francisco. Their itinerary included Austin, Carlsbad Caverns, the North Rim of the Grand Canyon, Zion, Sequoia–Kings Canyon, and Yosemite. All through the hottest parts of the country at the hottest time of the year in Kyle's twelve-year-old 300ZX, featuring a temperamental air conditioner. The universe was paying him back for swiping his dad's home office.

We'd done a lot of work during our month in Texas, and learned more than a few things about what needed to be done with our business. But somehow Kyle's arrival in San Francisco on July 7 seemed like the official start of Platinum Concepts, Inc., MouseDriver, and our whole adventure. This had less to do with a feeling and more to do with our place in the real world. We had an office, letterhead and business cards sporting our lofty titles under way at Kinko's, and product samples on the way from Hong Kong.

MAKING MICE
IS HARD TO DO

Time flies when you're way behind.

That was our first lesson on the West Coast. It came to us just a few days into our new office/apartment, sometime after we'd decided to temporarily reject outmoded social concepts like "unpacking" and "laundry" in favor of clearing avenues between unopened boxes and jumping into work on Platinum Concepts, Inc. There was so much to be done, and we couldn't wait to do it. Then, days later, when we'd run out of fresh socks and the stimulation of setting far too many projects in motion at once had worn thin, our second West Coast lesson hit home.

In manufacturing, there is no such thing as a simple product.

Kyle and I had always thought of MouseDriver's simplicity as one of its strengths. After all, what were we trying to put together? A housing device, with two buttons on top and a rollerball door underneath, an integrated circuit, a rollerball, and a cord with a plug at one end. Fewer than ten parts, and all but three were standard-issue plastics, ceramics, and electronics.

Only the "chassis" of the mouse—the housing device and the two click buttons—were specially designed. Assembling the whole package should have been easy as pie.

Except it wasn't. Making MouseDriver turned out to have more components than we'd expected. The samples (our first real, fully operational MouseDrivers) were still on their way from Hong Kong, courtesy of Carmine and Kenny, but in the meantime, Kyle and I were already swamped preparing for their arrival, chasing down answers to questions we'd never imagined caring about.

Like what kind of box to put MouseDriver in. Our Texas PMS experience turned out to be merely the first of too many run-ins with the worlds of printing and graphic design. Needing a box design proved to be another. Our 500 samples were scheduled to arrive packed in foam sheets in generic white boxes distinguished only by the words "The Original MouseDriver" printed on the top. Obviously, we had to come up with something flashier in the way of a box for our mass production runs. And of course, we already knew from experience that choosing the box wasn't the end of the packaging problem, it was only the beginning, a jumping-off point for all sorts of other peripheral issues, such as who would make (and do the printing for) the box, and who would put MouseDriver in the box, and where would this meeting of MouseDriver and box occur, and how much would all of this logistical magic cost. None of which was glamorous, but all of it had to be resolved, and soon.

Then there was the issue of handling specialty printing. Kenny had been able to do our PGA samples, but we had to be able to customize MouseDriver—postproduction—according to what corporate clients wanted to see on the product (Enormous Worldwide Holding Corp. might want its logo on

MouseDriver, for example). After some digging, Kyle and I learned that customized imprinting on a product like a PC mouse required a little-used heat transfer process called pad printing. It's the same process used to print letters and numbers on keyboards. That was great to know; now all we had to do was decide whether to pad print here or overseas, shop around for vendors, and learn the ins and outs of the technology well enough to know what we could or couldn't offer potential corporate customers.

Still more fun remained to be had. We needed a product code for MouseDriver, a partly important (but mostly ridiculous) number sequence for differentiating between design models. Never mind that we had a sum total of one design model; according to Hong Kong, we needed to come up with a product code as soon as possible.

And a warranty card, we needed a warranty card as fast as we could make one up. Hong Kong had to have it, ASAP.

What kind of box, what colors are the box, how does the product come out of the box, does the box have a clear window view of the product, does the product have a model number, what kinds of logos are on it, what kind of warranty does it have. Eight million details no one ever thinks about unless they have to. And we had to.

To attack these problems, we came up with a three-plan system. Before picking one, we'd first consult by phone with Kenny, our point person for East Asia Action Express. In all our dealings with EAAE, Kenny went above and beyond the call of duty. Though Platinum Concepts was an amoeba on his company's food chain of clients, he was unfailingly patient with us, approaching all of our panicked and unreasonable calls the same way he took in our calmer requests. Kenny would cheerfully plot out the full extent of the problem in MouseDriver production and engineering terms: It could wait, it was annoying but critical, it had to be done yesterday. Then he'd wish us good luck and leave us to work it through our three-plan system.

We'd always kick off with high hopes for Plan A—trying to take advantage of our network of contacts. Usually, after just a few minutes of researching the problem and brainstorming possible solutions, we'd have enough information to know Plan A wouldn't work. Generally speaking, Plan A almost never worked. We were just starting out in the world of specialty products, so our network of contacts was understandably unimpressive. It was a time to build contacts, not draw on them.

Then we'd move on to Plan B—hitting the streets to find a creative solution on our own.

Plan B turned out to be surprisingly effective. To figure out what kind of box we might like for MouseDriver, we hit the shopping malls and started looking at any and every conceivable package. I liked the color scheme of one in Brookstone, and the design of a jewelry box at Nordstrom caught Kyle's eye (it felt a little silly to us, even while we were blitzing through the malls, but that's the truth of the Harrison/Lusk box solution). Those two plus a few other comparables helped us come up with the layout and texture and overall look of our ideal box. We then ran it all by Kenny and settled on a five-by-five-by-two-inch box with a glossy finish and a transparent display panel, trimmed in three colors, black, green, and gold. Kenny put together a manufacturing package for it that worked, complete with a thirty-day turnaround, and with that we were off and running on all things packaged and boxed.

We also kicked the pesky warranty card and product code out of the way with Plan B. We knew nothing about warranty language and were complaining about this latest gap in our knowledge to our friend/investor/co-inventor/all-around-answerman, Ed McClung. He suggested we take a look at a warranty card for a similar product. It was a stroke of genius. Forty-five minutes, one small purchase, and one well-meaning act of near- (but not total-) plagiarism later, and we had warranty material fit to run past our lawyer.

The product code problem disappeared using a similar method. A quick trip to a computer store, some stolen glances at product codes, and bang! MouseDriver 2.0a was born.

And in those cases when Plan B failed, or simply wasn't appropriate for the task at hand, it was time for Plan C.

Plan C. Also known as working the Yellow Pages.

Plan C took care of the pad-printing problem. After a lot of dead-end calls along the "Uh, you said pad, right? Yeah hold on lemme check. Yeah. Can you hold? Okay, um, you still there? Because—wait, yeah—no we don't have any pads" variety, we found a local company called Graphatic that specialized in pad printing. Our point person at Graphatic was Anita, the woman who first answered when we called, who turned out to be very helpful to Platinum Concepts for months to come, and who we might never have run across if not for a search through the Yellow Pages.

All the legwork and telephone sleuthing that came out of executing Plans B and C taught us three valuable lessons.

First (and least important), from now on Kyle and I would scoff at jumbles of letters or numbers attached to product names. Thanks to our own product code experience, we knew the deal. In our eyes, a Harley-Davidson XLH 883 Hugger, a BMW Z3 Roadster, and a Hewlett-Packard Jornada 540 Series Color Pocket PC were only a motorcycle, a convertible, and a handheld organizer that, for all their words in strings, carried no more weight with us than a Snickers Bar 1.0.

Second, our own logistical runarounds served to deepen our respect for anyone who brought any kind of tangible product to market. We walked around with a newfound awareness of the hidden hassles behind the manufacture and packaging and shipping of everything from shaving cream to washing machines. Before we'd started, we'd directed most of our admiration toward entrepreneurs. Now we were catching ourselves marveling at the design of half the products we ran across, all the way down to the padding and wrapping materials from the boxes they came in.

Third, and perhaps most important, it was not lost on us how much more often the Yellow Pages came through for us than our Wharton network. Plan C was trumping Plan A on a regular basis, for a couple of reasons we found interesting. One was self-evident: We were in an industry that didn't place a premium on MBAs. While we thought this might work to our advantage over time, we also knew that few (if any) of our potential business school contacts would be able to help us tackle specific questions, like how to get the rights to use the PGA logo.

There was also a more subtle reason why our Wharton connections often fell short in helping us start up Platinum Concepts.

Business school has a split personality. Half the time, it's a forum for thinking through general business concepts, including issues surrounding start-ups. The keys to success and failure in start-ups crop up as often as any other subject in case studies, and professors often talk encouragingly to students about creating new businesses.

But the other half of the time, business school is a training ground for a handful of industries it feeds into naturally. It is quite rightly seen as an entry point into investment banking, consulting, and management in Fortune 500 companies. In this mode, business school is poorly named. It's more like job school.

Even when it focuses on start-ups, business school generally turns its attention toward new ventures with the potential to generate huge revenues and/or change the dynamics of an industry. This approach leaves out the majority of the world's start-up businesses, which have only a handful of products and employees and possess little or no chance of changing the course of any marketplace. When the Whartons and Harvards and Stanfords squeeze in time for these buzz-deficient new ventures—businesses like ours, for example—they tend to study them in aggregate. And where business school offered aggregate information, we needed the detailed scoop on where to find a reliable pad printer willing to do special orders on a moment's notice, precisely the kind of stuff business school ties couldn't provide us. All of which brought us back to the Yellow Pages.

*   *   *

Our first box of product samples arrived during the second week in July. There were only two MouseDrivers inside. One had a PGA logo, one didn't.

Looking at our first true MouseDrivers was a bittersweet experience. On one hand, it was thrilling to think something that Kyle had dreamed up years before was now resting in our hands. These working models represented the first fruits of our labor.

On the other hand, they didn't look like we expected them to. On the PGA model, the logo was crooked. Really crooked. The key reason: The top curvature of the mouse was not what we'd designed—somewhere along the line, it had changed without our approval. In fact, the topside curves and slopes of these mice made them too crooked for logos of any length to look good.

The color wasn't right either. After all that running around in search of a PMS color match, the MouseDrivers before us looked a bit off. We knew we would have to send another golf club head to Hong Kong and backtrack almost to the beginning of the process with Kenny, just to get the look and feel of MouseDriver the way we'd wanted it in the first place. "This is getting expensive," Kyle mumbled.

And while the MouseDrivers worked without software as advertised, their click buttons were flimsily attached and broke off easily after only mild pressure had been applied. We had no way of knowing whether this was a manufacturing problem or a result of the way the buttons fit together with the oddly curved (and unauthorized by us) design that sat before us on our kitchen counter.

Either way, we had a lot of questions for Kenny. We'd expected problems, and we still had faith in our Hong Kong connection. We just didn't expect so many flaws to hit us at once.

Several days after receiving our half-bungled mice, we reached Kenny by phone. He was cheerful as always, and still in the process of negotiating with GE Logistics for the transit of our next 98 samples, many of which carried the PGA logo. We told him about the crookedness of the logo on our one PGA sample.

"Oh yes. All the PGA samples have crooked logos," he said.

We asked him why.

"Oh, that's because of the design change. Any kind of logo you put on top comes out crooked."

We told him about the click buttons breaking off.

"Really? I'll look into it."

Then he told us the next 98 samples were almost ready to ship. We asked that he hold onto them until he could fix the logo problem. Kenny agreed, and was back to us within days, telling us the topside curvature had been corrected and the reapplied PGA logos looked much better.

At our request, Kenny switched the shipping from GE Logistics to Federal Express, and our next 98 samples arrived on July 26, kicking the worldwide total number of MouseDrivers in captivity up to an even 100.

Kenny was right: The PGA logos were much straighter, almost to the point of being straight. The color of MouseDriver was okay this time; it looked like what we thought PMS 429C ought to look like. The click buttons, however, remained flimsy. That was okay by us for now—we hadn't given Kenny any directions for fixing them before he'd shipped these 98 samples. We had worked up a design solution in between shipments, however, one that gave the mouse buttons more structural support.

We thought we were ready to call Kenny. Then a misplaced Kyle elbow sent a sample PGA MouseDriver flying off his desk and crashing onto the hardwood floor.

It should have been no big deal. MouseDriver was made of hard plastic, after all. But when Kyle picked it up and tried using it, our flying MouseDriver started making all sorts of new and ominous noises. When Kyle pulled out his tool kit and took it apart, with me looking over his shoulder, we realized that (to paraphrase Kyle) its guts were all broken. There was a little bit wrong with everything inside, from the integrated circuit connection to the cord.

There was only one thing to do: The time had come to smash a lot of MouseDrivers.

Kyle and I spent the better part of the day test-dropping mice, then taking them apart to review the damage. It was a weird sight to behold, even for the two of us in the middle of it—young entrepreneurs repeatedly dropping their first creations on the floor, then examining the damage from the crashes.

Many broken samples later, we had our answer: MouseDriver was way too fragile. An ordinary drop of a few feet (a fall anyone could re-create with a sudden loss of coordination at a typical workstation) consistently resulted in a lot of damage to the inner workings of MouseDriver. In some drops, the rollerball broke out of the housing on impact and gloomily rolled off to the far corners of our living room to hide between packing boxes.

We were upset that our samples were so easily broken. We wanted to position MouseDriver as a high-quality novelty item, and it was behaving under pressure like a cheap and flimsy throwaway. Our product had to be more durable. End of discussion. We packed up our MouseDriver debris with the idea that we'd FedEx it to Kenny so he could brainstorm with us on improving product quality.

The day after our mouse-smashing session, we called Kenny. We asked him if he'd made any further progress on straightening out the PGA logos.

"No, no more progress. All the logos are still a little crooked. I don't know if that can be fixed."

We asked him about implementing our redesign of the mouse buttons, to make them less flimsy.

"No, there's not a lot more we can do with the mouse buttons." He cited constraints having to do with the overall design of MouseDriver.

We told him about our crash tests and expressed concern over the rollerball flying out of the housing.

"The rollerball? The rollerball is standard. Nobody else has any problems with the rollerball."

We needed something positive to hold on to. We told him that we were concerned about all the problems, but that at least this time we'd liked the color of the MouseDriver samples.

"The color? Oh yes. The color's too dark. I tried to put a whole bunch of different logos on the mice, other than the PGA one, and you can't see any of them. The mice are too dark. We have to change colors."

We trusted Kenny, but the experience of manufacturing so far away was beginning to get to us. We talked about planning a trip to Hong Kong to take a look at the manufacturing operations, but we knew we wouldn't have the time or the money to go in the near future.

Looking back on it, Hong Kong travel talk was just a cover for our frustration. We wanted to do something to feel like we were in control, when in fact we weren't. We had to rely on Kenny, at least for now. The last of our samples, a shipment of 400, were due within three weeks. East Asia Action Express was now as aware of the kinks as we were. We would have to wait and see how much the last batch of our first-ever order would improve.

Kyle and I talked a lot about the fallout with our first samples. Before we'd received any MouseDrivers, we'd been eager to send them out to friends and family (our evangelists) and a few prospective clients almost as soon as we got our hands on them. Instead, we'd opened two boxes, one small, one large, and been disappointed by most of what we'd found inside. Not to mention the fact that we'd destroyed a good percentage of our existing inventory in the name of quality control.

We thought there were too many problems with MouseDriver to send it out to evangelists. We began brainstorming about ways to improve MouseDriver, including totally redesigning our product. We contacted Kenny a couple of times, running by him what, in retrospect, were overly ambitious product overhauls, just to get his reaction. Kenny would gently try to explain all the delays our proposed modifications would create and leave us on our own to talk ourselves out of making big changes.

It didn't take too many days of reevaluation and fretful phone calls to Hong Kong for Kyle and me to realize the trap we were falling into. Yes, there were immediate problems with MouseDriver, but we'd become overly obsessed with perfecting our product in the manufacturing stage. In that mode, we could have spent six more months holed up in our apartment headquarters, drawing blueprints for the perfect mouse. And there would have been no way Kenny could have pleased us. By focusing too much on getting everything right at the manufacturing stage, we were overlooking other aspects of introducing our product to the world, including things like, well, introducing our product to the world.

We remembered a lesson we'd come across while reading a book by Guy Kawasaki during business school. It was called *Rules for Revolutionaries: The Capitalist Manifesto for Creating and Marketing New Products and Services,* and in it Kawasaki wrote, "When your product or service is to existing products or services what toilet paper is to crumbled leaves, it's time to ship. S-h-i-p, ship."

It was great advice for us. We decided that if the 400 samples of our next shipment were at all passable—that is, they worked, they didn't break easily, and the logo problems were basically resolved—we'd send them out to our evangelist network and prospective clients as planned. We'd even send the few remaining unsmashed samples right now. There was no need to wait for perfection; we'd get more and better insights from the feedback of a few hundred interested parties than we could generate on our own.

We would ship and then learn, rather than learn and then ship. After being bloodied by rival Plans B and C, Plan A (drawing on business school resources) had come out of nowhere to help us, in the form of a half-remembered insight from an assigned reading. It helped us make one of the best decisions we would make in our opening months in business. We would receive great feedback from customers, retailers, distributors, old classmates, friends, and family as a result of Kawasaki's advice and the idea that sometimes good enough is better than perfect.

OUR FIRST SECOND
THOUGHTS

With the first batch of MouseDrivers finally settled safely in the United States, it was time for Kyle and me to get out and take a look around.

Kyle's mom Marsha had left an excited message in the Platinum Concepts voice mail telling us that *Condé Nast Traveler* or *Travel & Leisure* or some other dentist-office-type magazine like that had recently named San Francisco the number one tourist destination in the United States. "You must be having so much fun discovering it all," she'd said.

Sadly, we had hardly been further than a mile radius from our office/apartment. Many days, we didn't make it out of the apartment at all—taking a break meant leaving the kitchen to stroll around the living room.

We had gotten to know our own neighborhood, Cow Hollow, well enough as we foraged for meals, but it was only about twelve by five blocks. Its two main commercial streets, Union and Fillmore, were equal parts bars/restaurants (which meant sustenance) and clothing boutiques (which meant attractive women window-shopping). No complaints there. But everything beyond—Russian Hill, North Beach, South of Market, the Mission, Hayes Valley, the Haight, and so on—remained to be seen.

Through our Wharton network, we were hooked into a group of city/peninsula (south toward Silicon Valley) people. Work and social lives had huge overlaps, and everyone was involved with the New Economy. Our VC and investment banker peers were bankrolling it, and the dot-commers we knew were spending it.

Spending it defined the social landscape. You could display any given week in Microsoft Outlook on the average dot-commer's Palm Pilot and find: A B2C portal beta launch at the new Sony Metreon complex. Drinks at Bix, Harry Denton's Starlight Room, Absinthe, Bruno's, Café Monaco, Le Central, or Le Colonial. An Internet search engine IPO at the Palace of Fine Arts. Dinner at LuLu, Hawthorne Lane, Slanted Door, Betelnut, Aqua, Farallon, Zuni, or Rose Pistola. A comedy content Web site launch at the Caribbean Zone (this, we were to discover, was a kitschy umbrella drink bar whose most desirable seating was in the fuselage of an old airplane, with tropical islands and seas bouncing by on the television screen windows).

Not that any of it involved us.

A new gold rush was under way in California, 150 years after the first. Stock options and IPOs were the modern-day gold nuggets. Using our MBAs to stay home and make a novelty computer mouse out of our kitchen during 1999's dot-com boom was just about equal to tossing out the pick-axe and gold-pan at the edge of the mother lode and trying to sell monogrammed belt buckles to the 49ers instead. Yes, functional, but no real value added. And definitely missing the main event.

We knew all of this, and it didn't bother us. Not at first.

We'd chosen this path. We'd decided to go with Platinum Concepts and MouseDriver, to do everything ourselves. And we'd opted to put ourselves in the center of the New Economy action, even though we knew we were pursuing something different.

The differences were becoming clearer all the time.

Thanks to a friend of a friend of a Wharton friend, Kyle and I got on the guest list to our first official dot-com party, for the launch of a company that enabled nonprofit organizations to add online donation capabilities to their Web sites. Wearing our invitation-instructed "snappy casual" attire (we guessed that this meant the seasonal rather than staple Banana Republic corporate casual gear, which turned out to be on the money), our pockets stuffed with our freshly printed business cards, we squeezed into one of the elevators of the Bank of America building, the tallest in the city, and felt our ears pop as we rode fifty-two stories to the top. We stepped out into the Carnelian Room and 360-degree views of the whole Bay Area.

We were excited, partly just to be out in the world again, but also by the prospect of being able to talk to people about what we were doing with MouseDriver. We knew that we'd be able to generate a lot of interest, and possibly some sales.

We were wrong. Everyone was impossibly cool, drinking cosmopolitans from those difficult martini glasses and not spilling a drop. They spoke a completely different language— "turnkey," "ASPs," "first mover," "opt out," "scalability quotient," "click-through rates," "CPMs." We were familiar with it, but far from fluent.

I tried to start a conversation with a thin, dark-haired woman in chic librarian glasses and an olive-colored suit. Her name was Nadine, she was a content strategist at a Web consulting company and had come with her roommate, who was minister of culture at the host company. I felt suddenly self-conscious of my stodgy vice president of marketing title, but smiled anyway as I handed over my card.

"Platinum Concepts?" she asked, skeptical. "Is that some kind of credit card company?"

"Ah, ha ha, no, it's not. It's an upscale consumer specialty products company. Right now we're in the final stages of development of our premier product, a computer mouse that looks like the head of a golf driver." There, that sounded reasonably interesting, cogent, and weighty.

It failed to grab her, and she went after her own interests. "I don't know of it . . . is it a big company? Who does your Web consulting?"

"No, we're still in our first round of funding and growth," I said. "We'll probably roll out an enhanced site sometime in Q1-Q2 2000." Where did that come from?

I tried a different tack. "Do you live in the city?"

"Yeah, in Noe Valley." I wasn't sure where Noe Valley was, but I nodded. "How about you?" she asked.

"Cow Hollow," I said. "On Filbert, right off Fillmore." This territory I knew.

She looked at my card again. "So you live right by your work? Lucky you."

We had, of course, printed our business cards with our home address/office address—they were one and the same. We had thought we were being pretty clever by changing our apartment number to a suite number. Very official, we had congratulated ourselves. The only snag so far had been my mom, who couldn't figure out how to reach me. She would call our number, get the Platinum Concepts voice mail, and leave messages that always started with, "Hi, son, sorry to leave a message on your office line, but I still don't have your home number." When we forwarded calls from the office line to my cell, we lost her completely. "John? I thought that I called your office line. You know, I still need your home number." Was it that complicated?

"Uh, no. I . . . um, we, my business partner and I run our business out of our apartment," I told Nadine.

"Oh," she cooed. "That's adorable!"

My cheeks turned hot as she looked at me like I was a Labrador puppy. I had no interest in being adorable. "Yeah, thanks. Nice talking to you," I said, snatching a cracker piled with caviar from a passing tray, stuffing it in my mouth, and heading for the gigantic buffet. At least the caviar was satisfying.

Kyle, in rare form, had abandoned his post at the bar and was diligently working the buffet. He'd selected a few dainty morsels for a couple of women he'd been chatting up and assembled a mountain of skewered chicken, stuffed mushrooms, cheese cubes, and a couple million other things for himself. Every finger food from every part of the globe was represented in a display that would have put a cruise ship to shame, and Kyle was halfway through his own personal world tour.

"How's it going?" I asked, grabbing a plate and moving in for some shrimp before he cleared the table.

"Ig thunno, cubbee bether," he said through the chicken. Swallowing, he explained, "I'm talking to some women from the PR agency that helped stage this whole deal. They have some clients that would fit MouseDriver, but I haven't gotten them to set up a meeting or anything."

I followed Kyle past the dance floor and swing band to a small table by the windows looking out toward the Bay Bridge. He introduced me to Stephanie and Michelle, two attractive blonde women in their mid-twenties, who, after they thanked Kyle for their plates of sushi, told me that they were associates at the host's PR agency.

"So, this is your account?" I asked, thinking they'd be pleased to talk about their work.

"Oh, no," Michelle replied. "We do B2B IT. This is B2B2C e-transactions. We just came for the party."

"What kind of clients do you have in, uh, B2B IT?" I asked.

Michelle started to tick off clients. I'd heard of exactly zero of them and stopped paying attention as she and Stephanie traded gossip about their client contacts and executive interactions. This was going nowhere. Kyle and I tried to have an interesting MouseDriver conversation on the side, hoping they would overhear it and by some microscopic chance want to join in, but we didn't have the steam to keep it going. We tried asking Stephanie and Michelle where they lived, where they were from, where they'd gone to school. They were friends from un-dergrad at UC Santa Barbara.

Ah! Finally, an in. "That's cool that you guys ended up work-ing together," I said. "Kyle and I are friends from school too."

"Really, where?" asked Stephanie, mildly interested.

"We went to business school together," I replied.

"Oh, where was that?" she asked.

"Wharton."

They looked blank. "Wharton?" Michelle said. "Oh, that's one of those Ivy League business schools, isn't it?" She turned back to Stephanie. "Remember Jeff Martin, the CEO of eExsell? I think he went to Wharton. Did you ever hear what he said in Vegas when we were there for that trade show . . ." And they were off again. It was like Kyle and I didn't exist.

Looking around at all of the snappy casual people grazing the buffet and displaying ridiculous amounts of energy attempting to swing dance, we felt like outsiders. These people didn't seem to have a care in the world. The whole city was their party. The stock option money may not have been real yet, but there was more than enough of it to make up for that fact.

Part of the reason Kyle and I had decided to come to San Francisco was to be in an innovative environment, one that would embrace and support our venture. But we weren't getting that feeling at all. We were having to fight for every little thing, including respect. We had shown up eager and proud to join California's technology boom, but too many of our interactions with it were making us feel like we had something to be ashamed of, just for being small and new.

Now we knew how the small-college teams at the NCAA basketball tourney felt. Yeah, we played in a minor conference, and even our starters weren't looking at pro careers. But we believed in ourselves, we thought we deserved to be there. We expected to be somewhat of a Cinderella story, not the surefire losers on everyone's tourney pool entry. But looking at the seven-footers looming in front of us (I had just heard a guy next to me say that his company was looking to raise $25 million for its second round of VC funding), we could see why such thinking prevailed.

I looked over at Kyle, leaning back against the windows, taking in the room. He had heard the $25 million guy too. "Wanna bail?" I said. He nodded. We downed our drinks and headed out, enlightened on at least one thing: Dot-com we were not.

*   *   *

Usually, when you start a new job, people drop by your cubicle or office and chat or invite you to lunch. After a few weeks, most people have made some friends in the office and can manage to enjoy themselves as they socialize with their coworkers. Maybe it's a coping mechanism for dealing with the grind of the impersonal corporate world, but even if so, it's underrated. A friendship is a friendship, no matter where it originates.

Kyle and I were friends. We were roommates. And we were business partners. It was the last of those relationships, though, that took precedence. As we were getting all things MouseDriver up and running, friendships—especially new ones—were a luxury we couldn't afford. We had our heads down twelve, thirteen hours a day, working. Our only new friend was someone we hadn't even met—Kenny, 6,893 miles away in Hong Kong.

I remembered a friend of mine from undergrad at SMU who had gone on to medical school. For her senior thesis, she had worked with a neurology professor who studied the effects of different environments on the brain development of baby mice (the animals, not the computer accessories). The mice with rich environments—hamster wheels, lots of toys and distractions, I don't know, maybe some newspapers to read or something, developed these elaborate neural networks, with dendrites galore (dendrites, apparently, are kind of like brain wrinkles—the more you have, the smarter you are). The mice in the stark, empty environments paid a hefty price, developing only the brains they needed to navigate the cage from water bottle to food dish.

Kyle and I were feeling like the deprived mice. Being in the apartment all of the time, interacting with only each other, was stifling, no, killing any shreds of creativity we possessed. It hadn't gotten to us when we were in 500 mph set-up mode, but now that we were starting to execute our plans at a more sustainable 80 mph or so, we needed some outside stimulation to keep things from feeling like totally mundane routine.

Our office/kitchen window faced the street, and I would look out it some mornings, face practically pressed against the glass, at all of the dressed-up people hurrying to catch the bus to work. They all looked so, well, professional, in their bright blue shirts and dark gray suits. There Kyle and I were in our jeans (Kyle's intact; mine full of holes), T-shirts, and sweatshirts. I couldn't believe that I was longing for work clothes. Was I insane?

I'd confessed my envy to my (still single) friend Andrew, who was back at work in Dallas in full suit and tie. "You've lost it, Lusk," he said. "I'm sweating like a pig in this get-up. I've gotta wear a T-shirt under my shirt just to soak up all the sweat. You and Kyle have it made, sitting around in shorts all day working on your beer guts."

If only it were true. Late summer in San Francisco was anything but. The sun was MIA, and it was freezing. Most mornings, the fog wouldn't burn off until 11 A.M. or so, only to roll right back in six or seven hours later, bringing the wind along with it. On top of their blue shirts and gray suits, nearly every work-bound person passing our window each morning was also wearing a leather jacket.

To break the routine, we decided to add a formal conference room to our cozy office setup, namely, the corner table at Starbucks. We would gather our papers, pack up a laptop, forward our calls to my cell phone, put on thick sweatshirts, and brave the cold to trek the couple of blocks down Union to the café. It was great—being around people and caffeine resurrected our dendrites. We added Amy, the barrista, to our informal staff, running ideas by her. After all, she fit our main demographic— gift-buying women ages 25–75.

Soon, Amy knew all about MouseDriver. She called us "Kyle-mouse" and "John-mouse," which would have been annoying except that we were pleased to have someone remember our names. After seeing us at least twenty times a month for a couple of months straight, Amy asked, "Don't you guys ever get sick of each other?"

We'd heard this before, but the answer still surprised even us: No. We couldn't afford to get sick of each other. We needed each other, and not just because our lives were so entangled.

Who else could understand our obsessions with mice? Any time we came across someone using a computer, whether in an office, at Kinko's, or in a shop, both Kyle's and my eyes would immediately go to the mousepad and register what was resting there. We'd size up the workstation or the person using it and, just by looking at each other, agree on whether it was a potential MouseDriver home or purchaser. We'd evaluate people we passed on the street: The man in the striped polo shirt and khakis getting out of his 4Runner was MouseDriver to the core; the guy in the suit walking out of Kenneth Cole, probably not; the bachelorette and her bridesmaids waving from the limousine sunroof as they cruised the Union Street bars, very likely. Not only did each of us know what the other was thinking—we knew that no one else in the entire world was thinking that way.

In a nutshell, Kyle and I needed each other to validate our decision to do this. Second-guessing was beginning to creep into our enthusiasm. Yes, we were introducing a brand-new product. Yes, we were getting the firsthand experience of running our own business. But no, no one around us (except for Amy) cared.

We became a bit masochistic about our description of Platinum Concepts, Inc. One night, talking to a couple of women next to me at the bar at Left at Albuquerque while we waited for a table for dinner, I abandoned all efforts to describe MouseDriver adequately and just went for, "We make a novelty computer mouse out of our kitchen," then added, "Yeah, got MBAs for that." The women looked at us like we were freaks.

It was hard not to think about what our Wharton friends were doing. Working at home, we would go online and check the stock prices of their companies. Good thing we'd signed up for DSL service—we could learn that much faster which of our friends had become paper millionaires as their stocks went IPO or just up up up (we're talking 300% gains in a single day).

But we plugged along, making calls, soliciting feedback, talking to Kenny. Then one night we were driving back from the airport, where we'd gone to drop off our late-night package of broken mice to ship back overseas to Kenny. We took the Central Freeway, which would drop us a little further south in the city than it apparently would have before the end of it broke in the 1989 earthquake, and which was now a hot political topic for the November election between drivers who used it and activists who wanted to demolish the rest of it to free the neighborhood below of the dividing scar. (We were reading the *San Francisco Chronicle* daily, trying to get a feel for what was going on in our new home.)

Kyle saw it first, looming high in the distance just before the freeway ended. I heard him breathe in hard and spotted it immediately myself. There, all lit up over the freeway, 25 by 12 feet, was a billboard, just like any other. Except this one said, "PayMyBills.com." That was J.T.'s company, a company that was started at the exact same time as Platinum Concepts. MouseDriver was about a million miles from appearing on any billboards.

We decided to vote to tear down the Central Freeway.

Even though we had a clear case of dot-com envy, we didn't want to be dot-com. We were learning, all too painfully, that we couldn't do things on the standard six-month cycles of the New Economy. We were far from web-dependent; in fact, we were pleased just to be working toward setting up our Web site.

Once we did, we weren't expecting it to drive or even much change our overall business success. And we knew nothing about banner ads, other than that we could lose up to 30 pounds in three weeks just by clicking on one.

What Kyle and I did know was that we could talk about MouseDriver and what we were doing in concrete, understandable language. It was real.

Some parts of it were all too real. While the dot-coms were fueling outrageous spending habits (another *Chronicle* tidbit—the Bay Area Mercedes and BMW dealerships were wait-listing purchasers, most of whom were under 30), we were doing a monthly budget for things like postage. We'd hired someone to clean our apartment the first month, but after paying $111, it was off to the store for $5 worth of sponges and cleanser.

It wasn't just that we were paupers at the dot-com ball. We were also the serfs living in the flatlands under the castles on the hill. Not five blocks uphill from us, in Pacific Heights, were the billionaires' mansions, with sweeping views of the Golden Gate Bridge. People like the oil-rich Gettys, Oracle founder Larry Ellison, and San Francisco Giants owner Peter Magowan were technically our neighbors. Not that we were expecting them to drop by and borrow a cup of sugar.

Basically, we were surrounded.

We decided that all we could do was not worry about it. We had to keep our eye on the ball, stay on our path, don't worry about what they got, just sit and stir our own pot and all of that. We too were on our way up, albeit at a slightly slower pace than the rest of the whole damn city.

We had to give ourselves more credit. We'd not only solved our MouseDriver manufacturing problems, we'd taken an important lesson from the experience as well, learning that sometimes better is the enemy of good. We were ready to focus on our next big challenge: Sales.

Determined to keep our spirits up, we devised a plan that would break the monotony of our days and get us out of the apartment.

We joined a gym. We found a 24-Hour Fitness, ironically open sixteen hours a day, that offered a great package. We could work out at any 24-Hour Fitness anywhere, important since we anticipated doing a lot of business travel once all of our sales got under way. We could also get a substantial discount by agreeing to use the gym only during the "nonpeak" hours, good for saving much-needed cash and not a problem since we had flexible schedules.

Oh, and one more bonus. Kimberly, the cute trainer signing us up, told us that we could get a discount if we registered as partners. A business-friendly gym. That was cool. I turned to my partner. Kyle looked at me, then at her. "Partners?" he asked. "You mean partners-partners?"

Oh, partners-partners. San Francisco–type partners. Domestic partners. "How much of a discount?"

It was enough. Who cared? No one but Kimberly would know, and she didn't care—the rock on her hand showed that she was married, anyway.

Kyle was my friend. He was my roommate. But, like I said, more than anything, he was my partner. Business partner, that is.

DARKNESS, DARKNESS, DARKNESS, DARKNESS

They're nonessentials. Accounting and jargon and quarterly reports, e-mails, off-sites, and acquisitions, memoirs of boardroom melodramas and erratic CEOs, high-priced consultants and how-to books and analysts lobbing sound bites to fast-talking cable news anchors with stock tickers streaming across the bottom of the screen. Whirlwinds of words and numbers. Take them away, and what's left are the fundamentals of business.

Making and selling.

That's all any business is, really, from Boeing to a corner lemonade stand. The rest is dreaming, description, and distraction.

Making and selling. That's what our business boiled down to, for all our scheming and schooling, all our planning and diving in, all the lessons we'd learned from experience and advice and reading, and all the breakthroughs and setbacks we'd seen and were yet to see. As Platinum Concepts, Inc. neared the end of its first summer, that's how we defined our work, in terms any six-year-old could understand.

As for making, after a barrage of e-mails and telephone calls with Kenny, we had high hopes that we'd gotten our manufacturing problems under control. The final 400 units of our initial 500-unit order were due to arrive in the last week of August, at which point we would see how well our long-distance pestering of East Asia Action Express had panned out. Kenny had dedicated himself to correcting all the problems we'd discovered in the first 100 MouseDrivers we'd received, and his reports from Hong Kong had reassured us. The next 400 to come our way would arrive with sturdier click buttons, a better color on which to contrast corporate logos, and a rebuilt housing for the mouse, which eliminated any and all crooked labeling problems.

The good news out of Hong Kong encouraged us. We mailed most of the handful of MouseDrivers that we hadn't smashed on our living room floor to friends and family, just to get some feedback outside of our apartment, and planned to send out the 400 we'd soon receive to the rest of our evangelist network and a few prospective clients.

We also followed through with another step in our business plan, placing an order on August 5 with Kenny for an additional 2,500 units, securing it with 50% cash down, agreeing to pay the balance on delivery. We would follow up our August 5 order with an even larger order on September 8, this time for 25,000 units—jumping slightly ahead of schedule for growing our inventory, but still keeping in line (in terms of volume) with our original business plans, which called for a total store of just under 30,000 units by the end of 1999.

We were going forward with our production plans on faith. Though we found Kenny's reports from Asia reassuring, all we'd heard were descriptions and promises. The reality was that the only MouseDrivers we'd ever seen didn't look good and didn't work well. Committing financially to additional (and fairly sizable) orders meant taking on risk in the face of manufacturing uncertainty.

Why had we jumped ahead without any physical proof that our product had improved? Well, first, we felt a need to stick to our original business plan whenever we could, and that meant building up a modest inventory by the end of the calendar year. We couldn't sell what we didn't have, plain and simple. Even though we were no longer anticipating big sales for 1999, we needed to be ready in case the plan changed again. Also, despite the initial evidence, we trusted Kenny. Though sometimes his first responses to our complaints were mildly frustrating, he always turned out to be very receptive to what we asked him to do.

Finally, we knew we couldn't devote all of our time to making MouseDriver. We had to address the issue of selling it, as soon as possible. We were thousands of miles from our factory, and though it was great that we trusted Kenny, the fact of the matter was, we had no choice but to trust him. We didn't have the time or the resources to do otherwise.

As a result, when we weren't troubleshooting manufacturing problems that summer, we were figuring out how to bring ideas for selling MouseDriver out of our marketing plans and into the real world.

We'd followed our latest plan, doggedly pursuing upstairs retailers, but it had stalled—we had trouble reaching buyers, and the ones we did reach told us to call back when the product was finalized and we had plenty of inventory in stock. Determined to get somewhere, anywhere, we'd moved on, back to corporate promotions.

We were becoming experts on the underwhelming world of ASI, the Advertising Specialty Institute. We hit the phones, cold-calling more corporate promotional products buyers, and mixing in a few distributors, companies that hire sales forces to market multiple product lines (which they buy, rather than make) to corporations. After a few weeks of research, ASI had gone from being a nagging three-letter mystery to the obstacle in all our marketing paths.

If we wanted to put logos on MouseDriver (and we did, badly), there didn't seem to be any way around ASI. Every manufacturer of any promotional product anywhere seemed to go through ASI. Every dead-end corporate promotions marketing strategy session Kyle and I had seemed to end with those three letters. If we'd substituted the name Big Sal for ASI, it would've felt like we were in a fifth-rate gangster movie.

"Hey, what if we tried to set up our own network? We've got some contacts, right? People will buy from us. Let's do it ourselves."

"There'll be trouble. We'll get in a couple of places, sure, but sooner or later we'll run into Big Sal. And there'll be trouble, I'm telling ya."

"I don't care about Big Sal."

"You'd better care about Big Sal. Nobody in this business goes around Big Sal and gets very far, get it?"

Big Sal, Big Sal, Big Sal. On one hand, it would have been painless to join ASI. There was only a onetime fee of less than a hundred dollars, and we would have been embraced by ASI's vast network of distributors and suppliers of specialty merchandise as a member of the $16 billion logoing machine. We'd get an ASI number, sort of a stamp of industry approval for all the world to see.

On the other hand, we hated the idea of joining ASI. We hated what it was doing to our marketing plans.

The facts were these: Yes, we did have a few contacts in the corporate promotions industry, and we could make some sales, but probably not enough for our business to thrive. Generally speaking, the purchasers of promotional items at most corporations didn't deal directly with manufacturers like us. They worked with sales representatives from distributors, who sold multiple lines from multiple suppliers, who aggregated products from manufacturers such as ourselves. In other words, the core of our corporate market wanted us to be at the back end of a long chain of middlemen, all working under the blessing of ASI. It felt like a rigged game, and we hated rigged games.

This wasn't just an emotional response; the insistence of corporate buyers and ASI that we join in a manufacturer-supplier-distributor-sales rep conga line meant trimming our gross margins, a big part of the financial stronghold of our business plan. We couldn't know how deep the cut might be before entering negotiations with some suppliers and distributors, but even the idea was unsettling. The alternative—raising prices to incorporate margins for our new middlemen—didn't seem attractive either.

On top of that, we didn't like being defined solely as manufacturers. We were entrepreneurs. We wanted to do it all, to have the whole experience, to make and sell. Handing over the sales function seemed like no fun at all.

And on top of that, we still just couldn't get over how tacky ASI seemed to us. We didn't want our product affiliated with crappy coffee mugs and awful paperweights and horrible bobblehead dolls (okay, Kyle has a bobblehead doll and the thing is hilarious). Every time we talked about ASI, our inner snobs would rise up, joining forces with our pride of ownership and insistence on product quality, and leave us both in bad moods.

In addition to mapping out the world of ASI for us, the cold calls we made to potential customers and distributors gave us an education on another front, one we needed but maybe didn't want.

We'd tried to work our backgrounds into our pitch, especially when talking to distributors. The plan was to introduce ourselves, talk for a few moments about our MBA backgrounds, and then go into our spiel. Big mistake. It didn't take many phone calls to realize that in the promotional products industry, nobody gave a rat's ass about what graduate school we went to. In fact, 75% of the people we talked to hadn't heard of Wharton. Just the letters MBA put a lot of people off. Maybe they'd had some negative experience with a hotshot MBA consultant or manager who'd come into a company where they'd worked and laid everybody off. Who knew? Anyway, we ended up dropping the MBA angle in our opening conversations. We discovered that using that part of our story was effective later on, in follow-up conversations with distributors, after they'd grown comfortable talking to us and wanted to know a little more about who we were. Then it was an asset—they'd get interested in why we were doing what we were doing and begin to feel like we were including them in our venture, which we were. We were seeking their advice and opinions, and they became eager to help.

Unfortunately, what they told us wasn't what we wanted to hear. According to the distributors, the only way to get around ASI membership was to team up with a supplier who was a member of ASI. That way we could avoid our own product quality/inner snob issues about joining while still enjoying the benefits of being in ASI's network (or Big Sal's good graces, depending on how we looked at it).

We weren't thrilled with the idea of a supplier, but cold-calling corporations hadn't gone any better from California than it had from Texas. Corporate buyers of promotional products still wanted to pick and choose items from multiple product lines, all with the ASI seal of approval. We were losing our taste for cold-calling rejection, and decided to look for a supplier to team up with. We would have to rethink our pricing schedules and figure out a way to defend our margins, but we knew working with a supplier was our way in on the corporate side.

It didn't take much research into suppliers to find a catch, again courtesy of ASI. It turned out that almost all the best sellers among ASI products had been really strong retail products between 18 and 24 months prior to moving on to the corporate promotions circuit. Which meant we had to become a hit in retail before even approaching a supplier for ASI.

Let's review. First, we'd wanted to market to both corporate and retail at the same time. Then, Steve Little of Team Mouse had informed us in the middle of June that we'd missed the retail Christmas season. So we'd shifted our focus to corporate only. Then we'd gotten shut out of corporate when trying to sell direct, thumbed our noses at the ASI route, and backpedaled to the upstairs portion of our upstairs/downstairs retail strategy. Oops, not enough inventory for retail, so back to ASI to suppliers, who told us to get a hit in retail first. When it came to marketing strategy, we'd already flip-flopped on our flip-flops, and it was only our first summer.

Our prize at the end of all our about-faces was jumping back into retail, worse off than we'd left it. We were now certain we'd missed the boat for the rest of 1999. The new plan was to bring MouseDriver to retail storefronts in 2000 and then try to go big in ASI (corporate sales) in 2001–2002.

We also realized at this point that, if it were to succeed, MouseDriver wasn't going to be a two-year project. A month or so of phone calls and strategy reassessment had added at least a year to that total. We weren't going to sell 100,000 mice in twelve months. We weren't going to be millionaires in an 18- to 24-month time frame. Not the end of the world, certainly, but the end of some of our illusions.

We'd made a common entrepreneurial mistake, one that counterbalanced most of the things we'd done right so far. We'd come up with a great product, one that we could make and sell profitably. We'd secured financing and worked out reasonably solid business and marketing plans. But we'd spent too little time on distribution.

In a way, this was understandable. All we'd done was create one product. We had no prior experience or knowledge of the industry category our product fell under. We were confident that there would be demand for what we had and figured distribution wasn't a strategic problem but rather a logistical one. We thought distribution was just a step along the way.

Looking back, I'm not too sure why we thought that we could bring MouseDriver to market just a few months after graduation and sell something like $5 million worth of product during our first year. I could point to a mix of MBA enthusiasm and arrogance. I could lay it on the doorstep of the boom market all around us at the time. Everybody everywhere was under the spell of the New Economy, and spoke of building huge businesses out of nothing in six months flat. I know we believed in what we had; I guess we both assumed that once we had the product, it would just sell itself.

Whatever the reason, we were dead wrong. It turned out that in our business (as in so many others), distribution was the most important element of all. Every other part of the business played off it. In fact, you could make a reasonable argument for starting a novelty product business completely backwards from what we'd done, by lining up distribution first, and then moving on to trivial matters like inventing a product.

We'd focused too much on the big picture and strategy, and not enough on details and execution, and we were paying the price for our oversights. It was going to take time to build out distribution, build product awareness, and make money. We'd jumped into Platinum Concepts as an adventure, but now it was a real business. We would have to go back to the painstaking process of updating all of our models to reflect that fact.

                        *   *   *

On August 24, a box arrived from Hong Kong. In it were the final 400 units of our very first order of MouseDrivers. We were in trouble.

As promised, Kenny had taken care of a lot of problems. This time the curves and slopes on the top side of the mouse were as we'd envisioned them. The logos were no longer crooked. The click buttons no longer broke easily, and these MouseDrivers fared much better in the drop test we'd concocted with our first batch, surviving the crashes without any damage.

All of that was good. The only major problem that remained from the first shipment had to do with the color. Instead of having a single uniform color (like a golf club head would), these MouseDrivers were suspiciously two-toned—the top of the mouse was lighter than the bottom. It looked like someone had given the tops a poor corrective paint job. And though Kenny had been right about one thing—the new color served as a better backdrop for the PGA logo—overall, the mice looked terrible as a result.

Still, as problems went, the color was minor. Aggravating, but minor. We were in trouble because of what our evangelist network had been telling us even before the 400 MouseDrivers had arrived.

The friends and family to whom we'd sent the first few un-smashed MouseDrivers had come back to us with a number of insights, most of which we hadn't anticipated. They hadn't seemed to notice or care about the crooked labels or self-de-structing click buttons (perhaps they neglected to perform drop tests in the comfort of their own homes). What they had cared about was the mouse feeling too light in their hands. They wanted MouseDriver to be as heavy as a golf club head.

This was nuts. It was a PC mouse, not a golf club head. The gimmick was that it looked like a golf club head, but I guess the gimmick worked too well—now it had to feel like a golf club head as well.

A golf club head with a longer cord and possibly a scroll wheel too. Those two suggestions had also come back from our network. Again, helpful insights that were also just a tiny bit de-ranged. Our potential customers wanted a mouse that not only looked but also felt like the real thing, a golf club head. But they also wanted a deluxe mouse. Never mind the Zen question of what was "real" about combining two unrelated physical ob-jects into one. Never mind that neither I nor Kyle nor anyone else in the world had ever seen a golf club head with a scroll wheel or a long plug-in cord, but oh well, the market had spo-ken. We had to make some changes.

We'd gone about it like this: Just before Kenny was ready to ship our final 400 samples, we did what we'd learned how to do best that summer. We went into the kitchen and started breaking apart MouseDrivers. Only this time, we were creative rather than destructive. We opened up the rollerball housings, and then later the mouse itself, and put quarters inside MouseDrivers. We used different allotments of quarters to fool around with

MouseDrivers of different weights. It was odd, half-scientific fun, test-driving mice for weight and feel on the kitchen counter.

We decided six quarters per mouse worked the best, which translated to 32 grams of additional weight to be added to MouseDriver. We went online and shot an e-mail message to Kenny, trying to catch him before he shipped. He came back to us, agreeing to include two different weighted samples in the shipment of 400. We decided we loved Kenny.

So we opened our box when it arrived. We were pleased with the improvements, peeved by the two-toned paint job, and then we found our weighted samples. They felt great. We wanted our next two shipments—one for 2,500 we'd already locked into, and another 25,000 we were getting ready to order—to weigh the same as the two samples. We hopped on the phone to Kenny.

We told Kenny how much we liked the weighted samples.

"Yes, they're much different with the weight."

We asked how much it would cost to add the weight.

"Add weight? Oh, it should run you about a dollar per unit."

We asked about lengthening the cord, from five feet to six. And about adding a scroll wheel.

"Lengthening the cord should run you about twelve cents per unit. Adding a scroll wheel changes everything. That would double the cost of the whole product."

We didn't need to run any numbers. It was yes on the weighting, yes on the cord, no on the scroll wheel for now. We asked Kenny when he could get these things done.

"Get them done? The cord is no problem. But we can't add the weight. Adding weight changes everything. Add weight, add four weeks to every schedule. Forget about the weight."

We could wait for a better MouseDriver. We asked Kenny to add the weight.

"You can give me extra time? You agree to pay more? I can't add the weight anyway. You have to change your design."

This was very, very aggravating. We were staring at the MouseDriver people wanted to buy, and we couldn't manufacture it, not without major delays.

Kyle joked, "Hey, you know what? Kenny could ship us MouseDriver as is. Then we could put the weights in ourselves. Six quarters per unit. I estimate our costs would be, oh, around $1.50 a pop." I threw a two-toned MouseDriver at him.

The bottom line: We wouldn't get the weights in on our order of 2,500. And we'd also have to pass on changing it for our order of 25,000. No matter how quickly we changed our design, the risk of delays on our first substantial inventory investment wasn't worth it. We committed to our order of 25,000 in a call to Kenny on September 8.

That's how our production run of samples ended—with a slow slide from inspiration to frustration. We sent out most of the remaining 400 MouseDrivers in our possession to the rest of our evangelist network, holding back only a modest reserve, which we planned to take into a handful of California retailers to test-market and price our product.

The end of summer found us battered but still standing. We had survived a series of setbacks and strategic reversals in our marketing plans and come full circle to concentrate on retail. We had come out on the other side of a lot of production wrangles with Kenny, our prospective customers, and, frankly, our own expectations. We didn't get everything we wanted right away, but at least, when all was said and done, we would end the year with 98% of our inventory being the highest quality MouseDriver we could produce—an original-weight, long-corded, non-scroll-wheeling mouse in a single attractive color with perfectly applied logos. All in all, we thought we had weathered the storm.

Of course, we were wrong again.

It all came at us furiously fast. On September 16, just eight days after we made our final purchase order of 1999, Typhoon York hit Hong Kong. We first heard it from Kenny, then we clicked on CNN to find out exactly what a typhoon was. An uneasy stretch of a few hours passed as we waited for further information from Kenny. We expected him to give us a cheerful call and tell us our latest shipment had sunk to the bottom of the South China Sea (which, apparently, happens far more than you would think).

Kenny reached us with good news: No sunken ships to report, and the factory where our MouseDrivers were produced had made it through the typhoon in one piece. If there were any production delays at all, they would be minor, maybe only a day or two.

We were always told to expect the unexpected when it came to manufacturing, but we'd assumed that meant garden-variety production mishaps and governments collapsing. We'd thought natural disasters were more our territory, here in earthquake-friendly San Francisco. Silly us.

Six days later, a lonely little shipment of MouseDrivers arrived at Platinum Concepts, Inc. world headquarters. It was the first batch of 40 of our order of 2,500, and it sucked.

Somehow, everything had gone wrong with these MouseDrivers, in new and horrible ways. The white plastic trays in our flashy new boxes were all split apart. That was because something was wrong with how our flashy new boxes were put together in the first place.

The two-color problem had gone away, but its replacement wasn't any better—a splotchy, inconsistent paint job on every mouse. If we rolled the mice on any surface and then lifted them up quickly, the rollerballs would fly out of the mice in a desperate bid for rollerball freedom. And the two click buttons at the top of the mouse were suspiciously raised, as though another rogue redesign had taken place in Hong Kong without our knowing.

To top it all off, Dave Ramsey called. Dave had helped us out during the whole PMS color/golf driver runaround, and now he was one of our evangelists. He called just after we opened our box of truly awful MouseDrivers and said, "Hey guys, um. I got your thing in the mail. Yeah, I like it, the look and feel and everything, but overall, it's kind of cheap and plasticky, don't you think?"

Thanks, we already knew.

We spent a couple of days sorting through the wreckage and decided to gather our thoughts and come up with a plan before going back to Kenny. We were frustrated. We couldn't get our minds around the fact that we had an all-new set of production problems, right after we thought we'd fixed them all.

Then, September 27, 1999. What Kyle and I refer to as our all-time favorite day.

Our plan was to call Kenny and go through the production problems. But Kenny beat us to the punch. There had been an earthquake on the 24th in Taiwan, where the integrated circuits for MouseDriver were manufactured. Kenny was placing calls to find out if any damage had occurred, and what kind of production delays we might expect on our order of 25,000 units.

We hung up the phone and waited. Later in the day, we received another shipment of 40 mice. This time, some of the old problems reappeared. The click button ribs weren't reinforced (as they should have been from our redesign), so the button mechanism was easily breakable once again. And an extra screw under the label at the bottom of the mouse was missing. But we couldn't focus on any of that; we were worried about Taiwan.

We had a huge order on the way, and Taiwan was part of the production chain. Kyle pointed out that we hadn't finished filing for business insurance yet. If there were a natural disaster affecting our 25,000-unit order, we were screwed. I pointed out how there'd been two natural disasters in ten days, and we were still waiting to find out if we were screwed.

Then our friend Ed McClung called us. We told him about the earthquake and the typhoon, and he told us he had another disaster for us. We'd asked him to check out whether MouseDriver could be made compatible with USBs, a type of serial port in specialty PCs. The answer was yes, he said, for around $50 per unit, many times the cost for a regular PS/2 MouseDriver. Which meant the answer was no.

Kenny e-mailed us. He was still looking into getting a report from Taiwan, and said delays were possible for our 25,000 integrated circuits. Then he asked whether we'd received any new MouseDriver shipments. We let him have it, but gently. He'd just been through two natural disasters, after all.

He asked whether we'd gotten the Moon Cakes he'd sent us.

Kyle checked the mail and found the box. Moon Cakes.

We wrote back. What are Moon Cakes?

Moon Cakes, Kenny explained, were the secret mail system of Chinese rebels. Apparently the Chinese once hid notes in bread at dinner to coordinate a revolt against the government. Now the Chinese celebrate by eating cakes with egg yolk centers.

We didn't quite get it, but it was a nice gesture by Kenny. A novelty gift from China. One that hadn't been flattened by a typhoon or destroyed in an earthquake or compromised by button and rollerball issues or hamstrung by ASI.

We'd suffered some setbacks, but until now, we'd had a hand in our own troubles. We hadn't researched, we hadn't anticipated, we'd overestimated and underestimated. If we weren't making or selling effectively, it was because of something we'd done, and there was always something we could do to correct it. Now it was different. Now we were in a maelstrom of wildly bad luck.

We ate our Moon Cakes and wondered what would happen next.

GOOD GOD,
WE MAKE A SALE

Something my granddad used to say was finally making sense. You can't fall off the floor.

Mother Nature had beaten us up, manufacturing had been rocky, and sales and distribution had been at best incomprehensible and at worst impenetrable. Things could only get better.

They did. Shortly after we received the 40 splotchy MouseDrivers, followed by the 40 better-looking but weak-buttoned MouseDrivers, we heard from Kenny that the remaining 2,420 MouseDrivers of our 2,500 order were on their way, delayed just four days by their run-in with Typhoon York. Production was also going smoothly with our earthquake-endangered 25,000 order, which Kenny said we could expect to arrive by the end of October.

But that good news took a backseat to even better news. We had made a sale.

In our long-ago first MouseDriver sales strategy, Kyle and I had assumed that we would sell directly to corporations and retailers. We based this strategy on our expectation that sales would be next to effortless—once people became aware of MouseDriver, it would sell itself.

Our evangelist mailings supported the corporate promotions side of this strategy (and served the immediate function of gathering feedback on the product). So we'd put MouseDriver in the hands of our friends, family, and former classmates for them to in turn introduce it to all of their corporate colleagues. Initially, we'd hoped that the network would expand in no time, penetrating every big business with MouseDriver evangelists, followed closely by logo-plastered MouseDrivers themselves, all by word of mouth. Now that we knew better, we were gearing more toward 2000–2001 for moving mice in this market, via an ASI supplier. But our evangelist network could be a secret weapon—not only a way around ASI to the corporate promo market, but also potentially a quicker way in.

And now, lo and behold, the strategy had worked. Our very first corporate sale was to the Municipal Advisory Council of Texas (MAC), which expressed interest in purchasing 75 logoed MouseDrivers, then a week later placed an order for 100. Kyle drew a "Q4 1999 Sales" graph on our office/kitchen whiteboard, hatched the bottom axis with marks representing weeks, and connected the two figures with a fat red line. "Check it out," he announced, "That's a 33% increase in sales. Swee-eet!"

It felt great. We were finally using all of the structures we'd worked so hard to put into place—the pad printing, the packaging, the evangelist network. In fact, the MAC sale had come through our top evangelist, a financial advisor at UBS PaineWebber named Cathy Lusk.

Given that Cathy was also my mom, though, the sale didn't quite generate the same degree of excitement and gratification that Kyle and I had envisioned for MouseDriver's official entry into the marketplace. Yes, it felt great, but it didn't feel one hundred percent legitimate. It reminded me of a pathetic story a friend of mine told about working at a department store one Christmas break during college selling a contraption that would remove yarn pills from sweaters. She stood there hour after hour, day after day, ignored by every shopper, until her mom bought dozens of the things and shipped them off to distant relatives who probably complained about not getting the usual fruitcakes. When it comes to their kids, moms will do anything, especially for an only child like me. The MAC sale was definitely real—my mom didn't buy the MouseDrivers herself—but not real enough.

Fortunately, our first "real" sale wasn't far behind, courtesy of another key evangelist, a Wharton friend of ours named Caskie Collet. Caskie took MouseDriver to the head of Bank of America's investment banking recruiting department, then called us himself with the news. "Hey Lusk. It's Caskie. Put me on speaker," he drawled. I did. "Guys. How about y'all printing up 200 with the BofA logo?"

Yeeha! Now it was time to celebrate. We were psyched, for two main reasons.

First, the sale meant validation—a big investment bank ordering our product. One customer buying, we reasoned, meant others were sure to follow.

Second, we thought that all of our former classmates would be right on Caskie's heels, pitching MouseDrivers to their merchandising managers and selling 200 units a pop. With all of the people we knew in banking and consulting, we were poised to make a mint on referrals alone.

Since Caskie was one of the many Wharton alumni now residing in San Francisco—he lived just a couple of doors down from us—we kicked off our Platinum Concepts, Inc. Sales Rewards Program right then and there. As soon as he got home from work, we took him out for a few drinks.

Back in our office/kitchen later that night, Kyle drew another graph on the whiteboard. Skipping over the numbers, he made a quick, swoosh-shaped line. "Look at that steep demand curve," he admired. "Know what we need to go with it? We need some supply."

Kyle didn't miss a trick—the very next day, we got word that the 2,420 MouseDrivers had arrived. We'd arranged to have them delivered straight to the pad printers, who would store them so they'd be ready to fill logo orders for companies like Bank of America and the MAC at a moment's notice. After finding Graphatic and Anita in nearby Hayward (thanks to the Plan C Yellow Pages), we'd gotten a recommendation from some ASI distributors for another pad printer, Graphic Images Line in Nashville, Tennessee. We'd decided to give both of them a whirl and see what worked best—2,420 MouseDrivers to Nashville, 25,000 MouseDrivers to Hayward.

We'd already sent two MouseDrivers to Nashville ourselves for a quick turnaround printing of the logo for chipshot.com, the top golf equipment and accessories e-tailer, which we were planning to go after as a good fit for MouseDriver sales. They'd come back looking great, which was encouraging after all of the crooked PGA logos. Steve Little and Team Mouse, by the way, loved the PGA sample and would be all systems go on MouseDriver once they finished recapitalizing the company. Who knew, if things kept going like they were, we might end up needing both pad printers just to keep up with orders.

Chipshot.com marked the debut of our revised 1999 retail sales strategy, which, with three steps, was a bit more complicated than the "hit up friends and family" revised 1999 corporate sales strategy. We had planned to (1) schedule a meeting with chipshot.com's buyers, (2) hand the buyers the logoed chipshot.com MouseDrivers, and (3) close the sale.

Driving back up Highway 101 from Sunnyvale after completing steps 1 and 2, Kyle and I speculated. Chipshot.com had agreed that MouseDriver would be a great giveaway and retail item for them, especially for Christmas. We'd told them that our maximum shipping volume for 1999 was 20,000. Maybe they would order all of it.

Maybe. But for how much? Since we hadn't gotten into retail yet, we hadn't debuted our small-samples-at-different-prices test-marketing in stores, so we didn't have a definite retail pricing schedule. We weren't sure what the market would bear. We could consider the data from our two corporate sales, but even there our supply and demand graph was only a couple of days old.

Without a set retail price, we didn't know what base price we should sell MouseDrivers to retailers for, either. We'd decided to start at the top of our range. We'd told chipshot.com that, depending on volume, we could sell at $20 to $25 per MouseDriver, leaving them room for a healthy profit if they followed our current "MSRP" (manufacturer's suggested retail price, where, hey, we were the M!) of $39.95.

The numbers chipshot.com came back with were off—they wanted to buy at somewhere between $12 to $15 per unit, still sell for $39.95, and start with an order of 100. Initially, Kyle and I agreed that we wouldn't budge on the per unit base price. Then we budged. Honestly, we wanted the sale and were eager to work with a dot-com. We settled on $17 (along with a promise that we'd be featured on the chipshot.com homepage at Christmas) and didn't know if we'd won or lost. But at least we knew that $39.95 could work.

Our Wharton friend Nick Rothman, who was at PrizeCentral.com, heard about our feeling our way around retail pricing and the dot-com market, and he offered to help. He proposed that we put MouseDriver on the site's sports prize section. PrizeCentral.com aimed at online gamers, so it wouldn't hit our target market, but it could give us a feel for how people responded to our price. It sounded good in theory. (A month and a half and 1,100 entries to win later, the reality was that PrizeCentral.com had ultimately affected the fates of just two MouseDrivers—one prize and one purchase.)

Another haphazard swing at the dot-com world got us a deal with ChristmasGolf.com, without even showing them logoed MouseDrivers first. For the hell of it, we also stuck a MouseDriver on the dot-com to end all dot-coms, eBay. Bidding started at $10 and surged to $13 before topping out at $15.50. We tried the experiment a few more times, playing with higher minimum bids to learn more about our pricing. For the most part, the results supported our $29.95-$39.95 thinking.

*   *   *

Considering all of the switches we'd seen in our sales strategies, we were pleased overall with the beginning of our fall 1999 sales efforts. We had a decent start on corporate sales and a couple of dot-com deals. Similarly, we thought that our limited official marketing efforts to date—through evangelists and golf Web sites—were fairly effective. We couldn't wholly assess marketing, though, without looking at our own evangelizing, which Kyle and I did in all of our communications, every day.

I generally put next to no stock in "how-to" business books, but Guy Kawasaki's ideas on marketing and PR resonated with me—basically, position yourself, get it right, and make sure that everyone else gets it right, so that no one ever says about you, "They kinda do . . . uh, it's like that other company that does . . . "

So for our first big proactive marketing move, I created a synopsis of our story, something that we could easily explain to people on the phone or communicate in a paragraph or two via e-mail. Every chance that we got, we would tell the story. The story being: Why would two Wharton MBAs bypass the six-figure salaries of banking, consulting, and dot-com to manufacture a computer mouse out of their kitchen? People would conclude the answer—because they had a great product that they believed in.

Whenever we talked to anyone about MouseDriver—whether a supplier, vendor, sales rep, or bank teller—we always pitched the story, making sure that the person fully understood the origins of the product, trying to get them invested in its success. Everyone, we told ourselves, was a potential customer.

To help spread the story, we needed to get our Web site up. We weren't overly concerned about enabling it for online sales, since MouseDriver was so new that people would definitely want to touch and handle it before they purchased the thing, but we did need it as a marketing tool, a repository of all MouseDriver information.

Kyle, whiz that he is, wrestled with FrontPage for all of a day, and we were set. MouseDriver.com wasn't flashy, wasn't deep, and often wasn't available (we'd gone for the $7 a month Web hosting option, so its constantly being on the fritz wasn't a big surprise), but it was functional enough to do the job for the time being. We would spend more money when we had more money to spend.

Still slightly paranoid of competitors and knockoffs, we did go ahead and fork over the cash to monopolize the market on relevant domain names. Golfmouse.com, drivermouse.com, and justdriveit.com were ours, all ours. The last one had come to us during a brainstorming session for a new tagline and may have been partially inspired by the swooshlike shape of Kyle's whiteboard demand curve. To protect ourselves from any copyright infringement suits, we filed to trademark it. Again, more cash. Lots of cash, actually, since lawyers with hourly billings were involved, but there was no getting around it.

MouseDriver.com was the perfect vehicle for our second big marketing move—the creation of the *MouseDriver Insider* newsletter. The newsletter already existed in an ad hoc form, in all of our e-mail responses to former Wharton classmates who would write, "What did you guys end up doing after that golf-mouse thing?"

"Friends," I wrote.

"Since this venture began in July, we have received a number of inquiries from people asking us to keep them informed of our progress. Most of these inquiries have come from aspiring entrepreneurs currently working in the corporate world who want to 'live the entrepreneurial experience vicariously through us.' However, many of you have asked us to keep you informed simply because you're interested in finding out how this MouseDriver story progresses and ends. After all, some of you were around when this outrageous idea was first used as a class project at Wharton.

"So, we've got an idea . . . and we're hoping that this one generates as much excitement as MouseDriver. Kyle and I would like to keep everyone informed of MouseDriver's progress. On a periodic basis, we'd like to share our successes, our failures, our issues, our stories, and our feelings toward this entrepreneurial

*gig. We basically want to give all of you an opportunity to ac-
company us on this crazy ride.*

*"If you're interested, just reply to this e-mail and say 'I'm in,'
and we'll include you in the mailing.*

"Hope everyone is doing well."

I signed off with Kyle's and my names and sent it to a list of
nearly 100 people, wondering what I had gotten us into.

Like I said, we were happy with where our homemade sales
and marketing efforts had taken us. We looked forward to the
day when we could enlist some professional help, and we knew
we were going to have to get into ASI eventually, but at the moment we couldn't afford anything beyond do-it-yourself. Then
we stumbled upon Brian Fenton and Rick Connelly.

Plugging away, I was cold-calling Bay Area promo products
suppliers and distributors, still sounding out the industry and
looking for some companies to consider. I called one company,
Applied Graphics in San Rafael, and the woman there said that
the guy I needed to talk to was in Monterey. So I called him,
told him about MouseDriver, and sent him a sample along with
some literature. About a week later, the guy called back, saying
that we had a great product and that I had to talk to this guy in
his office.

He put on Brian Fenton, who said that he was an indepen-
dent golf sales rep. He wanted to rep MouseDriver into retail
stores. I was confused. I'd called to talk about the promo products industry and here I was talking to a golf sales rep. Whatever. Brian suggested that he come up to San Francisco
immediately to talk about what he could do for us.

This was completely out of left field. Kyle's and my only decisions on sales reps to date had been that someday, if it made
sense, we would consider having them. But I figured that if
Brian was willing to make a two-hour trip north to meet with a

couple of guys who had made a random product submission, then, hey, he must be serious.

We had no trouble spotting Brian the second we walked in to meet him at Perry's restaurant on Union Street. Only golfers, tennis players, and sailors were that tan. He certainly had a solid golf background—he was an ex-PGA player and pro, which went a long way with us. He'd been a golf rep for ten years, most recently for one of the biggest names in the industry. He asked about our pricing structure, heard our woes, and assured us that he could help implement our test-marketing plan, placing small numbers of MouseDrivers in lots of retail stores and gathering feedback to determine optimal pricing. His retail knowledge also included a very interesting tidbit of information for us.

All retail stores save some holiday shelf space for late-hitting products, i.e.—newsflash—we could still make the retail holiday season. Brian was our man, he could get MouseDriver in stores, he could help us figure out pricing, he could sell truckloads. We just needed to get him MouseDrivers, lots of them.

Not a problem, we assured him. We were expecting 25,000 by the end of the month.

"The end of October? We need them sooner," he said. "I can sell them sooner. We can't risk any delays on this. October means November. You never know what can happen with manufacturing in Asia."

That we knew. So we checked with Kenny to find out how much it would cost to fly rather than ship MouseDrivers to the United States. The importing charges were already impossible to understand—we were sure we were getting screwed, we just hoped not too badly. We also asked Kenny about getting a discount because of all the time we'd spent on the flimsy button issues, which were finally corrected after a few too many hassles.

"Sure, I can get you a discount," Kenny said.

Great! How much would we save?

"Oh, you won't save any money," Kenny explained. "The earthquakes made the costs of components go up. You were looking at a price increase anyway."

Kenny estimated the importing cost difference between ocean and air shipping to be $1.95 per pound. We were at 0.5 pound per mouse, so that meant roughly a dollar a mouse. $25,000, plus all of the customs duties. But if Brian sold all of them, Kyle and I would be looking at Christmas bonus checks to the tune of $100,000 each.

We switched the order from ocean to air and signed the sales rep agreement Brian had sent us. We had nothing to lose, after all—we weren't giving him an exclusive or any particular territory. We did, however give him a 20% commission, idiotically not knowing that was incredibly high.

Brian didn't waste any time. He was on his way to the PGA International Golf Show in Las Vegas and needed a brian@mousedriver.com e-mail account, business cards, MouseDriver samples, media kits, and corporate brochures. He promised to return with feedback on the product, feedback on pricing, and outright orders.

We were dying to get further in retail, but things were moving a tad too fast for us. We had been nurturing MouseDriver's story and image, and we had concerns about turning them over wholesale to someone we'd just met. Was our new sales rep Brian a legal representative of the company? If he screwed up, would we be liable? We equipped him with e-mail, said no on the business cards, and wished him (and ourselves) luck.

The show didn't generate much revenue, but a couple of stores ordered MouseDrivers, enough to get us started on test-marketing the product. Also, a picture of MouseDriver ended up in some golf newsletter, which was really thrilling at the time. Seeing somebody else notice the product that you've spent so much time and effort bringing to market is always cool. The best thing that the show brought us, though, was a phone call from Rick Connelly.

Rick was president of a company of one called Marketing Golf Resources, which specialized in developing marketing and PR programs for small manufacturers and companies in the golf industry. He knew Brian—they both lived in Monterey—and had seen him at the show with MouseDriver. Rick suggested that we all meet in Palo Alto to talk about our plans for the product. We drove down to the Palo Alto Golf Course and waited in the bar for Rick and Brian to show up, killing time watching the Cowboys getting drummed by the Giants on the big-screen TV.

Once we met Rick, everything became clear. Rick knew the golf marketing industry. We, on the other hand, didn't. He'd already put together a marketing and PR plan for MouseDriver that included not only strategies for preparing for the PGA show in Orlando early in 2000 but also a generic marketing strategy on how to tackle the golf industry. We were impressed with what Rick was saying, things like, "I can get your product into these magazines, I can introduce you to these influencers, I can help you get into the PGA shows." We weren't even sure what the PGA shows were all about.

Still, Kyle and I were inclined to be skeptical. We'd both been consultants, so we knew all about charging hours and selling people as experts in an area when they didn't know thing one. We didn't know if this was the case with Rick, and we weren't going to find out without spending $3,000 a month. It was worth the risk, we decided. Between Brian and Rick, if nothing else, we would at least learn a lot about golf and get to play a round at the exclusive Monterey Peninsula Country Club.

Besides, Kyle and I both liked Rick. Maybe not the most logical basis for a business decision, but let's face it, that's the way much of the world works. And here it would work in our favor. We soon found out that everyone liked Rick. He seemed to have connections everywhere in the golf world. And he was such a straightforward guy that it made perfect sense to us when we learned that, as a kid, he was the real-life model for the title character on the TV show *Leave It to Beaver*. His dad was a big-time Hollywood producer and creator of the show. The Beav was doing our marketing.

Brian and Rick took us under their wings, giving us a luxury tour of the golf world. With all of those manicured greens and 19th holes, it was more like a fantasy world. Brian even landed a deal with the National Association of Golf Coaches and Educators (NAGCE) to use logoed MouseDrivers as a fundraiser, with kids selling them door-to-door like cookies. It was surreal.

The fantasy ended, though, on the day that Brian and Rick finally took Kyle and me golfing at the Monterey Peninsula Country Club. Brian was chattering at the tee about how NAGCE was talking about dropping the MouseDriver price to $29.95 until he had threatened not to ship unless they put it right back up at $39.95 where it belonged. Then he stopped to watch Kyle's swing. Kyle awed us all by ripping out a four-inch divot and slicing the ball into the rough. My own divot was smaller, but I lost my ball entirely. Five hours later, we'd done our best to destroy the course. Brian shot a 71—two off the course record—and Rick shot an 83. Both Brian and Rick looked at us somberly and told us that if we were going to be in the golf industry, we were going to have to learn to play without crushing a course. We had to listen to Rick—he'd written a book on how to properly mix business and golf. We were going to have to take lessons.

*   *   *

Brian and Rick were taking us beyond homemade in sales and marketing—with good results—but those weren't the areas where we needed the most help. We still had a major issue to address, one that we'd been going at for a couple of months already and still hadn't tackled—distribution.

Distribution was the single most important part of our business. How were we systematically going to get MouseDrivers into our customers' hands? It looked like the answer was a supplier.

We'd reached that conclusion once we finally understood the depth and power of ASI. But it also fit our own requirements. In the short time we'd been filling corporate promotions and dot-com orders, along with the beginnings of retail orders from Brian, we'd discovered some things about ourselves. We hated invoicing, collecting, shipping, etc. We also hated coordinating the pad printing of individual customer orders on MouseDrivers. It was all tedious detail—getting the artwork from the customer, making sure it was in the right format, sending it to the pad printer, approving a faxed copy, checking to see that the client was ready to go forward, running the print production, doing spec samples, and so on. Kyle, who happened to be the one with all of the artwork software on his computer, especially hated it.

We'd thoroughly considered, then discarded, other options. Direct sales left most of the busywork in our own capable but reluctant and overcommitted hands. Outside sales reps hinged on finding the best reps and, on top of the administrative tasks, demanded too much management from us. Things were going well with Brian, but we weren't eager to build up a team of sales reps and spend all of our time making sure they pushed MouseDriver and watching out for overlaps. Stock-holding distributors would utilize their powerful sales channels and take care of everything we hated, except the awful logoing. And licensing would solve everything before we even started, leaving us with about 3% of total net sales and none of the fun.

A supplier would free us from all of that. Going with an ASI supplier meant we could outsource all of the things that we didn't want to do and focus exclusively on executing our marketing strategy.

ASI suppliers either sourced or manufactured all sorts of trinket-type items, then supplied them, already printed with company logos, to distributors. At that point, the distributors sold the logoed products to corporate customers. Distributors selected product ideas from all of the suppliers out there to feature in their catalogs, which they mailed to their corporate customers.

So, if we sold directly to a supplier, we gained (1) an immediate distribution network, (2) the advantage of reaching more customers while managing fewer, and (3) freedom from all of the routine tasks that were giving us giant headaches. We would expand the distributor network ourselves as we built more relationships, especially in retail.

Finding the right supplier—the next step—was another task entirely. There, we faced the same limitations we had recognized in considering sales reps—we didn't know the industry, so we didn't know which companies were best. We had no experience, no advisors, no class notes, no case studies showing us how to find suppliers. We had a lot of research ahead.

Maybe we would get as lucky as we had on sales reps. Brian was going strong, putting lots of things together for us. He knew a tech guy who could tie an online ordering page to our Web site to give us e-tailing capability. We didn't see any problems with that. If Brian wanted to try to sell MouseDrivers online, more power to him.

Brian had also gotten us approved as an official vendor for Edwin Watts stores, which meant that Edwin Watts headquarters had given the okay for each of the 48 individual Edwin Watts store managers to purchase MouseDrivers as they pleased. This was major. We would send each of them a sample MouseDriver, with a dual purpose—getting them to buy the product for their stores and enlisting them to help finally kick off our retail test-marketing.

We had run the MAC, BofA, and NAGCE printing through Nashville, but this time, for the quickest turnaround, we took 48 MouseDrivers (most of what was left from our first order of 500 samples) straight to Anita to print with the Edwin Watts logo. Then we brought them home to pack for shipping to the 48 Edwin Watts stores. We figured we might as well do it ourselves while we still could—once the order of 25,000 MouseDrivers hit Hayward, we were going to be gunning for Anita, suppliers, anyone but us to handle invoicing, collecting, shipping, and so on.

We spent most of a day assembling boxes, collating ordering information and test-marketing instructions, sealing packages, and printing and sticking labels. After a while, we'd built a sizable MouseDriver package pyramid in the middle of our living room.

They were ready to scatter in the different directions of the 48 Edwin Watts stores, but they needed help getting there. We couldn't exactly stick stamps on them and leave them at the mail slot for our regular postal person. Kyle hauled a huge duffel bag out of his closet, I pulled my old soccer team bag from under my bed, and we started stuffing.

Two dozen each and they were full. We slung our bags over our shoulders and set off for the post office. By appearance, we could have been on our way to the laundromat, except that we were strolling easily rather than stooping under the dead weight of a couple weeks' worth of dirty clothes, and there were a lot of sharp corners poking through our bags.

Walking down Fillmore, right past all of the hot-spot bars gearing up for happy hour, we made quite the spectacle. Kyle had the distant, slightly stunned look of a proud dad on his face, but he was inexplicably carrying a huge sack. I kept forgetting that my bag stuck out a foot and a half on either side of me and nearly took out a few other pedestrians, including Kyle, every time I turned.

We reached the P.O. in less than ten minutes. Taking our places at the end of the long line, we let our bags thump to the floor. It looked like quite a wait. I thought about all of the responses we'd been getting back from our invitation to subscribe to the *MouseDriver Insider,* and all of the people who wanted to hear about our entrepreneurial experience. We had a few stories to tell them.

LOOKING FOR MR. WACKY
WALL WALKER

Our business was shifting again.

We felt the change in our everyday work. We'd begun by taking our ideas and wrestling with them until they made sense on paper. Then we'd struggled to pull our plans back off paper and turn them into a product, which meant financing and double-checked designs, fretful phone calls and shipping orders, with the odd Moon Cake and natural disaster thrown in, courtesy of Kenny. And while we still needed to stay on top of our planning and manufacturing processes, our days were definitely shifting away from paper and product toward people.

People were coming out of the woodwork. Friends of friends, friends of contacts, referrals from evangelists, people who'd met people who'd met us at a party, every one of them calling us about MouseDriver. We were beginning to live life on the phone, setting up meetings, weighing opportunities, and returning to the phone again to set up more of the same.

Our business was telling us something.

It was exciting to have a product up and running and talk to new contacts about marketing deals and alliances, but it was also somewhat bewildering. We'd moved through the paper and product stages and on to the people stage of our business in less than six months, and we needed help. We needed a mentor.

It's not that we hadn't been dealing with people all along—certainly Kenny, Carmine, and Steve Little qualified as people. Until Brian and Rick, however, almost all of our interactions had been about accomplishing concrete tasks, like making MouseDriver. Now our interactions with people were about possibilities for MouseDriver. We needed to gauge people and opportunities with almost no background information. People would call from companies we hadn't heard of and ask for exclusive distribution rights, and we had no idea whether to leap up and say hell yes or hell no. Our interactions with people now had real opportunity costs; going down one road meant never taking another. We'd filled our brains with two years of case studies for just such occasions, but we still needed a guide.

We'd needed one from the beginning, truthfully. We thought we'd find one easily in San Francisco, but like so many other things we'd misperceived about our new home, we'd been off target about identifying an instant local mentor. There may have been some great people, but because we weren't a dot-com, we weren't meeting them. So we'd moved ahead without one.

Certainly we'd survived without a mentor, but when Kyle and I looked back on our first few months in business, we couldn't shake the thought of how much time and money we might have saved if we'd had someone on board advising us. We might have known what to expect in our first encounter with overseas manufacturing. We might have avoided a lot of hassle and re-thinking if someone had helped us to nail the distribution issue a lot earlier. With almost anything that had taken too long or cost us too much, we'd wondered how a mentor might have helped.

Mentor is a tricky word. Everybody has a personal idea about what it means, varying from the sensible to the fantastic. We weren't looking for Merlin from King Arthur's court or the gruff-voiced trainer from *Rocky* (although having someone like Burgess Meredith certainly would have helped). Instead, we wanted somebody with industry experience who could help us get up to speed, make some introductions to key retailers, help us understand distribution, and maybe make a small invest-ment in Platinum Concepts just to have some stake in the game. We didn't want or need someone who could see the fu-ture or tell us what to do step by step. We were hoping for something a lot simpler: Someone we could bounce our ideas off of. A sounding board, a veteran in the kind of entrepreneur-ial experience we were pursuing. A part-time participant, will-ing to take one or two calls from us a month.

Len Lodish met a lot of our mentor requirements. He'd made an investment, and he was great for bouncing our strate-gies off of. Plus, he was like a human refresher course for busi-ness school, helping us frame business problems as they arose.

Len Lodish was also a top-flight entrepreneur, having founded Management Decision Systems, Inc. (MDS) in 1967 with only $2,000 in equity capital. By 1985, he'd grown MDS to 300 employees and merged it with Information Resources, Inc. to become a premier international decision support and mar-keting data supplier, and a real business-to-business success story. He'd followed up by launching another venture in 1991, Shadow Broadcast Services, a broadcast-based provider of traf-fic information, which he sold to Westwood One, Inc. seven years later.

Unfortunately, Len was not the ideal mentor for Platinum Concepts, for one big reason: He lacked retail contacts. Len's entrepreneurial experience had been almost entirely in the business-to-business arena—he didn't know retail. He also didn't know our industry, which meant he couldn't really open doors for us.

Len understood what we were after, and offered to set us up with an entrepreneur with more direct retail start-up experience. He suggested Ken Hakuta, a Washington, D.C.–based Harvard MBA who had started a number of successful businesses. Hakuta's most notable achievement had been the commercialization of the Wacky Wall Walker, a rubberized toy that, when hurled violently against a wall, makes a squishy sound as it sticks, and then walks slowly and spiderlike down to the floor. Hakuta had run across the toy while traveling in Southeast Asia and bought the rights to it. Though his business was privately held, the rumor was that he'd sold 250 million Wacky Wall Walkers, and pocketed in excess of $20 million along the way.

We couldn't believe what we were hearing. Len Lodish was going to set us up with Ken Hakuta, a minor legend among entrepreneurs, a man who sold a quarter of a billion toys to hyperactive eight-year-olds. Mr. Wacky Wall Walker himself.

We asked Len to call Hakuta, and then we did some followup research on our own. Our prospective mentor had moved on from Wacky Wall Walker to create other ventures, including a company that sold cereal box toys and yes, a dot-com—All-Herb.com, an online shopping center for herbs and herbal products. He was a bit of a showman, but he knew how to sell. He had a syndicated children's television show with a live studio audience, in which he would appear before squealing kids, five foot eight, bespectacled, fortyish, and energetic, wearing a solid-colored sweatshirt covered with assorted Wacky Wall Walkers, jumping every few minutes to another toy or game or contest. To promote AllHerb.com, he'd hired an African shaman to host a chat forum and recommend medicinal herb combinations for various ailments.

Despite obvious differences in industry and style, Hakuta seemed like a perfect fit for us. He had retail experience, distribution expertise (and probably contacts), and a good handle on the novelty retail industry. Once we'd heard from Len that Hakuta was interested in talking to us, we sent an e-mail to introduce ourselves to Mr. Wacky Wall Walker.

Then we waited and waited and waited. A week went by with no response. We were busy enough with other tasks, but we'd been eager to talk with Hakuta and were puzzled when nothing had happened. Finally a short e-mail came across our screens.

"This sounds like my type of product. Give me a call."

Exactly what we'd wanted to hear. We thought Hakuta could help us with our greatest fear—the prospect of knockoffs coming out of international markets. He'd had a lot of experience with the knockoff problem, and we thought we'd run our preemptive strategies by him as a jumping-off point. So Kyle called Hakuta and left a message.

But he didn't call back. So Kyle left another message. Again, no reply. We called Len, who'd said he'd talked again with Hakuta about our business, and insisted that Hakuta was interested in speaking with us. So Kyle called again to leave message number three.

Hakuta's lack of response was puzzling and frustrating, but runarounds on the telephone were nothing new to us. We e-mailed him an ultimatum: Contact us soon, or we'll move on to other advising prospects. It worked. He called and we talked for about twenty minutes about MouseDriver. He said he was interested in working with us, and asked that we put together a company overview and investor package for him. Kyle planned a trip to Washington, D.C., to meet with Hakuta in person. Mr. Wacky Wall Walker would see MouseDriver for himself in ten days.

We scrambled to put together a package for Hakuta, and soon Kyle was off to D.C. Kyle called right after his meeting with Hakuta. I was excited. Kyle wasn't.

"How'd it go with Mr. Wacky Wall Walker?"

"Well, he's wacky alright. I got to the coffee shop where we were supposed to meet and he was an hour late. And he left early."

"So what'd he say?"

"He said MouseDriver was a good product but not a great one. And he said he thought knockoffs are going to be a *huge* issue for us."

"Great. Did he have any suggestions?"

"Um, no. Not really. He didn't say anything we didn't already know."

"What'd he say about advising us?"

"Um, he'd said he'd have to talk it over with Len."

Now I felt like Kyle. Hakuta had said he was thinking about investing, but no more than $10,000 (a nominal amount, at best), and he expressed interest in being on our board. Of course he wanted to check on everything with Len first. (We didn't understand this; hadn't he already checked with Len?) It was nice to hear he was interested in what we were doing, but we'd never mentioned our board, partly because it met only once a month—to go over the formalities and reports a board goes over—and also because we were more interested in him as a mentor, a concept he didn't seem to grasp fully.

Mr. Wacky Wall Walker turned out to be a kind of wacky we didn't understand. Kyle never got a feel for his sense of humor.

("He told a lot of stories and laughed a lot for no apparent reason.") And the more Hakuta talked, the less sure Kyle had been that he could help us out with distribution and sales contacts—he was concentrating on AllHerb.com, and his retail contacts seemed a little dated.

Still, when Kyle returned, we both decided to go a little further with Hakuta. We sent him our strategy for defending against knockoffs. Most of it revolved around our patent and our plans for a licensing deal with the PGA. We also proposed a plan for product redesign, to expand our product line just as knockoffs might start to encroach on our markets. A lot of it was speculative, but we wanted to see how Hakuta would respond.

Of course, Hakuta didn't respond. We didn't hear anything for two weeks, until we'd e-mailed Len Lodish and asked him what was the deal with Mr. Wacky Wall Walker. Len came back to us a day later, telling us that Hakuta had wanted his blessing before working with us. Len had given it, and now Hakuta was on board as an advisor.

That was great, except we hadn't heard anything from our new advisor. We couldn't reach him ourselves, except by relying on Len as a go-between. That was totally unworkable, not to mention weird. What good was an advisor we couldn't reach on our own?

And just as we were speculating about what to do next to catch Mr. Wacky Wall Walker's attention, a surprise offer came our way and took our minds off him entirely.

Our friend J.T. had called from PayMyBills.com to say that Doug Baron, his CFO, wanted to talk to us. Doug took the phone from J.T. and proceeded to tell us what a phenomenal product we had. He had all sorts of ideas for blowing out the product for Christmas '99 and asked if we were looking for investors. We were flattered to hear the word "phenomenal" associated with the word "MouseDriver" and eager to gather more suggestions for a major holiday offensive, but we were quick to tell Doug that no, we weren't looking for general investors. That, it seemed, was the end of that. We continued on with our daily sprint through telephone calls and e-mails.

Then a few days later, Doug's brother called. He introduced himself as John Baron, and explained that he worked with some former professional golfers who were "really interested" in meeting with us. He named names, including three we recognized immediately: John Schroeder (an ex-pro and a cofounder of Cobra Golf), and Senior Tour pros Chi Chi Rodriguez and Gary McCord. We'd seen all of them on television as players and commentators for both the PGA and Senior Tours. McCord had even been in one of our favorite movies, *Tin Cup*. Baron invited us to fly down to San Diego to meet him for a drive and a meeting at John Schroeder's house in Rancho Santa Fe.

We'd never heard of Rancho Santa Fe, but we were still excited. In truth, we were kind of star-struck; we were only a few months into our venture, and already some big names in the golf field were noticing our product. We didn't expect anything would come out of it, but we were definitely interested in what Baron and his stable of golf pros had to say. We assembled another company overview package and booked a flight to San Diego the following week. Just for fun, we left a message with Hakuta before we took off.

"Hi, Ken. John and Kyle. Huge deal in the works here at Platinum Concepts. Would really appreciate getting some of your insights. Catch you later."

John Baron picked us up at the San Diego airport in a black Jeep Grand Cherokee. He was in his mid-thirties, a few years older than Kyle and I, and our first exchanges with him seemed nice and relaxed. The plan was to head to Schroeder's house in Rancho Whatever and then head out to a waterside restaurant in posh La Jolla, where we'd talk business.

By the time the plates had been cleared, Kyle and I had heard the pitch. John Baron's group thought MouseDriver was a great idea, and they wanted to make a $500,000 investment in Platinum Concepts, Inc. They wanted most of that money to be directed toward shooting an infomercial about MouseDriver that would star Gary McCord and possibly also Chi-Chi Rodriguez, which Baron's group would produce. Between the infomercial and their contacts in the golf industry and retail, they claimed they could easily sell MouseDriver to large department stores and mass merchandisers. The bottom line: We would be looking at selling one million units in the next 12–18 months. The catch: There was no way they'd do the deal without the infomercial.

That was some lunch. Kyle and I flew back to San Francisco with way too many thoughts about a deal that had come out of nowhere. For starters, John Baron had mentioned the figure of one million units with a straight face. That would have put our gross revenues at five times the size of our most optimistic estimates for two years into the business. That was thrilling, but also hard to believe. Baron's group certainly brought the golf celebrity firepower. Not Tiger Woods, but still good—for starters, John Schroeder's mammoth house was full of trophies and pictures of him with every other famous golfer who ever lived. But one million units, well, that was more MouseDrivers than we could imagine selling in a 12- to 18-month time frame. We weren't even sure our manufacturer—that is, Kenny and his connections—could make that many that fast.

The infomercial strategy also made us uneasy. We'd started out making a simple product; if we accepted this deal, we'd suddenly be in the television business. With Gary McCord and Chi Chi Rodriguez. With a half-hour infomercial on a computer mouse. How could anyone spend more than a couple of television minutes demonstrating how MouseDriver worked?

We had visions of ridiculous infomercial skits. Like Chi Chi Rodriguez losing his grip on a golf driver, watching it fly off the course and crash through the window of a nearby house into the hands of an unsuspecting home PC user. The PC user would look at the driver, scratch his head and say, "If only someone could come up with a mouse that looked and felt as good as this golf club head. . . ." Really awful stuff. The kind of thing you only see late at night on infomercials, preferably at the end of a lot of drinking.

Cheesiness aside, no matter how we came at it, the Baron group's insistence on the infomercial didn't make sense. Unless, as we both suspected, they also had some prearrangement with an infomercial production company.

Parts of the deal were tempting. We had no doubt that bringing these guys into the picture could help sell MouseDriver. We were especially interested in working with John Schroeder, who had helped Cobra Golf flourish. And we daydreamed of ending up on all sorts of fabulous golf courses in San Diego to talk business with these guys on a weekly basis.

Still, we kept coming back to the infomercial. Baron's group wanted a lot of equity for their investment, and their infomercial strategy ran counter to a lot of what we'd planned for MouseDriver. We saw MouseDriver as a niche market item, targeting affluent customers, women buying gifts, impulse purchasers, and the like. The television approach seemed too broad and likely to miss the mark. It also ran counter to our idea of building up loyalty in a defined niche before rolling out MouseDriver to the mass market. The infomercial not only seemed like a huge waste of money, but it also seemed likely to undermine our ability to go to the high end of the market first.

Despite our misgivings, we could also see Baron's offer another way. We wondered how we'd have felt if this offer had cropped up two years into the business, instead of in the first few months. We could make a good argument that—assuming these guys would follow through on what they were saying—accepting the offer would be winning the entrepreneurial war without ever having gone into battle. We would have a major investor and marketing firepower beyond anything we'd anticipated in our original plans, all without lifting a finger. We could give up equity, take a smaller piece of a much larger pie, watch the sales and profits roll in, and move on to another adventure, years ahead of schedule. Game over.

There were a lot of arguments to weigh on both sides of the deal. It was perfect material to run by oh, say, a mentor maybe.

We called Hakuta and left a message. We e-mailed him too. No reply.

We couldn't wait for word from Washington. Kyle and I decided to run an alternative proposal past John Baron. We put together a pricing schedule that paid Baron's group royalties for every sale. It was an accelerated scale that would have generated $2 million in profits for Baron & Co. if they moved anything close to the one million units they'd promised. We would not accept the $500,000 investment offer, meaning we retained all our equity, and we killed the infomercial. We figured that if their contacts in retail were anywhere near as strong as they'd claimed, Baron and his partners would be gathering a tremendous return in exchange for a few introductions to retailers. Basically, we wanted them to put their money where their mouth was.

The reasoning behind our offer was philosophical as well as financial. We didn't want to turn over the keys to our business so soon. We realized that the Baron offer, no matter how appealing, was a test of our entrepreneurial resolve. We had told ourselves we wanted the full entrepreneurial experience, not a shortcut. Turning down Baron's initial offer was proof of our concept. We wanted to stumble and succeed on our own terms, and continue to actively manage Platinum Concepts the way we saw fit, even if it meant passing on a lot of money.

We faxed our offer to San Diego and waited.

The response came quickly. John Baron hated our offer. In fact, it angered him. He refused to do any deal without the infomercial. He insisted that we didn't know anything about the business we were in, and that we were making a huge mistake.

We had no problem with someone disagreeing with us, but the more Baron talked, the angrier he got, and the more he began to creep us out. During our brief visit to San Diego, we'd grown to like John Schroeder, but John Baron's charm had worn thin. Now it was completely gone; he seemed as desperate as Tom Cruise's character in *Jerry Maguire.* We'd had mild suspicions that Baron had some hidden agenda with us, and now he was confirming them. Rejecting the infomercial proposal sent him into an extended rant, very little of which made any sense to us. The angrier he got, the more we felt we'd made the right decision by walking away from his offer.

We hung up the phone with a sense of relief. We'd faced an ambiguous situation, an offer that had some attractions and some pitfalls, and we felt like we'd done the right thing. And we'd done it without the help of Mr. Wacky Wall Walker (who never called us back, by the way).

John Baron called back, however, about two weeks later. It was another angry call, only this time it was premeditated, with an "I-told-you-so" twist. It seemed that Gary McCord had just won the last Senior PGA Tour event of the year, in Spain. Baron wanted to let us know about all the exposure McCord was going to get—more proof in his mind that we'd missed the boat by not signing up for his infomercial scheme. He truly was Jerry Maguire, without the happy ending with Renee Zellweger and her crazy-haired kid.

At the same time our ex-golf-pro adventure ended, we decided to close out our nonrelationship with Ken Hakuta. We called Len Lodish to ask about other advisor prospects, and guessed he would get back to Hakuta with the news.

We still wanted someone to talk to a couple of times a month who could open doors in retail distribution and help us think through challenges in our particular industry. But we'd also proven to ourselves that we could survive without someone looking over our shoulder, helping us make our way down the path. Mr. Wacky Wall Walker hadn't worked out. Neither had the chance to immortalize MouseDriver in a Gary McCord–Chi Chi Rodriguez infomercial, running until the end of time late at night on a cable station near you. Without any help, we'd stuck to our business principles, and come out of all of it in one piece.

MUST WE DO
EVERYTHING OURSELVES?

The bulk of our rush shipment of MouseDrivers arrived at Graphatic in Hayward in early November, a few days behind schedule. Just a few weeks before, we'd have been alarmed by the lateness of the shipment. Now we didn't care. Brian had already let us down.

Steve Little of Team Mouse had told us we'd missed Christmas 1999 in the middle of June; Brian had talked us back into the holiday rush in September. Kenny at East Asia Action Express had told us sending 25,000 MouseDrivers by air freight would set us back a dollar a pop; Brian had talked us into taking the plunge. Brian had told us that even in September and October, most retailers left shelf space open for hot products that had just come out. He believed MouseDriver fit the hot product profile, and that he could clear out our inventory by the end of the year. Brian was so sure we'd move that many units over Christmas (provided we had them on hand by late October) that he'd offered to buy out the rest of our inventory at the end of the year if he were wrong.

Brian was wrong.

At first, we'd been happy with Brian. He'd lined us up with the Edwin Watts shops within a few days of signing on, and he'd been kicking around a lot of other leads, including setting up an online ordering system and toll-free number out of his home base of Monterey. The Edwin Watts duffel-bag trek to the post office had even paid minor dividends. Six of the 48 shops we'd mailed samples to had immediately put in orders for more MouseDrivers.

But it hadn't taken us long to learn that when it came to MouseDriver, Brian was better at casting lines in the water than reeling them in. He'd gone to the PGA International Golf Show in Las Vegas in September and talked about all the leads he'd generated by circulating with the golf vendors there, but few sales came in. He'd gotten us started with NAGCE and set our heads spinning with sales possibilities, but NAGCE's way-past-due check hadn't arrived. Overall, Brian was on pace to close out the year with a total sales figure of around 500 units, nowhere near the level he'd sold us on.

Sold was the key word. It's not that we weren't wary of Brian (from a business perspective) when we'd first met him. We knew going in that he was a sales rep, and sales reps are all about making the sale here and now. We expected him to be shortsighted about our product, to push for volume over any nuances in product strategy, to blow past issues like the product life cycle and optimizing every sales channel in favor of selling more immediately on his own behalf.

But somehow we'd overlooked the fact that the first thing sales reps do is sell themselves. We'd never imagined he'd be as poor at generating sales volume as he'd been. We had another classic start-up mistake to chalk up in the lesson column:

Never, ever trade money for words.

In the business world, trading money for words is done millions of times a day. It's called financing, and there's nothing wrong with it, except if you happen to be an entrepreneur. An entrepreneur has to guard whatever cash is on hand and always covet more, because it's the lifeblood of a start-up. An entrepreneur has to peddle ideas and business plans and equity— words spoken and written, basically—for cash. Other people are supposed to finance them.

We'd gotten it all backward with Brian. He'd sold us on the idea of himself, and he'd used tantalizing bait. We'd fronted more than $25,000 to rush shipment based on his words. He could guarantee sales. He'd buy our inventory if he were wrong. And the sales would mean something on the order of an extra $400,000 in revenues to book for the end of 1999. The guarantees didn't come with a signed contract. The inventory purchase offer had no money down, no cash in escrow. The extra $400,000 shot to the sales column came with no receipts. It was only words.

Our commitments, on the other hand, had been real. We'd paid out of pocket for rush shipping, and now we had around 25,000 MouseDrivers sitting in Hayward with few sales on the horizon. We were going to miss the big Christmas season just like we'd thought we would back in June. Only the way it turned out, we'd wound up financing Brian's sales and marketing plan, not our own.

Or, as Kyle put it, "Crap, we're dumb."

Of course, we should have known better. We'd successfully dodged a bullet with John Baron's wonderful world of infomercials, and we were well into the process of learning where we stood on the mentor front with Ken Hakuta. In both those cases, we'd spotted the problems early. Baron's group hadn't bought into our vision for MouseDriver, and Ken Hakuta hadn't bought into the concept of returning our calls. Brian, on the other hand, had taken our own vision for MouseDriver, put it in racy sales rep packaging, and sold it back to us. He'd agreed with everything we'd wanted to do but felt we couldn't—break into retail and build market enthusiasm—and told us it could all be done faster than what we'd been told. We wanted to believe him.

Brian hadn't conned us, he just didn't know what we'd learned about our own product through trial and error and hard work. But we were swayed by his belief in the product, and deferred to his vision. Big mistake. Between Brian's 500-unit sales pace for 1999 and our 25,000 unit order, the three of us were on our way to missing our dream holiday sales estimate by a whopping 98%. William Blake said it best: The road to hell is paved with good intentions. Kyle said it quicker: "Crap. Crapcrapcrap."

In our case, William Blake was a little off the mark. For us, good intentions had paved the road to Hayward. By the time our shipment reached Hayward in November, we knew we weren't going to turn it around quickly with immediate sales. The bulk of it would have to be transported across the country to our warehouse/pad printer facilities in Nashville, where it would camp out cheaply as our stockpile of blank units, waiting for corporate sales. We'd also arranged with Anita to keep a few thousand on hand at Graphatic, just to clear any local sales we (or Brian) happened to make.

By early December, however, Brian was causing trouble in new ways, forcing us to come up with another plan for our remaining units in Hayward. In his holiday haste, Brian had urged us to build the ability to fulfill online orders into our Web site. Again, this hadn't been part of our original plans—we were in no rush to begin offering single-sale MouseDrivers directly, online or otherwise. Kyle and I were wary of fulfilling individual orders ourselves—there was so much else we already had to do, like gearing up for the new year (when the real selling push would begin). But when Brian offered to set up and run the system on his own, we agreed.

So Brian had set up his own toll-free number, built an order page that resembled our Web page and then had some tech guy build links between the two. We put an order button on the homepage, and bam—we had online ordering. Then Brian agreed to purchase nearly 1,000 units at a wholesale discount and ship them to his office in Monterey, where he would carry the inventory and take care of fulfillment for his sales with his assistant, Brett.

Just a few weeks after it debuted, the whole online ordering plan was in a nasty downward spiral. It seemed like the order page was never up and running. Some bug would always take it down for hours at a time. Worse, Brian had failed to pay the bill for his toll-free number, so customers who called to order only got an error message. We went through the roof when we found this out—nothing would kill potential sales quicker than being unavailable to customers.

Brian quickly tried to rectify the situation, sending out a mass e-mail explaining that there was a new toll-free number for MouseDriver and encouraging recipients to call and place orders for "the hottest golf gift item on the market."

It was hot all right. We had no idea how hot until I answered a call to the Platinum Concepts main number about a week later from a customer who had tried calling Brian's new toll-free setup. She had first tried to order online, she said, and that hadn't worked. I told her we were sorry, that we were taking the necessary steps to fix the online ordering capabilities, and that I'd be happy to fill her order right then and there over the phone.

Not so fast, she said. She wasn't finished with her story. I held my breath and waited to hear the rest. When she couldn't order online, she had tried the original toll-free number, only to get the error message. Yeah, yeah, this I knew. What else?

Irritated, but still determined to acquire her MouseDriver, she had gone back to the online ordering page, noted the customer service e-mail address, and shot off a note. That put her on the list for Brian's mass e-mail. Receiving it confirmed that there truly were people behind www.mousedriver.com, making her confident that her third try at purchase would be the charm.

Dialing Brian's new toll-free number had not, however, finally connected her with her very own MouseDriver. Instead, it had offered her hot, hot talk from naughty, naughty girls. By writing 888 where he should have written 877, Brian had sent out the number for a phone sex line.

I was horrified and furious, then mostly furious. So was she. I managed to convince her that we were not a pornography company, gave her a long apology, which made her happy, and sent her a free MouseDriver with a personal letter on the spot.

Kyle and I drove to Monterey and reclaimed the remainder of Brian's MouseDriver inventory. He wasn't pleased, but he could hardly argue with us; he'd only sold a couple dozen units online, and he'd yet to reimburse us for any of them. Brian hadn't e-tailed any better than he'd retailed.

Brian had turned us into financiers in the early fall. Now, two weeks before Christmas, he'd also turned Kyle and me into a two-man warehouse/fulfillment outfit. We had to take our remaining MouseDrivers in Hayward off Anita's hands and get them to our apartment somehow, because now we had to take care of any late 1999/early 2000 noncorporate orders all on our own—Anita only dealt with large orders, not individual ones.

We hadn't settled with any distributors or suppliers yet, and Brian had botched the online process with our blessing. Now we'd have to sell direct from . . . our apartment.

We couldn't bear spending any extra money on shipping our already costly MouseDrivers from the East Bay into San Francisco, so Kyle and I forked out $100 for a rental truck and made a day of it.

We hit Hayward and loaded 60 twenty-five-pound boxes of MouseDrivers—a total of about 2,500 units. Anita was cheery and professional as always (just like Kenny, only without the bad news bulletins). We kept around 2,000 units with Graphatic in Hayward, because Anita could offer quick turn-around pad printing, and we headed back home with the rest. Of course, it was slower going in San Francisco, trudging up a flight of stairs to our place. I took up more boxes than Kyle, who "paced" himself.

We had enough space in our apartment, and we were glad to be tackling our latest Brian problem head-on. We were also amused that we'd solved a nerdy business school problem—keeping inventory holding costs down—with a U-Haul. But honestly, we were up to our necks in MouseDrivers. Both of our bedrooms were stacked to the ceiling with boxes. My bay window was covered and the whole placed smelled like cardboard. All of which was fitting, I guess; our bedrooms weren't bedrooms anymore. They were order and fulfillment rooms, where we happened to sleep.

We didn't have long to wait before packing and shipping our first apartment units. Brian's phone services may have crashed and burned, but ours were working fine, and the phones had been ringing steadily for weeks before we'd trekked to Hayward in search of MouseDrivers to pack and ship. Our own telephone work and contacts had yielded a handful of corporate sales, and Rick had generated our first real PR. He'd placed an article about MouseDriver in some regional golf publications, which apparently had a sizable readership, since people were calling Platinum Concepts directly for orders and more information.

Rick's efforts had also landed us an interview with a guy named Ed Abrams, who hosted a golf radio show on KYW News Radio 1060 AM out of Philadelphia. He did a show every weekend on golf accessories, and he wanted to chat up MouseDriver and ask us a few on-air questions. That was great. The call for the show came in at 6 A.M. West Coast time. That was bad. Kyle and I were slightly on the sleepy side. The interview went well, except we overpitched our telephone number (probably a result of our toll-free number trauma with Brian) and underpitched our Web address (which worked fine without the Brian link).

Not that it mattered. The calls were coming in. When somebody ordered, it was off to one of the bedrooms for packing. We had a UPS account, and it didn't take long for our regular UPS guy to get the hang of our state-of-the-art, real-time point-to-point shipping system. Every weekday, the UPS guy would stop his truck in front of our place and honk. We'd go to one of our two remaining box-free windows and give a thumbs up (yes, we have a shipment) or a circling index finger, the international hand symbol for "We have zero to ship out today."

We were also getting a lot of general inquiry calls as a result of our own PR labors. Following Rick's advice, Kyle and I had put together and mailed out 400 media kits a few weeks before. Each one had a press release and color picture (of MouseDriver, not us) and synopsis of the product and company story, and we'd sent them to writers and publicists in the golf industry. Now a handful of people were phoning in, wanting to interview us (evidently they'd missed our stellar crack-of-dawn performance on live Philly AM radio).

And here and there, we'd get customer service calls. One guy called from Sydney, Australia, to figure out how to guarantee delivery of two MouseDrivers by Christmas. Our irate sex phone customer called back, and sweetly said how pleased she was with the MouseDriver we'd sent her free of charge. She told Kyle we had the best customer service she'd come across. "Thanks," Kyle said, "I'll pass that along to our president."

And that was how it went. Kyle and I would sometimes, well, let's say "exaggerate" about the extent of our customer service department. We may have told customers things that weren't exactly true, like insisting we had a customer service department. I'll admit that I even told one customer that the head of our training department lived in a town near her own (not a complete fabrication—she lived near Kyle's parents, who had certainly trained him in something). We weren't trying to joke around with MouseDriver buyers, we just wanted to present Platinum Concepts, Inc. as an established company that took interest in their customer service needs.

So yes, there were some lies, but we thought of them as white ones. And sometimes we paid for them in the form of mix-ups: Once we had a local phone network-switching problem and lost a lot of phone messages. Some of these lost callers made follow-up calls, and when we pleaded ignorance, we got clobbered over the phone. We had to remember that every interaction anyone had with any aspect of MouseDriver became part of the product image. Which meant that we had to fix not only our own mistakes, but also other people's (especially Brian's).

In some ways, fielding every imaginable call and chasing down orders was a great experience. We got feedback from customers, members of the golf press, and people who were just curious about MouseDriver but still hadn't purchased. But we couldn't keep going like this. We needed to get warehousing and fulfillment out of our apartment. It was the same old distribution issue smacking us in the face again. Once we'd assured the quality of the product itself (which we'd done), finding distributors and suppliers was the real root of customer service for us. They would handle every order and track every customer call for us. We needed to free up our time for marketing and raising funds and generating revenues and . . . figuring out what to do with Brian.

We were down on him to be sure, but we hadn't thrown in the towel yet. On one hand, the rush shipment had been costly. But on the other hand, we now had inventory, and our first big marketing opportunities would follow fast on the heels of Christmas, most notably the giant PGA show in Orlando in early February. The plan was to give Brian another chance to redeem himself. We would give Brian specific goals for the show—key contacts to make and reasonable sales targets to reach—and, unless he met them, we'd let him go.

We'd decided on one more chance because we had nothing to lose. The inventory had already been made and paid for. Setting up goals for Brian was in fact an exercise in trading words for the prospect of cash, which is something every entrepreneur should be willing to try.

We wound up passing through the Christmas season unscathed by huge orders. It was all about cleaning up our own and Brian's bungles, and making slightly higher margins on our modest sales by selling, packing, and shipping from our bedrooms and kitchen. We'd been entrepreneurs, financiers, moving men, PR flaks, press secretaries, warehouse hands, shippers, and switchboard operators. It wasn't a disaster. Parts of it had even been fun.

Nevertheless, we had to make our warehouse-in-an-apartment setup go away as fast as possible. And we had to apply our newest hard-earned lessons. We would hang on to our cash, and we would hang on to our plans. We had to make the final calls about MouseDriver, no one else. We had to be confident about what we were doing and ready to succeed or fail on the merits of our own thinking. No mentor, no dealmaker, no sales rep could be allowed to make the final call for any decision in our business.

THE ART OF LOW FINANCE

At the end of 1999, while most people prepared for the dawn of the new millennium, our crack team of accountants (Kyle and I) met with two high-ranking Platinum Concepts, Inc. officials (John Lusk and Kyle Harrison) to conduct a thorough financial review of our first few months in business, for the purpose of providing an accurate financial picture for the company's major shareholders (us).

That's the longest way I know of to say "we did our books," which itself is slang for figuring out how much money we spent and how much money we earned in 1999.

That's the problem with accounting. It's clogged to the gills with jargon and incomprehensible language. It's also a confusing, boring mess that only an accounting professor, financial analyst, or CFO could love. Or an accountant, I suppose. Between local and federal reporting requirements (completely different for private and public companies, of course) and approximately eight billion state, local, and federal tax implications for every line item on an income statement, doing the books for a company is about as much fun as filling out tax forms for an entire neighborhood.

Of course, none of that mattered to Kyle and me. We were eager to do the books on our own company's first fiscal year, even though Platinum Concepts, Inc. had only been in existence for seven months. There were several reasons why Kyle and I didn't want to wait for a full calendar year to pass before we did a financial review.

First, accounting gets a bad rap. If you take tax implications out of the equation (which we did) and your inventory expenses are easy to understand (which ours were), then business accounting becomes an exercise in applying mostly sensible and straightforward rules.

Second, we may have been bored to death working through accounting case studies in business school, but the idea of running through our own numbers was a different story. It felt like we were grading ourselves, which was a lot more interesting than evaluating other people's businesses.

Third, we hated companies whose fiscal years ran March to March or June to June, all because of arcane reasons having to do with taxes, public relations, purchasing seasons in different industries, and the deep need to drive analysts and investors completely mad. So we resolved to have our fiscal year coincide with the calendar year. Besides, we wanted to get through the whole process our first time, just so we could tell everybody we knew that yeah, we'd already completed our first fiscal year. When you own your own business, it's amazing what amuses you.

In accounting terms, the heart and soul of our venture to date was the income statement, a simple add-and-subtract scorecard of all our sales and expenses across the past seven months (or fiscal 1999, to be technical about it). It featured all sorts of subcategories, running from the technical (Amortization Expense and Product Development) to the inescapably dull (Health Insurance and Postage). Some of our categories were intended for use in 2001 and 2002; items like Advertising and Point-of-Purchase Displays (we hadn't bought any) and Income from Accessory Sales (we didn't have any accessories to sell) posted big, fat zeroes for 1999. And some very official-sounding categories were cover-ups for very ordinary expenditures, like our lone overpriced experience with a cleaning lady, which (plus our subsequent purchases of cleaning supplies) landed under the expense category of Janitorial, to the tune of $135.

Once every imaginable source of income and expense had been put into proper categories, finishing off the income statement became a simple matter of addition and subtraction. At the end, our fiscal 1999 amounted to this:

Total revenues booked: around $35,000
Total expenses booked: around $65,000

So we'd spent roughly $30,000 more than we'd taken in. What did it mean?

On one hand, it was a net loss no matter how we sliced it. Generally speaking, the world doesn't smile on businesses that spend more than they take in. And in our case, the income statement reflected our initial ignorance of our industry—we'd missed the big holiday selling season, we'd struggled to manufacture a quality product, we'd gone back to the drawing board more than once to hammer out a workable marketing strategy. Obviously, we hadn't ramped up nearly as fast as we'd thought we would.

On the other hand, being out of pocket $30,000 wasn't so bad considering all we'd accomplished in our first seven months. We knew who we were going to market to, we had a sales rep

(Brian, sort of) and fledgling PR (Rick), and we had an inventory of over 25,000 MouseDrivers ready to go in California and Tennessee. We were prepared to do some serious business. We may have been a few months behind our original schedule, but we had enough money left in the bank to hold us over and a lot of income potential from the MouseDriver inventory we'd already committed to. So all in all, we could make a solid argument that we were entering 2000 in pretty good shape.

Even though our sales and expense figures were tiny, there was still some valuable information to be found in our income statement. For example, our gross profit margin was healthily in excess of 50%, right in line with what we'd anticipated in our pro formas. This meant that the cost of producing MouseDriver was well less than half what it generated in sales, even in our first few months in business. So while Platinum Concepts, Inc. had lost money overall in 1999, MouseDriver itself was a reasonably profitable product.

Our net losses had come as a result of including all of our other expenses—like interest expense and the cost of attending trade shows (more Brian's expenses than ours, to date, but so what). If we could sell more MouseDrivers at the current gross margin, and we became a more efficient marketing and operations machine—that is, if we generated a lot more sales per dollar spent on items such as office equipment, phone bills, and travel expenses—our promising gross margins would turn into healthy net margins, and we'd start making money.

It was also encouraging to realize that a good portion of our net loss for 1999 came from investing in things we needed to have immediately, but that we would use for months to come. Printing brochures, for example, had set us back about $7,000—nearly 25% of our total net loss for 1999. This was a onetime expense that occurred in 1999, but would pay dividends over time, as we used the paid-for brochures throughout 2000 and possibly even 2001.

We also knew other costs would decrease as a percentage of the volume of MouseDrivers we ordered from Carmine and Kenny. Liability insurance, cargo insurance, commercial insurance, importing expenses, and shipping charges would drop on a per unit basis the more product we ordered. Every percentage drop in categories like these translated directly (in our favor) into our net margins.

There was a lot to be encouraged by, looking at the numbers as a whole. The potential for MouseDriver to take off in 2000 was all there in our first fiscal year results. We just needed to push more MouseDrivers through the system.

The downside of our first accounting results for Platinum Concepts, Inc. carried exactly the same message: We needed to push more Mouse Drivers through the system. We'd booked only a couple thousand MouseDriver sales in our opening seven months in business, far short of the 17,000 units we'd forecasted, and even further short of the 25,000 we'd thought we'd move during a brief pre-Christmas mania in the late fall. It wasn't the end of the world that we'd fallen so far off our original estimates, but it was a perfect reflection of the difference between putting a business idea on paper and trying to execute it in the real world.

Put simply, when we started our business, we didn't know what we didn't know. We made mistakes in understanding distribution, and it had cost us time. We wrestled with manufacturing, and our product had arrived a lot more slowly than we'd anticipated. We'd had run-ins with acts of God (typhoons and earthquakes) and acts of weirdness (noncommunication with Mr. Wacky Wall Walker, total miscommunication with John Baron and his posse of faded golf pros). Everything took more time than we'd expected, which eventually translated into lost sales. Time truly was money; it was right there in our first results.

In retrospect, we could see how overly optimistic we'd been. Kyle and I joked about the Rule of Four, a new estimating method we'd come up with that we were beginning to swear by. If we'd have taken our first estimate for how many MouseDrivers we'd expected to sell in 1999, and divided it by four, we'd have been a lot closer to predicting what eventually happened. If we'd have guessed it would take four run-throughs with Kenny (instead of our prediction of one) to get our manufacturing process in line, we'd have been right. If we'd taken almost every time allotment we built into our plans for almost any learning process (distribution, marketing, building contacts, acquiring a mentor) and multiplied by four, we would have been a lot more realistic. The Rule of Four, our first homemade metric for understanding start-ups.

Now the question was, how did the Rule of Four apply to our predictions for 2000 and 2001? In our first pro formas, we'd anticipated selling somewhere in the neighborhood of 500,000 MouseDrivers. Did the Rule of Four cut that number to 125,000? Or did we have the right sales estimates, but the wrong years? The Rule of Four could multiply our time horizon from two to eight years; under this application, we'd sell half a million units, but we'd do it in 2007 and 2008. That would add up to nearly a decade in the novelty PC mouse business, long enough for us to lose our minds thinking about what might have been, if only we'd said yes to making an infomercial with Gary McCord and Chi Chi Rodriguez. . . .

Of course, we had high hopes that the Rule of Four wouldn't apply in 2000 and 2001. Maybe we'd taken most of our start-up lumps in 1999, and, going forward, the Rule of Four might turn into something more manageable, like the Rule of Two or the Rule of One and A Half. We were okay with having missed targets in our seven-month debut because we'd learned a lot, and also because the numbers on both sides of the ledger (sales and expenses) were so small. It all felt like practice, in a way. Our first full-fledged fiscal years, 2000 and 2001, were another matter. We wanted our initial estimates to be close to the truth. Half a million units in two years. We'd have to sell, sell, sell to get past the Rule of Four.

*   *   *

We'd matched our first real-world results against our pro formas and lived to tell the tale. That didn't mean there weren't still financial challenges ahead—in addition to ramping up MouseDriver sales, we had to pay a few bills in the first two quarters of 2000. Tops on the list was a final payment for our shipment of 25,000 units (roughly $50,000). This alone just about matched the remaining funds we had in the bank at the end of 1999.

Not that we were worried. First, we knew we'd be booking some revenue (hopefully a lot of revenue) from sales, which would solve the most important problem underlying our income statement—cash flow, money in the bank, the lifeblood of any start-up.

Second, we'd learned a lot in our first months in the start-up world, not only about making and selling MouseDrivers, but also about the art of low finance.

Low finance had nothing in common with high finance, the world in which our dot-com counterparts lived. High finance was all about reputation and potential; a well-respected team of engineers and MBAs could talk their way into VC money and investment bank money, if their ideas held the promise of a huge upside. Low finance had more to do with anonymity and repeatedly reaching modest goals; the less the issuers of our credit cards and our lines of credit understood what we were doing, the more access to capital we could get, provided we paid on time.

Low finance had taught us several valuable lessons, most of them counterintuitive. In low finance, banks were risky and credit cards were safe. In low finance, the best time to apply for a loan was when you didn't need one. In low finance, the more thorough the paperwork, the worse the quality of the loan.

Our first lesson in low finance was discovering that for start-ups, banks suck. A lot of banks like to advertise that they're eager to work with small businesses, but what they mean by small business is a company that's been around for ten years and has $10 million in revenue. Which eliminated us right off the bat.

Even when we tried to use commercial banks for specialized services, they drove us nuts. We once had a MouseDriver order come in from a customer in New Zealand, and, in order to speed the financing of the transaction, we tried working with a bank to get a letter of credit. It was supposed to work like this: A buyer opened a letter of credit with his bank, in the seller's name, by filling out some forms and committing the funds for the purchase. The bank then held the funds until the buyer received the product, at which point the money was released to the seller. It was a system for guaranteeing a transaction.

It was a great idea, until Kyle started the paperwork. There were hundreds of lines to be filled out in the forms—things like where the product would be delivered, the method of delivery, the exact delivery date, the documents that would accompany the shipment, and so on, down to nauseatingly minute detail. If any one of the stipulations weren't met, the money would have been frozen in a New Zealand account. Which is exactly what happened—our factory in China shut down for a couple of days and delayed the shipment. We wound up paying penalty fees and sent a lot of product at extra expense by air just to satisfy the customer and get out of the letter of credit mess. Overall, an all-out fun banking experience—one that, Kyle said, I would get to learn firsthand next time.

There's a reason banks are so conservative; they're working with federally insured money, so they're under a lot of regulatory restrictions. They're risk averse because their mission is basically to make a steady return without risking capital. Start-ups, of course, are the complete opposite: They bet all their capital in hopes of a sizable return. Ergo, banks and start-ups don't mix.

Where banks were terrible, credit cards were wonderful. Credit card companies make money two ways. The first was by getting a percentage of every purchase from the vendor. If we bought office supplies from Office Depot with a MasterCard, then MasterCard picked up a small percentage of the sale. The other way credit cards make money, of course, is by charging interest on balances. The net result of both of these methods is this: Credit card companies will do everything they can to encourage you to use their cards as often as possible. If a start-up is smart, it can beat credit card companies at their own game.

We built up a tremendous reserve of credit just by charging our everyday business expenses on personal credit cards, and then paying off the balances at the end of the month. Cycling $3,000 or $5,000 or $10,000 through a credit card in a month did wonders for our credit line. As credit card companies watched us run up sizable bills and then pay them all off, they started to treat us like moguls. Our annual interest rates dropped substantially—from 18% to a lifetime rate of 9.9%.

Our maximum credit limits rose, to an average of roughly $20,000 per card.

On several occasions we even took advantage of credit cards dangling cash transfers at a fixed six-month introductory interest rate of 4.9%, an absolutely senseless offer. It meant that we could borrow cash from our credit cards and deposit the funds in a bank or money market account earning almost the same rate. In other words, we were giving ourselves nearly interest-free six-month loans, without filling out any paperwork, courtesy of our credit card companies.

No, we were not trying to run up huge credit card debt. The key to the plan was clearing the debt after the six-month introductory period was over so that we wouldn't get charged normal interest rates. The maximum reserves and low lifetime rates, however, were readily available lines of credit in case of emergency. In essence, we were building our lines of credit precisely at the moment we didn't need them, for later use as temporary sources of funds for shipping or whatever expense jumped out at us unexpectedly.

Another credit reserve had come courtesy of my stockbroker. For part of our first inventory investment financing, I took out a $30,000 loan against the value of my portfolio (a very fancy word, considering how small my account was). Kyle and I cosigned an agreement that made each of us responsible for half the loan amount. It was a cheap way to finance, provided we could stomach the fact that we were now personally in debt. If the market tanked and my account value went with it, the loan could have been called, which would have meant paying some or all of the principal back on the spot.

Unlike commercial banks, neither the credit card companies nor my broker cared what we did with the money we borrowed. They didn't know anything about us or Platinum Concepts, Inc.

We were anonymous borrowers who paid our bills on time, and that was all that counted in the world of low finance.

The ways of low finance were fine by us. We entered 2000 knowing we had enough leeway in our credit and our cash on hand to handle the growth we'd anticipated or weather a storm we hadn't predicted. We could pay the bills, invest in a little more inventory if we needed to, and generally stay the course entering the new millennium. Or, as we liked to call it, our second fiscal year.

SUPER BOWL SUNDAY

As the New Millennium began, we were tired of learning. Not that we were worn out or developing bad attitudes—it just felt like we'd been behind schedule from the word go in 1999, and while taking our lumps and learning our lessons had been invaluable, we wanted 2000 to be about learning a little less and doing a little more. Once we realized Y2K hadn't totaled our phones and computers and that the radio was once again safe from Prince's "1999," Kyle and I opened the Next Thousand Years of MouseDriver with a fresh burst of energy.

While everybody else stumbled out onto the streets and into cafés to get lost in a swirl of meaningless theories about the dawn of a new age, Kyle and I knew what the year 2000 A.D. was all about: The PGA Merchandise Show in Orlando, Father's Day, and Christmas. Our first full calendar year in business would focus on retail after all, and each of these three events would be critical to our success. The PGA show was the golf industry's most important sales convention of the year, and Father's Day and Christmas were the essential holidays for impulse gift purchases like MouseDriver. Our big three were spread across the calendar, falling in February, June, and December, respectively. They felt to us like the three major PGA events of the year might feel to a golf pro—they were our Masters, our British and U.S. Opens (yeah, we know the PGA Championship is a major championship, but honestly, it doesn't have the same feel as the other three).

First up was the PGA Merchandise Show, four thrill-filled days in Orlando, Florida, in early February. Everybody in the golf world would be there, from manufacturers, distributors, and retailers to the golf media and the PGA Tour professionals, all in the shadow of Disney World. We'd heard and read that approximately 75% of all the golf retail purchases for the year were made at the show. If that figure were anything close to the truth, then the PGA would be a debut, a springboard, and a make-or-break opportunity for MouseDriver all rolled into one package.

We had tons to do to get ready. First, we had to secure booth space at the show for Platinum Concepts, and we had to construct a Platinum Concepts booth to fill that space. A couple of calls, and it looked like game over—booth fees and materials added up to way more money than we had. Then Rick bailed us out by squeezing us into a shared space with a couple other of his clients. Onward. We had to come up with giveaway packages and write and perfect a media spiel in case we were interviewed during the show. We had to create media kit folders and customized point-of-purchase displays to go with our, um, booth. We also had to order button-down oxfords and T-shirts with MouseDriver logos, captain's chairs for those all-important meetings, business card and brochure holders, promotional mousepads that had MouseDriver printed on them, computer stands so that we could display our Web site, and MouseDriver folders that would hold all of our media information, because you can never have enough promotional stuff for shows. And we had about a month to get it all done. The whole process felt weird, like gearing up for an incredibly strange cross between a prom and a wedding and a small-town parade.

Aside from all the giveaway gimmicks we needed to create for the PGA show, we also wanted to come into Orlando with other kinds of retail momentum. We hoped to set up meetings with distributors and retailers in advance of the show. This meant more cold calls and hitting up our small but proud network of contacts, looking for new points of entry into the retail world, especially since Brian had (to date) created more problems than he'd solved on the retail front. We'd put Brian on a kind of probation, giving him a chance to redeem himself at the PGA show by hitting set numbers, but we couldn't just put our faith in him and hope for the best any longer. We needed to create some of our own luck in sales.

Fortunately, we'd learned a lot in 1999. One of Len Lodish's business school lessons had hit home for us: When you're an entrepreneur, fighting to get your product recognized, you have to try a lot of things. It seemed dull and obvious when we'd heard it in class in Philadelphia, but less than a year later in San Francisco, it made perfect sense.

We had to try as many tactics as possible to get attention in the retail world, our small budget notwithstanding. Obviously, we didn't have VC money. We had a small product; inking Tiger Woods and Bill Gates to endorsement deals would have put us in debt for the rest of our lives. We didn't even have the where-withal (cash) to advertise in most specialty golf magazines (just a quick look into magazine ads told us all we'd needed to know—a half-page ad in *Golf for Women* magazine, for example, ran a breathtaking $23,000). But there were still a lot of ways within our reach to get people interested in MouseDriver.

One of them was to submit blind samples to large department stores, mall retailers, specialty golf stores, and catalog companies. Kyle and I sent off samples and information packets to places like Dillard's, Brookstone, Golfsmith, Herrington, and Hammacher Schlemmer. The idea, of course, was to catch a buyer's eye and land a big account. We knew the chances of success were slim. To get in most stores, we knew we needed some sort of personal contact to get the ball rolling, not because the retail game was rigged, but because big retail chains get thousands of unsolicited product samples each year, most of which wind up unopened or discarded by a bored assistant to an assistant buyer. It was a shot in the dark, but it didn't cost us much to try, and it gave us another chance at success.

We also didn't want to repeat that old 1999 feeling of always being behind, so we put in time on a few things that would pay off down the line. Like finally setting up our ASI distribution. Although we knew our focus for 2000 lay in retail, we stepped up our efforts to get everything set up in ASI so that we would at least have a channel where people could logo our MouseDriver product.

We also didn't want to repeat the 1999 experience of trying to do everything on our own, especially when it came to putting a logo on MouseDriver. There were companies out there who were experts in all the things we despised, like selling, printing, and shipping logoed products. After a lot of digging, we entered into negotiations with a couple of suppliers we'd identified in the promotional products industry. Both were members of ASI, which we were finally looking at as an advantage. One was Burkhouse, one of the best-known and largest suppliers in the business, out of Los Angeles. The other was Techpad, a smaller, less well-known company out of Salt Lake City that focused primarily on computer peripherals—mousepads, keyboards, and other computer accessories. Techpad had a reputation for being creative marketers. We entered our negotiations thinking it was a beauty contest between the two, the winner getting the right to market our wares (mostly in 2001) to distributors, who would then sell to the corporate market.

Then things got a little confusing. Both companies wanted our business. And both companies wanted us to commit to them in the form of granting an exclusive. It wasn't an unreasonable demand; in fact, it was fairly common in the industry. An exclusive gave a supplier more of an incentive to market our product, because it wouldn't be competing against other suppliers when marketing to distributors, who in turn sold to corporations. The ideal setup, we were told, was one producer (us), one supplier (either Techpad or Burkhouse), scads of distributors, and many, many corporate clients.

Granting an exclusive, however, was a demand that started a back-and-forth with Platinum Concepts, the two companies, and the airlines that linked us. We flew to Los Angeles to meet with Kip Rogers of Burkhouse. He told us MouseDriver looked like a winner, and he wanted an exclusive to put it through Burkhouse's distribution channels. He wanted to introduce the product at the Promotional Products Association International (PPAI) show in Dallas at the end of January, just a few days before the PGA show. We were all for the idea of a supplier jumping into the fray so quickly with our product—a year ahead of our new schedule.

Then, a couple of weeks later, we flew to Salt Lake City to meet with Art Harris of Techpad. We went into the meeting thinking Burkhouse was the place for us, no way could Techpad change that, and then Techpad gave us something to think about. Kyle and I both took to Art Harris, and Techpad's offer was attractive. Art promised a lot of promotion and he seemed to have his act together. We liked the idea of Techpad sales reps pitching our product alongside their mousepads and other peripherals. Of course, Techpad, like Burkhouse, wanted an exclusive.

Burkhouse. Techpad. Techpad. Burkhouse. We had to decide. One specialized in PC products. One was the big dog in the industry. Both were financially stable, with good reputations, and were willing to spend money marketing our product. Both were in the same range with regard to the price we'd charge for MouseDriver. And both wanted us to swear our undying allegiance to them and them alone.

So Kyle and I did what any entrepreneur would do in our situation. We tried to bend the rules.

What about a co-exclusive? We ran the idea of Burkhouse sharing an exclusive with Techpad past Kip Rogers. He went for it; Burkhouse's main point was that it didn't want more than one supplier in the picture because of price pressures. If Platinum Concepts could settle on competitive prices with both suppliers, Burkhouse would be on board.

We were excited. Having both Burkhouse and Techpad would mean that, for suppliers, we would have both the computer peripherals and the gift markets covered, all before the end of January 2000.

Then we ran the co-exclusive idea by Art Harris of Techpad. His response was, well, underwhelming. He explained that he didn't like the idea of doing the promotion and advertising he'd planned to do for MouseDriver and then having Burkhouse possibly benefit from it.

Okay, good point. We spent a few days mulling over what to do next, and jumped back to other projects in the interim. We purchased most of our stuff for the PGA trade show booth—arranging for the shirts and promotional items to arrive on time in

Orlando. We drafted a press release and ran it by Rick for comment before deciding to take the plunge, invest $1,000, and put it on PR Newswire, a multi-industry publicity service. Putting a release on the wire was like sending blind samples to department stores—another marketing tactic that had a small chance of working out, but was still worth doing.

We fielded calls from our evangelist network, with one guy calling in for a friend whose fiancée's father was a golf enthusiast and also the CFO of Office Depot. He wanted a couple more samples to send through his ties to get to this CFO character. We obliged. We made our first contact with Peter Mc-Quaid, editor of *Golf Retailer,* a magazine we hoped and dreamed of advertising in somewhere down the line. It was all small stuff with potential for big sales in the distant future.

And then, much to our surprise, Art Harris called back. Techpad was in. A co-exclusive with Burkhouse was fine by Techpad.

We had benefited in our negotiations by using the age-old tactic of Don't Just Do Something, Stand There. Techpad wanted our product and felt reassured by what we'd promised in the co-exclusive. They'd only needed time to think about it.

This was great. We had two first-rate suppliers in the fold, and we were on track for the PGA show. We'd even lined up another agreement, this time with a company in Reno, Nevada, called United Delivery Services (UDS). UDS would be our fulfillment house for direct sales—stocking inventory, integrating secure online ordering via our Web site, and offering 24-hour customer service, ordering and shipping through our toll-free ordering number and Web site. And, in case we wanted to be nerds about it (and we would, from time to time), UDS offered 450 inventory reports for tracking MouseDriver—who was buying, how much, and when. UDS's services came at a premium, but the whole package was worth it—Kyle and I would be freed from the rigors of shipping mice out of our apartment, our customer service would jump instantly from at-best-just-us/at-worst-Brian into the big leagues, and we could focus on the most important challenges in front of MouseDriver (sales and marketing). All that, plus the fact that UDS lay "conveniently" on the way to a time-share Kyle and I had recently splurged for in Lake Tahoe.

We were in such a good mood about our progress that it didn't set us back at all when Kyle's mom called from Texas, all excited about an ad she'd just caught on television for PayMyBills.com featuring our old friend J.T. We knew she must have thought we were certifiable for still selling mice out of our kitchen when our friend was pitching on TV, but we'd gotten over a lot of our PayMyBills.com/dot-com trauma. We were into our own business now, and not looking over our shoulders as much at what our colleagues were doing.

In the middle of January, Kyle and I dropped our final contract offers in the mail to Techpad and Burkhouse and loaded the SUV we'd rented with 720 MouseDriver units. We were headed to Reno/Tahoe to drop off the units at UDS to get them started. Okay, it was also a quick ski trip at the time-share. We were on the road, just outside of Sacramento, when Kyle's cell phone rang.

It was someone named Scott Rubinstein, calling from Brookstone. He said he'd gotten a hold of the blind sample we'd sent just a couple of days earlier. He loved MouseDriver. He wanted to put it in Brookstone stores for Father's Day.

I nodded furiously. "Yep. We can do that. Not a problem," said Kyle.

Kyle chatted a bit more with Scott, and within a couple minutes, the signal began to break up—we were leaving the range for Kyle's phone. Kyle and Scott hung up.

That was it. The greatest call in the history of Platinum Concepts, Inc., that we'd almost missed by being out of cell phone range, that we'd almost missed by trucking units to Reno and skipping out for a quick ski holiday.

Kyle and I rode the high of the Brookstone call all weekend. It was the reverse of the typhoon experience; someone had called out of the blue with incredibly good news for a change. Someone who mattered in retail had validated our business. Our product was wanted in the marketplace. Our hard work and hopes and bumbling and firsthand lessons were paying off, it seemed. It was just a great feeling, one of our first real entrepreneurial highs, the kind we'd imagined, the kind that would keep us coming back for more.

A few more days, a handful of conversations, and we had the Brookstone scoop: We would be in all 210 of their stores for Father's Day, provided we could come in with a price somewhere in the $12 to $15 range. And Brookstone wanted to have MouseDriver packaged as a Brookstone product, bundled with a mousepad. Not a problem. For now, the deal was more important than spreading our own name, we knew their packaging would look good (we'd used it as a reference when designing our own), and we'd figure out the mousepad problem with Kenny and our friends in Hong Kong.

Brookstone also wanted to be the exclusive retail outlet for the bundled MouseDriver-mousepad package and the only retailer of its type for MouseDriver. But what if The Sharper Image called? We started negotiating, but quickly recognized that we had no leverage. We were either in or out, and we definitely wanted to be in.

Negotiations were more successful elsewhere. We needed promotional mousepads for the PGA show; Techpad specialized in mousepads and wanted MouseDriver samples from us for marketing purposes. So we bartered—and settled on 2,000 mousepads in exchange for 400 MouseDrivers. Then we drove out to the nearby Presidio golf course, looked like mental patients for a few minutes as we took photos of a golf ball on a tee from a few different angles, sent the negatives to Techpad to print the grass and golf ball image on the mousepads, and our problem was solved.

The MouseDrivers-for-mousepads success spurred us to start wheeling and dealing everywhere we could in the barter economy. It was funny to think that Kyle and I had taken negotiating courses at Wharton, full of theory and game simulations, and we were putting it all to use with MouseDrivers as our main currency. Basically, anytime we dealt with a small company that sold a product, we tried to cut a noncash deal. A surprising number of companies were on our wavelength. In the end, our bartering scorecard ran like this:

4 MouseDrivers for 2 SlotLine putters

24 MouseDrivers for 2 Oregon golf vacations (from a travel agency)

24 MouseDrivers for 1 Canadian golf vacation (another travel agency)

5 MouseDrivers and 5 mousepads for a round of golf

2 MouseDrivers for 2 customized driver shafts

1 MouseDriver for 2 tickets to Hootie & the Blowfish at the PGA show

That last one was our favorite. First, we couldn't believe we landed two Hootie tickets for one MouseDriver. Second, we couldn't believe Hootie was still around, let alone playing a golf convention. Ah, Hootie.

Bartering wasn't just fun for us, it was resourceful. Paying with MouseDrivers was less costly than paying retail because all we had to sacrifice was the direct cost of the product. It wasn't any different than trading wholesale for wholesale, a good deal for everyone.

The only place we drew the bartering line was with advertising space. There were a lot of smaller publications offering to write about our product if we sent them $1,000 worth of MouseDrivers. The implication was that our "donation" would spur a favorable review. We always passed. We didn't like the feel of it, and our hearts weren't in buying fabricated reviews. It all felt cheesy and unethical.

Our only gray area with respect to advertising came with golf tournament sponsorships. We would trade MouseDrivers for ad space in tournament programs, but that felt different to us than buying reviews—there was no fake third-party commentary on MouseDriver, only our ad.

And while we bartered away, another pleasant surprise surfaced: Our casual e-mail newsletter, the *MouseDriver Insider,* was starting to take off. While we still only had about 100 people on the distribution, we were starting to get a lot of positive return comments. People were reading our informal rants and raves about being entrepreneurs, and we were keeping them awake and amused enough to get feedback. A lot of our former Wharton classmates would write to ask how we handled certain business situations. Kyle and I, who hadn't been able to figure out what ASI meant, who thought we'd never manufacture a MouseDriver without a crooked logo, who'd misunderstood our first sales rep situation, were suddenly being sought out for advice.

There were even a couple of our own Wharton professors, Len Lodish and Wes Hutchinson, who had begun handing out the *Insider* issues in class—having students look over our musings on distribution before launching into lectures on the same subject.

Were they kidding? The *Insider* was an educational tool. And MouseDriver was hotter than Hootie. All very strange.

After two weeks of getting steady responses to our newsletter, I began thinking about how the *Insider* might become a part of our marketing plans, a way of getting the message out about our company. It was genuinely gratifying to discover that we weren't alone in our entrepreneurial hopes and headaches, and it was exciting to think about something we'd launched with only a tiny particle of an idea turning into something bigger.

But our plans for the *Insider* would have to wait. There were other worlds to conquer. With a few days left in January, we flew to Dallas for the PPAI show, where Techpad and Burkhouse both had booths featuring MouseDriver. Although the PPAI show was the premier event in the promotional products industry, we sort of viewed it as a sneak peek of what might be in store for us at the PGA show. Also, we wanted to show Burkhouse and Techpad our support for what they were doing with our product.

What can I say about the PPAI show? On one hand, Kyle and I were thrilled to see MouseDriver on display in a booth setting for the first time. For a couple of single-product entrepreneurs like us, the show provided lots of moments of slightly geeky fun. Kyle and I would go back and forth between Techpad and Burkhouse, looking at MouseDriver in the display cases, then zipping around the corner, out of sight of the booths, to high-five each other. It wasn't pretty, but that was the truth of how fired up we were. Kyle especially liked what Techpad had done, putting MouseDriver on a pedestal in a slow continuous spin, like a moon rock in a museum.

On the other hand, the PPAI show was incredibly cheesy. We'd never seen anything like it. A woman in a bikini jumped out at us from behind one of the booths, doing an odd little dance and trying to hand us condoms. Logoed condoms. The perfect corporate gift, for sure. To save her from further embarrassment, we accepted the condoms, mumbled thanks, and shoved them in our pockets. We chucked them in the trash as soon as we were out of sight.

Any and every imaginable logoable item was on display—coffee mugs, pens, T-shirts, posters, Frisbees, hacky-sacks. And we were part of it. In between our bouts of self-congratulation about the MouseDriver displays, the PPAI show planted a few seeds of doubt. How cheesy would our own booth look at the PGA show? Would the PGA show be as weird as the PPAI show? Would we flop, like logoed corporate condoms?

We flew back home for our last few days before the PGA show. We continued to cold call, negotiate, wheel and deal, barter, and brainstorm. We also took time out to watch the Super Bowl, featuring the St. Louis Rams and the Tennessee Titans, a team that had abandoned Kyle's near-hometown of Houston a few years before.

The original plan was to root hard for the ex-Houston team— once a Texan, always a Texan. But that quickly changed as we locked on to the long parade of splashy dot-com television commercials.

We couldn't believe what we were seeing. Companies that had launched with VC start-up money just a few years (or sometimes even months) before were dropping $1.4 million a pop for thirty-second spots during the Super Bowl, the most expensive advertising media buy in the world. Amazon.com. AOL. Pets.com. There was even one incomprehensibly brain-bending ad from a company called LifeMinders.com, which featured nothing more than a blank backdrop and lettering.

"We didn't have time to make an ad so we're just putting our name up here. LifeMinders.com."

Was it a goof? A $1.4 million goof? Or the truth? Either way, it was mad money—we had no idea what LifeMinders.com was about before or after the ad. (Kyle, the thorough one, pulled it up on the Internet the next day. "It's some kind of e-mail newsletter/reminder service," he said. "Who's going to use that?")

We forgot about the game and started talking about the ads (pausing every so often, of course, to take a stab at "Wassssuu-uup?" and then roll with laughter). It hadn't been all that long ago when we'd have been nothing but green with envy. But now we weren't all that jealous. To us, a lot of these companies looked like they were expensively learning lessons we'd already been through. Sure, it would have been great to have had the resources some of these dot-coms had, but we felt like we knew what we were doing. We were becoming resourceful. We were getting the hang the industry. We had distribution and a good product. And with a lot of the dot-com ads, we couldn't figure out what they were, what they were doing, or how they were going to make money. Strangely, with our tiny budget and our unglamorous, non-earthshaking MouseDriver, we felt a bit ahead of the game.

And, speaking of games, it was fun to watch Kyle moan and roll as the clock ran out on a Tennessee player, one yard short of scoring the winning touchdown. It almost made up for the loss. But we really couldn't complain—it had finally been a true Super Bowl instead of an overhyped blowout. Besides, with so many things already going our way, we didn't want to get greedy.

WE DO ORLANDO

"So this thing is some kind of computerized driver. Right?"

Well, no. It's a mouse, not a driver.

"So you're telling me I can't put a shaft on this head here and take a swing?"

Well, no. It's a mouse, not a driver.

"Someone told me this thing has a chip in it so I can tell how hard I'm striking the ball."

No, no, it's a mouse for your computer. You can't hit a golf ball with it. I mean, I guess you could, but everything would break, and the ball wouldn't go very far.

"I don't get it. You're saying I can take a swing, but just in the air? I can't hit a golf ball with it?"

Um, never mind. Let's start over.

"Okay, tell me again. What's your MouseClub do exactly?"

That's MouseDriver, not MouseClub. It's for your computer. It looks like a golf driver, but it's a mouse you plug in and use with your PC.

"What are you, are you like the R&D guys for the company or something?"

Um, yes, we're like the R&D guys for the company.

"'Cause I gotta tell you, this thing's never gonna fly. You better call your boss and tell him it's just never gonna fly. I mean, who's gonna want a mouse for golf? You see what I'm saying?"

We see what you're saying.

"So what else you got here?"

All we have is MouseDriver today.

"Okay fellas, well, easy come, easy go. Hey, have you seen the booth with the computerized golf driver? Can you tell me where that is?"

That was how it went at the PGA Merchandise Show in Orlando. At first, anyway. Our rite of passage into the wild world of face-to-face golf retail began with a light warm-up of total humiliation followed by comprehensive sessions of ego crushing. Maybe we were on the hypersensitive side, but every negative comment we heard from browsers at our booth stung us. There were lots of people who understood and liked what we had to offer, and we garnered many more positive responses than negative ones, but every rejection seemed to burn.

The PPAI show in Dallas just ten days before simply hadn't prepared us for Orlando. First of all, we were tourists at the Dallas show—Burkhouse and Techpad were running the booths and doing almost all the work. Kyle and I had spent most of our time buzzing with excitement over seeing our product on display for the first time, in the hands of suppliers with whom we'd successfully negotiated. Watching people working to showcase MouseDriver felt like a small but satisfying payoff for a lot of effort we'd expended in December and January.

And let's face it, we were tapping into our inner snobs in Dallas. We thought most of the rest of the PPAI show wares were incredibly tacky, especially in comparison to our cleverly conceived and engineered product. We had no expectations for that show—we hadn't even planned to go until just three weeks beforehand, so everything positive that happened there was pure bonus. All the PPAI show meant was we were proceeding well ahead of schedule for our aggressive entry into corporate promotional products in 2001.

In sunny Orlando, where we had a lot more at stake, we were humble going in, and humbler still at the end of the first day. Our "booth" was more like a time-share; we had a third of the total space. Rick had set it up so that we were sharing with two of his clients, Dave Stephenson of Swing Systems and Roger Gunn of CyberGolfPro. We didn't have much room to maneuver, and our five-by-five-foot MouseDriver sign (about the size of a hockey net) kept flopping to the floor as we tried to put it in place. The overall effect of our one-third booth: Well, it was cheesy-looking, with an image of a golf hole draped over the top of the display. All in all, it wasn't PPAI-woman-in-a-bikini-passing-out-condoms cheesy, but still, we weren't psyched about it.

Even if it had been great-looking, our booth had no chance of giving us any confidence. Not when it was a minuscule display in a giant hall of booths and lights and posterboards and people hawking anything and everything you could imagine having to do with golf. We were lost in a sea of product pitches in the Orlando Convention Center, shuffling on the thin, gray-colored carpeting stretched over concrete across an impossibly huge space, basically a fieldhouse masquerading as a room. It took fifteen minutes to walk the Convention Center end to end, and God knows how many booths populated the main room. We felt like small-town kids bringing a will-the-mouse-find-the-cheese maze to a national science competition, setting up next to a bunch of whiz kids who'd unraveled the mysteries of the Big Bang and mapped the genome for extra credit.

And what a set of whiz kids. There were tons of golf-related dot-coms, some of them with very slick setups, and all of them, seemingly, with money to burn. We had gained some confidence with respect to dot-coms in general, but these guys were in it right alongside us in the golf world, and some of them, uncomfortably, were peers. There was a Stanford MBA grad at the show that both Kyle and I knew named Jim King, who had started a golf dot-com company at the same time we did. We crept by his booth, saw ten of his people working their way through an absolute swamp of onlookers in front of their gigantic display, and felt pretty low. And embarrassed. Jim had the same credentials, the same background, the same starting point, and there he was, looking like he was on the verge of an empire. We didn't even have the nerve to say hello. The fear of repeating the nightmare "So what exactly does MouseClub do?" conversation was too great.

And it didn't help that we were directly across the aisle from the Taj Mahal of convention booths, courtesy of a company called Greens.com. Frankly, Greens.com's setup wasn't a booth, it was a . . . house, and a great-looking one at that. It had great furniture, and it doubled as a bar. It was manned by fifty Greens.com employees. Naturally, it was mobbed from the first minute. Kyle said he'd heard someone talking about how the house had taken three days to assemble and had set Greens.com back about $200,000. Or, just around double our entire start-up budget.

Greens.com was far from the only dot-com splash at the show. It seemed as if every third booth was Internet-related, and a lot of them were architectural wonders. Double-decker booths with fully stocked bars on the second floor. Booths loaded with PCs and all sorts of cool games software to jump through and play around with. Meanwhile, Kyle and I were just glad we'd figured out how to keep our MouseDriver sign from flopping onto the ground.

More humbling still was knowing that we wouldn't have even gotten as far as we had with our own setup without a ton of help from Rick. It hadn't taken a lot of work in early January for us to realize what complete novices we were at the trade show game. Rick had saved our asses on more than one occasion. We'd thought of the show in strategic terms—we wanted to meet and set up relationships with stock-holding distributors and large retailers, get a smattering of media attention, and generate some product feedback. Rick had preached getting our ducks in a row. Things like figuring out a booth display, determining what promotions to run, deciding whether to offer show specials, learning about potential attendees, setting up meetings, and marketing the fact that we were attending the show ourselves. Things we either didn't know how to do or weren't doing very well.

Fortunately, Rick jumped right in and took over. He figured out our booth situation, be it ever so humble, and helped us put together a shared marketing program with CyberGolfPro and Swing Systems. With his help, we'd walked into the show offering individual MouseDrivers at a show special of $20, $18 a pop for an order of a dozen, having already issued a press release to the golf industry talking about our appearance at the show, mentioning our booth number. Plus, he'd lined up a couple of meetings for us, and showed us how to prepare and what to expect.

Rick even suggested an ingenious guerrilla marketing tactic that paid off almost immediately at the show. About an hour before opening, we walked the main floor, offering to set up anybody's display PC with a MouseDriver with a label of our booth number on the top. A few companies took us up on our offer,

including Greens.com, which had a row of PCs in front of its
monstrous house. It was a sweet way of turning traffic from
other companies in our direction. Rick was brilliant. Without
him, we'd have been tourists at another show, this time with serious consequences.

Where Rick delighted us, Brian troubled us. We'd had him
come to the show, along with his assistant Brett, to help run the
booth. We'd met with Brian a couple of weeks beforehand, going over his targets for Orlando and trying to jumpstart his enthusiasm for selling MouseDrivers by offering him a bonus on
top of his commission if he met them. Brett took to the booth
right off, keeping it organized, cracking jokes, and . . . selling.
Brian didn't follow suit. He acted as if he were just along for the
ride in Orlando.

That wasn't the plan. We'd discussed how one of the major
motivations for Kyle and me to attend the show was to find
stock-holding distributors. We'd run this by Rick and Brian,
and they'd both agreed that it was a good idea. Kyle and I
would hunt for distributors first and sell second. Brian and
Brett would sell first and last.

Then, at the beginning of the show, as we began to approach
distributors, Brian seemed miffed. He had it in his head that he
was Platinum Concepts' sales manager (he was not—Brian was
our sales rep), and that we didn't need distributors. His plan
was to build out an extensive network of golf sales reps consist-
ing of all his friends in the business. So while we were trying to
build alliances and sell, Brian opened the show by trying to set
up meetings featuring him, us, and potential sales reps.

It was mildly horrible. We would sit down with sales reps
who approached our booth and introduced themselves, saying
Brian had suggested we meet. We'd say, as politely as possible,
that we weren't in the market for more reps. Naturally, they'd

ask why they were even talking to us in the first place. We'd say we didn't know; there'd been a mix-up. It was better than saying our sales rep had jettisoned the master plan, but it didn't make it any less awkward for either the sales reps or us.

From his skewed view of himself as our sales manager, Brian seemed to think that he was entitled to kick back at the show and manage other people's sales (meaning Brett's full-time, and ours part-time). Kyle and I wondered where he got this notion. It was inexplicable and frustrating.

So there we were. Just hours into the show, feeling lost in a bazaar of golf-mad marketers. Bummed about our booth. Gun-shy about saying hi to Jim King, our friend. On pins and nee-dles with Brian. Traveling across the country to a town where, no matter what we did, our mouse would always run a distant second to Mickey.

Another lone browser headed up to our display. "Hey, you got any mice that look like Tiger Woods?"

I needed a break. I walked out of the main room, through the lobby, out into the Florida sun. A beautiful day. I'd just turned twenty-nine, having spent my birthday running down last-minute details on the booth I now wanted to avoid. Run-of-the-mill (but still effective) doubts ran through my head. What the hell was I doing? J.T. was running ads on TV. Meanwhile, I was at a golf show with a novelty computer product. What would I do if Jack Nicklaus came by our booth and hated MouseDriver?

I knew the answer to that one. It was simple. I would look Jack Nicklaus straight in the eye and say I was just working the booth as a temp, trying to earn my way to a thousand-year-old Turkish monastery, where I would live out the rest of my days in silence, contemplating God and eternity and why man should never mix golf with computer peripherals. And making goat cheese.

I walked back into the convention center, but remained in the hall outside the main floor. Kyle found me.

I'd like to say I rebounded instantly from my brief mood drop because Kyle had made a humongous sale. I'd like to say my sense of resolve was restored because I remembered our mission at the show, to find distributors and retailers. Or that I came to some epiphany about what it meant to take a real risk to go after something I believed in.

But all Kyle said was, "Hey, where you been? We just got invited to a party."

I never said I was deep.

Besides, I wasn't really that down. It was just another temporary entrepreneurial mood swing, a hazard of the profession. I could have just as easily been unreasonably sunny about our place in the show. It wasn't a stretch to say we were doing a lot of things right. We'd gotten Brookstone, so we had one big retailer for MouseDriver, albeit under a private label. And we'd been talking to distributors, some even before we'd arrived at the show. So we were making good, steady headway. We just needed to build some ties with a few retailers to market under our own Platinum Concepts–MouseDriver name. And we still had most of the four days in Orlando ahead of us to do it.

Back to the party invite. It was the first of many, and the beginning of that classic all-American trade show tradition of mixing lots of business with lots of alcohol. We had gotten our first hint of what was in store during the flight to Orlando. The plane out of San Francisco was full of conventioneers, their spouses, and their children. In addition to chattering about who would be at the show and what companies they wanted to see, everybody (except the children, for the most part) started drinking right after takeoff. And continued drinking all the way across the country. The beverage carts never stopped moving up and down the aisles. We half expected a champagne reception at the gate in Orlando.

The golf industry is sort of like one big happy family, one that's strangely comfortable with how important alcohol is to the family dynamic. Everybody knows each other. Everybody likes to have a good time, if by "good time" you mean "drinking a lot." Of course, there were other activities, like golf scrambles and the Hootie & the Blowfish concert. But we drank at those too.

Mostly, though, there were parties, both corporate and private, some of them borderline out of control. Close-of-business happy hours, sponsored by magazines. Hotel suites rented out. Private rooms reserved at restaurants. Awards ceremonies. Whatever. Word would get out on a party, and it would crowd to the point of being out of control. People would offer us extra passes, or let us make copies of their passes, just so we could overcrowd parties alongside them. The important thing for all concerned, it seemed, was to keep drinking.

Between the twilight, night, and late-night (and let's face it, sometimes early-morning) drinking and the honest-to-God twelve hours we put in each day hawking MouseDrivers and chasing down Brian and trying to make inroads with distributors, the four days in Orlando blurred together. Convention food combined with a lack of sleep can do a number on your ability to temporally sequence events in memory, or remember at all, for that matter. My recollections of the show hung together like the blobs in a lava lamp, floating out of sequence and relation.

Like watching Kyle doing his silly Kyle dance in the front row of the Hootie & the Blowfish concert. Or drinking my way through the International Network of Golf Industry Honors, an Academy Awards–style show at the Peabody Hotel, where I watched Brian's NAGCE contact, Frank Weinhausen, walk off with one of the night's awards, and wondered when the hell Frank was going to pay us. NAGCE, another Brian promise turned into a headache, a hoped-for big sale turned into a perpetual outstanding accounts receivable.

Other PGA show memories: Running into Michael Clark, a friend of a friend of mine from Southern Methodist University. It turned out his father was founder and president of Sherwood, the company that owned Burkhouse, our newfound supplier. Small world (and a great contact for us). Or the last night of the show, when Greens.com blew through at least a million dollars to rent out the "adult" section of Disney World, a collection of Disneyfied bars and clubs. Anyone sporting either a pass or a Greens.com hat could get in. Thousands of people attended and enjoyed free food and alcohol. Everybody danced and drank too much and negotiated things besides business that sometimes happen after dancing and alcohol. And everybody wore Greens.com hats. It was a weird, expensive, oddly conformist scene, with too many hats. Kyle and I paid homage to our decadent hosts by dancing with a couple of female Greens.com employees. Well into the evening, when we spotted the actor who played the J. Peterman character on *Seinfeld* moving through the crowd, blurring the all-important line between television and reality, Kyle and I knew it was time to go.

For all the alcohol-fueled strangeness, our three favorite offbeat convention moments were entirely sober and all MouseDriver.

The first happened across the last two days or so of the show. By then, the word had gotten out that a couple of Wharton MBAs had a booth. Once we were spotted, we had a number of different people approach our display, introduce themselves, and ask if we would review their business plans. I'm not too

sure why we inspired such confidence. We knew there weren't
a lot of MBAs in the golf industry, but still, it was a peculiar request, repeated many times over. Maybe they'd taken the info
we'd put in our media kit a little too much to heart. We could
have been smart about it, donning our old consulting firm hats
and charging by the hour. But we were hungover and sleep-
deprived, and we didn't have the hours to spare. We tried to
smile and chat our way out of each request.

The second brush with oddness came courtesy of a camera.
In the middle of the show, while I was speaking with a potential
customer, a small group of Korean gentlemen came upon our
booth and, after spending a few moments looking at our sample
MouseDrivers, began to set up a tripod a few feet from our display. Maybe they were with a Korean magazine and just wanted
a few shots for an article. Or maybe they were working for a
Korean manufacturer and were collecting information to knock
off MouseDriver. All I know was the show was overcrowded, I
was busy, and they were moving in for photographs awfully fast.
My sense of knockoff paranoia kicked in. I excused myself from
my conversation and practically leapt in front of the camera. I
asked questions, but all I got out of the group was that they
were from Korea. They packed up and left quickly. I never figured out whether I'd been incredibly rude or I'd just saved the
future of Platinum Concepts. Either way, Kyle couldn't stop
laughing at me.

Our third (and Kyle's favorite) odd moment came courtesy of
Brian. There was a moment during the last hours of the last day
that Kyle and Brett and I were overloaded working the booth—
there were just too many people checking out our display (a
nice problem to have). The whole room was booming with
noise. I'd been pulled away from a casual conversation with a
Greens.com employee by Brett to help with the overload.

Back at the booth, Brett asked Kyle if he knew where Brian was, saying we could really use his help just then.

"He's in the meeting area."

The meeting area was a triangular space created out of the intersection of the three parts of our booth. It was tiny.

"He's where?"

"Brian's in the meeting area. He's sleeping."

And sure enough, he was, right in the middle of the bustle.

The inappropriate nap seemed like the perfect ending for the story of Brian. He was good-natured, and we got along with him on a personal level, but we'd misunderstood and disappointed each other too many times. Brian had gotten into arguments with us in the last two days of the show. He had thought the deal was that we'd tasked him to set up a sales rep network as he saw fit. We'd said no, we'd never committed to that—we wanted to build up relationships with distributors. Then he'd started talking about not wanting to bring his lawyer into the situation.

I had gotten red-faced angry enough that Kyle, who always kept calmer in those kinds of situations, quickly stepped in and took over the conversation. All I knew was, I'd run out of patience, and Brian had run out of motivation.

Kyle had talked with Brian for a good half-hour, asking him why he'd want to spend money suing us when he could make money selling for us. From a safe distance, I had seen Kyle holding up his hands, palms up, in a mock scale. "Spend money on lawyers"—his right hand went up as his left went down. "Make money by selling"—left up, right down. Brian had looked at Kyle's hands and just shaken his head. He was like a mouse who knew there was cheese at the end of the maze but couldn't be bothered with all of that pesky running.

After the arguments, Kyle and I had decided to let Brian go, giving him a gradual 45-day workout schedule, during which he could still sell and receive commissions as he saw fit. His response, it seemed, was to nap.

We closed out Orlando with nearly $25,000 in direct sales, and we'd laid the groundwork for a lot of other sales that would pan out later. The PGA show had cost us around $10,000 all in all, so we felt we'd done well, both in the short and long terms. We'd also gotten enough immediate feedback to know what our firm retail price would be going forward. We left Orlando knowing MouseDriver would list for $29.95, ten dollars off our wildest-dream estimate, but only a few dollars off our most educated guess.

And we'd laid the groundwork with a handful of distributors, just as we'd planned. Between the PGA and a much smaller golf convention in Los Angeles at the end of February, we'd signed on with a couple. One was CJP Company, out of Dallas, referred to us by a retailer we worked with, MacBirdie Golf Gifts. And through Rick and Peter McQuaid, a friend we'd made at *Golf Retailer* magazine, we met Ryan Howard of Golf World, a big mass merchandising retailer. We also met with the Bookpeddler, a California distributor that was big in the golf industry. Plus, running into Michael Clark of Sherwood/Burkhouse fame would prove to be a real boon. He would teach us a lot of the ins and outs of the 2001 stage of our business, marketing to corporate accounts.

All told, the PGA had been a success for us. We'd survived the initial assault on our egos that came with our modest jump into the outsized, overfunded, bustling beauty pageant that is the trade show world. We'd been embarrassed for what we were doing, but gotten over our shame and hangovers to become engrossed in selling and wheeling and dealing. It wasn't fun to hear people telling us our product was stupid or lousy, but I learned a lot from watching Kyle, who was miles ahead of me in keeping his cool in difficult personal interactions, even though I knew he took MouseDriver criticisms as hard as I did. In the end, we both took comfort in the fact that the naysayers were far outnumbered by those who'd liked MouseDriver.

To top it off, people who saw MouseDriver at the show but didn't purchase at our booth were calling our toll-free number and ordering, according to the report we got from the home office. We'd flown an old friend of mine from SMU, Phil Nikpour, out to San Francisco for the week to man the phones and fill any orders that came in outside the UDS setup. Phil, who was working on becoming a sommelier, could charm anyone out of anything, so some of the bigger orders were perhaps due more to his sweet talk than to our showmanship—not only did Phil respond to customer inquiries, he made friends with the customers. He still keeps in touch with some of them.

Egos, deal-making, and showdowns notwithstanding, our biggest take-home lesson from the PGA Merchandise Show was that we were going to have to go into training to survive the big trade show pace. The mix of work and social interaction and alcohol with no regard for sleep, while lots of fun, would definitely kill us if we weren't careful. We were going to have to develop a preconvention regimen, like speed schmoozing at a half a dozen happy hours every night. We had to think of something. Maybe we could get Greens.com to pay for our training supplies.

YES, OF COURSE IT'S
MAC-COMPATIBLE

We came out of the PGA Merchandise Show with something else besides contacts, orders, and monster hangovers. Something had coalesced, something that had been floating around in pieces of what Kyle and I believed Platinum Concepts, Inc. was about.

We knew that word had gotten around at the show that there were these MBA guys with a clever golf product, but that place was such total pandemonium that basically all we took in was the realization that some people were noticing us. As it turned out, they were noticing the right things.

Our company identity had emerged.

The business world calls this "branding," and most people think of it as a luxury only large corporations can afford. You don't hear the mom & pop grocery on the corner worrying about whether or not it's building its brand—if it did, you might refer to the mom & pop shop by its name rather than "the corner store." But small companies who want to become big companies should pay very close attention to branding.

At Wharton, we'd read plenty of case studies that demonstrated the value, growth, and mismanagement of brands, all in association with the major players of the corporate marketing world—Coca-Cola, Pepsi, Ford, Kodak, American Express, McDonald's, and so on. Branding is an amazing concept. Essentially, when exercised properly, it allows you to break the rules of business.

A successfully branded company can go outside the parameters of the standard price/value equation. In considering a branded product, the customer decision goes from "Do I want to buy a dollar's worth of caramel-colored, caffeinated sugar water?" to "Do I want a Coke or a Pepsi?" and all of the images that go along with that. (Except, of course, in Texas, where all soft drinks are Cokes, as in "What kind of Coke you want? We've got Dr Pepper and root beer.") Branding gets customers to think nothing of going to Starbucks instead of 7-11 for coffee that costs three times more and is, realistically, maybe only twice as good. One of my personal favorites is Clorox, which, simply because of its name, can charge a premium over other brands, despite the bottom line that bleach is bleach.

Better yet, having the name brand in a product category means that companies can force the hands of their competitors. The branded company gets to look at how much the product costs to make, decide how much it can charge for it, and go to town. When one brand becomes the automatic choice, there's no room for the competition except at the lowest possible price. That's what store-brand colas are left with.

Given that branding brings all these advantages, the obvious question is not why should companies build brands, but how? Often, it's luck and timing—their product matches an emerging market need. But branding also has two key, controllable factors: Relentless marketing (primarily advertising, along with some public relations) and consistent, worldwide quality control.

With these two factors covered, every customer experience should lead to positive associations with the product. A Coke should always have the same fizz, whether in Mexico or Belgium. A McDonald's in Japan may have more fish choices than the standard American menu, but the Big Mac is going to taste the same. Ultimately, branding success depends on making sure that people always get the same high level of pleasure out of using the product, then strengthening those positive associations through advertising.

Kyle and I had tried to take these big corporate branding lessons and apply them to Platinum Concepts from the outset, discussing how we wanted the company to be regarded. There were some small company examples to look to as well, ones that had gone big partially due to successful branding. Ben & Jerry's started as a small player among many other regional gourmet ice cream makers. What made it come out on top in the mid-'80s was a quality product (apparently, consumers wanted rich ice cream with lots of chewy and crunchy hunks thrown in) supported by an appealing brand—smiling Ben and Jerry, two average, approachable guys, looking out from the lid of every pint. Nantucket Nectars took the same approach as it went from regional to national, building a brand based on identifying the product with its founders. Every bottle tells the story of how these two "juice guys" started selling fresh-squeezed juice off of their boat in Nantucket harbor in the summers.

We thought that a similar approach might work for MouseDriver (if everything went very, very well) and had played with some ideas for getting our own "story" out there more. But, since (1) we were just starting to hit customers, (2) we certainly didn't have any money for advertising yet, and (3) there weren't any direct competitors to differentiate ourselves from, we mostly thought of the Platinum Concept–MouseDriver brand in an abstract, future-oriented way, making decisions about whether or not MouseDriver belonged in an infomercial or among logoed condoms according to what image we were pursuing for the company. Everything was geared toward how Platinum Concepts would be perceived when it "grew up," when MouseDriver hit big. We hadn't stopped to look in the mirror and see what Platinum Concepts looked like in the here and now.

Then one day early in March, we caught a glimpse of ourselves as reflected in the eyes of Pancho Epstein (yes, his real name), sports columnist for the *Santa Fe New Mexican*. Pancho had heard about MouseDriver from a sports psychologist friend who saw it at the Orlando PGA show and got a kick out of the MBAs-making-mice story. He checked out our www.mousedriver.com site, liked the quirky information he found there, and called us for an interview.

In just 333 words, Pancho's article, "Computer Mouse Keeps Your Mind on Golfing," both hit the essence of what made Kyle's and my path from Wharton to MouseDriver unique and reviewed the product itself. "Everyone who ventures into this office is fascinated with it," he wrote. "MouseDriver puts smiles on people's faces. For the computer-using golfer, this is a must gift."

Not only did Pancho give us the perfect product review (even if it were made to order, it couldn't have been better), Pancho got what Platinum Concepts and MouseDriver were about. He wrote about Kyle's and my choice in contrast to those of our classmates, and he spotlighted how we'd taken a simple product and set it up to be all that it could be. Reading in print the story we had been trying to tell gave us a great "Yes, that's it!"

charge. Kyle popped open a couple of Dr Peppers to celebrate (even a month later, the PGA show debauchery had us steering clear of alcohol), and we clinked cans.

Up until that point, the only other person who'd really gotten it was Rick. The half dozen or so article placements he had secured for us in golf publications for Christmas and surrounding the PGA show almost all mentioned the unlikely entrepreneurs angle. Rick himself affectionately referred to us by our background, saying, "You can't fool those Wharton boys!" when a potential distributor at the show tried to talk us into a less than favorable arrangement or "Those Wharton boys are fine golfers (wink, wink)," when we pled work commitments in declining invitations to complete foursome after foursome on Orlando's deluxe links.

The best of Rick's hits was the recent news that MouseDriver would appear in the March–April issue of *Golf for Women* magazine—a bull's-eye in our target market. What a score! Rick was working his tail off getting people to pay attention to us, and he'd gotten great results, results that supported what looked like the beginnings of our brand.

The one downside of successful branding is that it puts you in a position where you always have to protect your brand. Anything negative—new Coke, the Arch Deluxe, exploding SUV tires—damages your reputation, staining your brand. This is especially true for small companies—flat out, your reputation equals your brand. For us, each and every experience people had with MouseDriver had to be positive, as it would all reflect on the brand.

With this in mind, Kyle and I decided to become the kings of customer service. We'd laid out ambitious plans along those lines before, back in early December when we'd had some free time and set out to write an individual thank-you note to each and every person who had ever bought a MouseDriver. We did write quite a few, but we got busy again, and now with all of the PGA show orders and the fact that we were no longer selling each MouseDriver ourselves, such personalized service was no longer possible.

That very fact made us nervous, as our outsourcing experiences with Brian and his order fulfillment fiascoes had been less than optimal. All had gone basically fine with UDS in Reno so far, but we figured that at this point, with everything getting so big, we couldn't be too careful. We couldn't tolerate the fallout of anyone screwing things up for us. So we redoubled our commitment to customer service. It was going to be flawless. At least all the aspects we handled, anyway.

We saw customer service as a place where we could differentiate ourselves, where we could build the Platinum Concepts–MouseDriver brand through accountability, respect, and commitment to customer satisfaction. The ultimate customer service, of course, was to have people plug MouseDriver in, have it work immediately, then happily "Just Drive It" for years to come—in branding terms, kind of a Maytag repairman approach. But if the slightest glitch occurred, we wanted to correct it as quickly as possible and leave customers feeling nothing but positive about having bought into this unique product. At this stage of our business, positive referrals and word of mouth from happy customers could have a major impact on our success.

Besides, customer service was fun, especially since UDS was now handling the bulk of ordering, and we were no longer swamped with calls. It was gratifying to get firsthand feedback from customers. Even when we heard complaints, it gave us a sense of accomplishment to be able to do something to fix the situation. People were so used to hanging up in defeat after going through hellishly intricate voice mail menus or talking to agents at some call center who knew nothing but what the standard scripts told them that they were overjoyed right off the bat just to talk to a live person who could do something.

So whatever the problem, whether it was our fault or someone else's, we were always quick to apologize and try to make amends via a free mousepad, a MouseDriver T-shirt, or (like in the porn number incident) a free MouseDriver. We just wanted the customer to be happy. One woman e-mailed to complain that she had ordered two MouseDrivers, but only received one. Kyle checked with UDS. They'd shipped two, just like she ordered. What could have happened here? Did one get lost in the mail? Did one arrive earlier than the other and someone else in her household forgot to give it to her? Did aliens abduct it? Who knew, but we couldn't imagine why anyone would make something like that up, so we sent her another one along with an apologetic note.

Even when the worst happened, we paused briefly to swear, then went to work on fixing things. Like in late January, when Kyle wondered aloud why inquiries to info@mousedriver.com had picked up so much lately and subsequent comparative research revealed that the e-mail account had been down for the entire month of December. Kyle swore creatively, something truly original about copulation and idiocy and laundry issues, then he hunted around our server to see if he could retrieve some of the lost messages. He found quite a few, to which I replied with deeply apologetic e-mails. As for whatever messages were lost, I ventured, "Maybe it was just NAGCE telling us that the check was in the mail." Still no check from NAGCE.

Or like when, shortly after we made a deal to offer a few test MouseDrivers on BravoGifts.com, I logged on to check out their cool program that gave product info via live chat and typed the no-brainer question, "Does MouseDriver work with a Mac?"

The customer support rep typed right back, "Yes."

What the . . . ??!! "No, it doesn't," I replied.

"I think it does. Do you want to buy one?"

"No," I replied. "I already have several hundred MouseDrivers sitting in my apartment right now, and not one of them will work on a Mac, even if I had a Mac, which I don't. Please tell your marketing department and all the rest of the customer support reps that *MouseDriver is not Mac-compatible* and that you heard that straight from the Platinum Concepts VP of marketing. Thank you. Good-bye."

Sometimes, customers wanting to place an order would just call the first toll-free number they saw on our Web site, dialing our 888 customer service number (which rang in our apartment) instead of our 877 ordering number (which used to ring at Brian's office, but now at UDS). Instead of telling customers to call the other number, we would just say, "Sure, I can help you with that," and then enter their info directly into our online ordering page for UDS to fulfill. It was a no-lose proposition—we gave the customer immediate service, and we didn't have to do any packaging or shipping.

I have to admit, there were times when answering the phone proved to have been a bad idea, unless we were up for killing some time listening to imaginative people's misperceptions of what should constitute a MouseDriver. I don't know where these people came from or how they managed to avoid all of the information out there describing what MouseDriver really was, but, if nothing else, they could be funny.

For some reason, it seemed like I was the lucky one who managed to answer almost 100 percent of these calls. There was the woman who was all excited to get her MouseDriver and, midway through the ordering process, asked, "What does the mouse's face look like?" I wasn't exactly sure which side of MouseDriver you would call the face, so I just answered generally, figuring maybe I'd hit the info she was looking for.

"It's all smooth on top, and the driver face is grooved like a real club."

"Oh," she said, sounding perturbingly unenlightened. "What color is it?"

"It's gray, like a driver."

"Oh," she replied. "Gray, like a mouse?"

We were on parallel tracks, obviously not connecting. And we never would. She wanted to buy a real golf club (apparently for actual golfing) with a head that looked like a mouse. An animal mouse, with whiskers and everything. So, almost five minutes into that call from the Twilight Zone, I went back and canceled the sale. "Good luck," I said. "Sorry we couldn't help you."

Another time, Kyle brought back lunch and heard me repeating a caller's question back to her. For half a second, he wondered if in some weird reversal the phone sex lines were mistakenly promoting our number.

"Ma'am," I continued, deliberately turning from the snorting, doubled-over Kyle. "It's not any length. There is no shaft. A shaft would make it unwieldy and a bit dangerous around the computer screen."

She wouldn't settle for a computer mouse that looked like just the head of a driver; she wanted a computer mouse that looked like the whole club, shaft and all. Again, I had gone through the entire order process and was answering the "Oh, I have just one more" question. Cancel order. Recovering from his laughter, Kyle handed me a sandwich, and the engineer in him wondered if she had planned to maneuver the complete MouseDriver by the head or by the shaft grip.

"Call her back," I encouraged, biting into the sandwich. "Talk to her about all the possibilities. Knock yourself out." I tasted roast beef and peered between the slices of sourdough. "Oh, hey," I said, handing it back and grabbing the unopened sandwich. "This is yours."

Eventually, I got smart, and just in time. Before I could even finish saying, "Platinum Concepts, this is John," a caller started asking why we hadn't branched out into other mouse concepts and telling me that he had this incredible idea that would sell millions of mice. "Just a moment," I said. "Let me transfer you to our R&D department. I'm sure they'll be eager to talk to you." I put the phone on hold, turned to Kyle, who had been working diligently at his computer, and smiled. "It's all you, dude."

Kyle scowled at me, then picked up the call, letting his Texas drawl come through. "Platinum Concepts research and development, this is Kyle Harrison. What can I do for y'all today?"

I grabbed my gym bag and headed for the door, pausing to mouth a couple of choice words of my own at Kyle before I left. "Check ya." When I came back—an hour later, at least—he was still on the call. He punched the mute button and gave me the scoop.

"This guy wants to manufacture a mouse that looks like a human ear. He thinks it'll sell huge to otolaryn . . . gologologismists . . . you know, ENT doctors. Like they're big computer users. He's got tons of data and a hundred million questions. Call me crazy, but it is kind of interesting . . . "

Nutty people calling with nutty ideas, if nothing else, loosened things up in our office/kitchen. We'd be all worried about some price negotiations or Brian's latest antics or the ever-rising fortunes of our dot-com brethren, when someone would call and ask if he could get a whole set of mice, one for every club in the bag. After politely responding to him (um, no), we would let the absurdity of it all get the better of us.

It was in such a state of mind that I started cold–e-mailing journalists, telling them our story. Why the hell not, right? I mean, if the ear mouse guy could do it, so could we. So anytime I read an interesting story in a golf or business magazine, I'd dash off a quick e-mail to the writer, praising the story and telling him or her about Platinum Concepts.

The March 2000 issue of *Inc.* magazine had dot-com this, dot-com that, more dot-com, and a story on an entrepreneur who had developed a special razor for guys who were shaving their heads (this growing trend was often accompanied by a little goatee). It talked about his manufacturing and distribution issues and all sorts of other problems like the ones we had run into ourselves. I was fascinated. I was elated. It was like a breath of fresh air. Here was a real business selling a tangible product to solve a genuine problem. Not another VC-funded dot-com with a ridiculous IPO making everyone who was not me or Kyle rich (which is how it felt in our insulated San Francisco microcosm—as the dot-coms flourished, so did the publications that covered them, so there was always an old *Wired* or *Red Herring* or *Upside* or *Business 2.0* left on the table at Starbucks to remind us of what we were missing out on).

I thought that it was incredibly cool that the journalist had chosen to write about this. So I chose to write him.

From: John Lusk
To: Mike Hofman
Subject: Wharton MBAs and MouseDriver

Mike,
    Many kudos on your recent article about Todd Greene and HeadBlade. It's nice to see publications such as Inc. covering

non–e-commerce related entrepreneurs … especially when I can relate to Todd's journey.

My business partner and I had every intention of leaving the Wharton MBA program last May and joining one of the many dot-com start-ups out here in the Bay Area. But some marketing professors at Wharton encouraged us to take a classroom project and turn it into a company. So now, instead of wheeling and dealing in the Internet world, we're focused on bringing MouseDriver (a patented computer mouse shaped as the head of a golf driver) to market … pretty whacked out!

Many of our classmates thought we were crazy, but wanted to hear of our progress nonetheless. Most of them are bankers, consultants, or e-commerce people who say they want to live the entrepreneurial experience vicariously through us. We send out a mailing every month informing such people of our triumphs, failures, fears, experiences, etc. I've attached the first two below, thinking you might be interested in seeing how a couple of MBA graduates are struggling with a non–VC funded company. Let me know if you'd like to be added to the distribution.

Again, it's great to see you covering companies like Todd's.
Regards,
John

A long shot for sure, but certainly worth a shot.

* * *

Anyone remotely interested in golf knows that it originated in Scotland. And while other United Kingdom sports like cricket, rugby, and soccer made isolated, occasional jumps to the U.K.'s English-speaking former colonies, golf was the most successful transplant. Personally this was a bummer for me, as I was a big soccer fan as well as a lapsed player. But professionally it was a boon. We'd met a lot of international golf people at the PGA Merchandise Show in Orlando (funny, since we'd thought that they would all have gone to the earlier Las Vegas show, officially titled "PGA International Golf Show"), and a lot of them had expressed interest in MouseDriver.

A small U.K. company called OCL Golf had called back and wanted to retail MouseDriver, as they say, across the pond. We remembered the OCL guys, and the idea of trying to hit the U.K. market on a limited basis appealed to us. Going with OCL would be a good test. Plus, we could direct all European inquiries to OCL and have them fulfill orders, making things much, much easier on us and much, much cheaper for customers in Europe trying to obtain the product.

Only one issue: OCL wanted an exclusive. They basically had one—we weren't in discussions with any other U.K. companies, and we had no plans to start any—but there was no way we were going to start granting exclusives now. I wrote OCL a letter outlining our strategy, trying to reassure them by explaining that we wanted to keep distribution limited so that (1) price competition didn't become an issue with MouseDriver and (2) Platinum Concepts could spend time marketing the product and pulling it through channels rather than managing a bunch of distributors. The chaps at OCL said, "Sounds fair," and ordered 1,000 units.

We were thrilled. OCL was eager to add to our marketing efforts by running its own campaign and even built a www.mousedriver.co.uk Web site. Nick, our main OCL contact, e-mailed us a draft of the press release they had prepared to announce the site debut and product availability. I only had one edit—rather than writing "sole" U.K. distributor, could he change it to "preferred"? I felt like a broken record.

Canada came calling as well, in the form of a Vancouver retailer, followed by some one-off Australian purchases. Kyle had fun figuring out different pricing for different countries and currencies, while I checked back with Nick at OCL to make sure they'd received the product.

They had and thought it was smashing. Just one small concern. Damn, I thought, not the exclusivity thing again. Nope, not that. They were "slightly uneasy" about the "<" we had printed on MouseDriver. (On our nonlogoed products, we had put the mark just below the MouseDriver name to indicate what would be the strike point on a real driver, adding to the whole "authentic driver look and feel.") Nick wondered politely if our "less than" symbol didn't look rather too similar to the trademarked Callaway "arrowhead." Callaway, the famous golf company whose Big Bertha had led the way in popularizing a whole class of oversized titanium drivers—the very type of club we'd designed MouseDriver to resemble.

A couple of booth browsers at the PGA show had mentioned this too, and I told Nick the same thing I'd told them. It wasn't a problem, and if a large number of retailers truly believed that our MouseDriver computer mouse would take away from Callaway sales of Big Bertha clubs, we would change it. Nick was satisfied and wished me a good day. "Thanks, take it easy," I said, and turned to Kyle, who was analyzing recent currency fluctuations. "We've gotta change the arrow."

Kyle had heard the whole thing. "Yeah, on the next printing," he agreed. "I'm thinking solid isosceles triangle, maybe with a slightly curved base . . . "

Just as we inked the deal with OCL to gain our first international golf industry retail distributor, we were close to securing one for the domestic market as well. On Rick's recommendation we'd met with a local distributor (conveniently headquartered about halfway between San Francisco and Tahoe in a small town called Grass Valley) called the Bookpeddler at the

PGA show. After talking for more than a month, we were close to an agreement.

We knew we needed stock-holding retail distributors to help us bring MouseDriver to market. With something like 10,000 golf-related stores in the United States, the golf industry defined the word fragmented. The Bookpeddler would be a perfect fit—it had distribution into most of the major national golf retailers and was well known as the primary distributor for golf books and videos, which we thought matched our golf gift item category quite nicely. Adding MouseDriver to its line would give the Bookpeddler a chance to expand to a new type of product while using the same promotional strategies. And given its already existing relationships, the Bookpeddler could get MouseDriver out there fast.

All of the pieces were coming together. We were closing in on the ideal setup—us as the one producer, Burkhouse and Techpad as the almost-one supplier, well on the way to several distributors, and many corporate and retail clients sure to follow.

But the Bookpeddler, like Burkhouse, like Techpad, like OCL, like everybody, wanted—all together now—an exclusive. We were getting sick of everyone asking for exclusives, even if it was just lip service. Kyle was having enough problems with his own personal exclusive (long-distance dating was not going well), and I myself had just started seeing a woman who was sounding progressively more exclusive-oriented.

We had been told by everyone in the golf industry not to give an exclusive to anyone. Even some people affiliated with the companies asking for exclusives had told us not to give them. Exclusives, we heard, were done only if (1) the deal was so sweet that you absolutely, positively, no way in hell could pass it up, (2) your product sucked so bad that no one would carry it unless they had at least that one advantage, or (3) you had no idea of how to sell, market, or promote your product, so you wanted someone to have an incentive to do those things for you.

We had no intentions of giving any exclusives, but we were also wary of working with competing distributors. Competing distributors would try to undercut each other on price to make the sale, consequently opening up the opportunity for retailers to discount the product, and we wanted to maintain our newly cemented $29.95 price point for now. Plus, overlapping distributors meant lots of phone calls complaining that the guy in Illinois was calling on the guy in Washington's account. We definitely didn't want to referee situations like that.

That said, distributors have to ask for exclusives. They don't want to deal with competition any more than manufacturers do. And there's no harm in asking. After all, there's bound to be the occasional dumbass manufacturer who will say, "Um, okay," and then the distributor has an instant monopoly as the sole distributor of the product. Talk about competitive advantage.

We understood where the Bookpeddler was coming from, and we wanted them to feel good about working with us. We set a date to meet with them in Grass Valley to explain our retail strategy and how they fit into it. We didn't mind—we could meet with the Bookpeddler on a Friday afternoon, maybe again (to take care of any leftover agenda items) the following Monday morning, and somehow fill the days between. The Bookpeddler's location, like the snow just beyond it, was perfect.

In the meantime, we gave the Bookpeddler a great win-win deal. Through our PGA show exposure and some success with our random mailings, we had been selling to a number of different golf stores, including some of the major ones. We would turn these accounts over to the Bookpeddler, which gained active or even new accounts, freeing ourselves of the headaches of fulfillment, billing, collecting, and so on. We gave up some margin, but it was definitely worth it. Our only caveat was that we would turn our accounts over in stages—upon the Bookpeddler's first order of X number of MouseDrivers, we would transfer Y number of accounts. That way, there was a built-in incentive for them to keep pushing the product.

Within a week we got a bitter phone call from Brian, complaining that the Bookpeddler reps were selling in Sacramento, which he considered part of his (actually nonexistent) "territory." "Hey, Brian," I replied. "You're gonna want to talk to Kyle about this one—he's got more of the details. Just a sec." I put him on hold and grinned at Kyle, who was poring over "unique Web visitor" logs. "This one's yours."

Kyle glared at me and took the phone. "Someone from Callaway spent twenty minutes surfing our site last week," he said as he pressed the line button to pick up the call. Uh oh.

SCHADENFREUDE

Everyone responds to risk differently. Some people cower and try to find a way around it. Others hedge their bets and cautiously proceed. A few (mostly entrepreneurs and stunt men) cross themselves, cross their fingers, and jump.

It's impossible to know how risk-averse you are until the situation strikes—when you're faced with the possibility of losing something you really care about (money, reputation, life) as part of the opportunity to gain something else (more money, better reputation, experience of a lifetime).

What Kyle and I found for ourselves was that once we took some risks, taking more risks came easily. It even felt natural. Ultimately, there are people who like to eat good, and people who like to sleep good. Apparently we went for eating.

When you accept risk, you have to also accept that you're going to lose sometimes. You sign up for the roller coaster. Ups and downs. The good with the bad. Highs and lows. Or, as they say on the West Coast, the yin and the yang.

And that's where we were, trying to take a Taoist approach to the wild fluctuations of start-up life, trying to ignore the needle on our mood meter, which was swinging from end to end several times a day, even more often if we checked the stock market numbers online.

We'd have days where we'd field calls from dozens of companies wanting to be affiliates, to sell MouseDriver from their Web sites, followed by days where the phone wouldn't ring once. Days where journalists would e-mail us, wanting to know more about MouseDriver, then days where I'd e-mail fifty and not a single writer would respond.

It was during those days that Kyle and I realized that having our own business was like owning a home. As a renter, if the faucet's leaking and the heater conks out and the toilet stops responding to that special jiggle that makes it flush right all in the same day, it's no sweat. You just call the landlord. But once you buy a home, it's you who calls the plumber and the electrician, and it's you who pays them.

But homeowners get tax breaks, pride in ownership, and the sense of permanence associated with having fixed or built something, no matter how mundane. Whenever someone expressed big MouseDriver appreciation, we could reflect, hey, without us the world would have no MouseDrivers.

Risk, roller coasters, and renters. Whatever. The point is we were getting comfortable with these ideas. We were getting the hang of the pacing of our business. We were even finding ways to take advantage of it.

We had changed our meeting with the Bookpeddler in Grass Valley from Friday afternoon to Thursday midday, and we set out east across the Bay Bridge Thursday morning with our retail strategy PowerPoint on the laptop in the trunk of my car and our snowboards in the rack on top.

The Bookpeddler's offices were like a mini PGA Merchandise Show with the amount of golf books (hence the name), golf videos, and golf paraphernalia they had. Kyle and I were impressed, and all the more flattered that the Bookpeddler was so pleased to be promoting MouseDriver. A receptionist directed us to an empty conference room, where we set up our Power-Point on a table whose centerpiece was several foot-high stuffed plush golf bags with eyes, all different colors. Kyle reached over to pick up a red one and nearly flung it across the room when it came alive, bursting into song. Nothing I recognized, but I could detect a slightly Scottish lilt.

Dain Miller, our contact, appeared in the doorway, with a few other people behind him. "I see you've met Chip, the 'Singing and Swinging' Golf Bag," he said, laughing. No wonder the Bookpeddler was happy to have MouseDriver in its collection. Chip was insane.

We told the Bookpeddler group that our first goal was to sell MouseDrivers in the golf, gift, and specialty store industries, building awareness and momentum within our target market. Next slide. Once we had proven sales, we would hit the larger upscale department stores, extending awareness to the upstairs retailers of the mass market. Next slide. At the appropriate time, we would take our current product downstairs and sell to the mass merchandisers—the Costcos, Wal-Marts and Mervyn's.

A few more slides. At that point, MouseDriver would become a $20 (or, rather, $19.95) item. To keep our $29.95 price point in the high end, we would introduce a new and improved MouseDriver for those channels—golf, gift, specialty, and upstairs. That way, our high-end retailers (and distributors, like the Bookpeddler) would not only continue to make margins, but they would also offer a differentiated, superior product from the mass merchandisers.

We'd be getting revenue from all of the available channels, and better yet, we'd give the impression that a low-end version of MouseDriver existed—essentially, knocking ourselves off. If we threw our original MouseDriver to the discounters just as we introduced a better product, other manufacturers would be discouraged from trying to copycat with their own ClubMouse or whatever. We hoped.

When we finished our presentation, the room was silent. Not a single question. They thought we were geniuses. We came clean and admitted that a lot of the strategy's components were based on case studies we'd read in business school. "Wow," Dain said. "That means that they'll probably work."

We also showed the Bookpeddler a letter we'd drafted to send to all of our golf retailers, telling them that from the time of receipt forward, they would need to purchase MouseDrivers through the Bookpeddler. To us, this letter represented freedom from all of the sales, invoicing, order fulfillment and collection hassles of the retail world—the same kind of freedom UDS had given us from individual orders. It was set to go out to the fifty or so small pro-shop retailers we'd picked up at the PGA show, as well as the nice handful of larger retailers (Edwin Watts, Don Sherwood's, Golf Galaxy, and Golf Town) that we'd reached through direct mailings and follow-ups at the PGA show.

Then we went over the unique, original part of our strategy once more, the part that made us proud. Give us an order for X number of MouseDrivers to send to your retailers, and we'll transfer Y accounts to you. Order more and we'll hand over Golf Galaxy. Order more and we'll hand over Edwin Watts. The Bookpeddler was completely on board and told us about the marketing efforts and sales calls they had already been making (which, thanks to Brian, we were already aware of). "Great!" Kyle said. "Sounds like you guys have got it all covered."

We kept heading east to our time-share, and spent Friday at Squaw Valley. It was phenomenal. Fresh snow, 70 degrees, not a cloud in the sky. All of the lifts were open and there was no one around. We got the equivalent of a full day's boarding in before noon. At one point we had the Riviera pipe all to ourselves and held our very own jump contest (the winner was debatable, with Kyle arguing for upright finish and me for degree of difficulty).

After quick burgers and beers for lunch, we went for the new Headwall Express lift to the 8,900-feet top of Squaw Peak. Over our shoulders we could see the deep, sparkling blue of Lake Tahoe. We were completely comfortable in T-shirts (mine said MouseDriver, Kyle's said Greens.com), and the only sound was the occasional schussing of a skier below.

We spoke of our friends who were indoors at work or joining the clogged artery of cars making the slow journey from San Francisco to Tahoe on a Friday afternoon. There was a lot to be said for being your own boss.

On the way back from Tahoe at the end of the weekend, we marveled over California. Here it was, early April, and we were leaving perfect skiing conditions, cruising into a warm Central Valley covered in wildflowers, on our way to the lush green hills that served as the gateway to the always-temperate Bay Area, all within a three-hour drive. Hell, if we'd wanted to, we could have gone straight to the beach (so long as we limited our time in the 55-or-so-degree water to, say, three seconds). Philly in April could be cold and gray, maybe even with some dirty, slushy snow hanging around the gutters.

And Texas . . . actually, Texas was gorgeous in the spring. It wasn't too hot, and you might get an early thunderstorm, where the sky went black, the wind picked up, the temperature dropped 20 degrees, and all hell broke loose, flooding streets and testing trees and power lines. Lightning and thunder with next to no time in between, every ten seconds for about twenty minutes, then back to normal as if nothing ever happened. We both missed thunderstorms and, although California was growing on us, it wasn't Texas.

We stopped at the Cattlemens restaurant in Dixon to try to console ourselves with gigantic steaks. Eating among men in cowboy hats speaking a mixture of English and Spanish in a tiny town surrounded by ag lands, it almost worked. But the steaks weren't nearly as good, and they didn't have Shiner Bock beer.

When we got back home to our office, there was a letter from Callaway. Probably interested in getting logoed MouseDrivers, I offered, trying to keep a brave face. Kyle opened it. It was from Callaway's lawyer. He expressed the company's concern that we were using their trademarked arrow and included a magazine clipping of some of our prized editorial coverage praising and picturing MouseDriver. He'd circled the arrow in red.

I called him the next day, explained that we'd already changed the logo in response to concerns people voiced at the PGA show, that we were no longer selling the stock with the arrow, and hoped that was it. Kyle calculated how many MouseDrivers we had left with the Callaway-like arrow. Fortunately, just a few dozen. "Let's send 'em to Callaway," he said. "Get 'em hungry to maybe buy some."

The publicity that made Callaway notice us had made a lot of other people notice us as well, and they were all hungry to buy MouseDrivers. The number of hits to www.mousedriver.com was skyrocketing, we were making some Internet sales, and we were hearing from all sorts of interested retailers. The golf-related ones we passed on to the Bookpeddler, the gift-related ones in the Southwest to CJP in Dallas, but the rest we handled ourselves. More retailers were of course a good thing, but I have to admit that sometimes we felt a bit overwhelmed.

All in one day, we heard from buyers for The Sports Authority (199 stores in 32 states) and Stein Mart (239 stores in 29 states, huge in the South and Texas). These were major, major national chains. Excited as we were, we kept our cool and turned them down. Next year, we told them—they were discounters, part of our mass merchandise downstairs strategy, and we weren't ready for them yet. Just months before we'd been scrambling, trying to reach buyers, and now they were calling us.

We also heard back from Ryan Howard of the big mass-merchandising retailer Golf World, whom we'd met at the PGA show. It was the same deal. Golf World sold to department stores like Sears, as well as a lot of sporting goods stores, not much on the high end. We talked about getting in with them for 2001, in time for the January–February period when all of their major clients purchased most of their product for the holiday season eleven months later. We were finally understanding just how long sales cycles could be.

Golf World had an interesting sales strategy, similar to the one we'd designed for ourselves. For nearly all of their products, Golf World sold two lines of the same thing—one in their colorful "Ultimate Gift" packaging, the other in their standard black-and-white Golf World packaging. They sold the Ultimate Gift package to the higher-end stores for a slightly higher price and the standard package to lower-end stores for, yes, a slightly lower price. The idea sounded good to us—the more differently packaged MouseDrivers out there, the more protection we had against knockoffs. Who would want to enter a market that already appeared to be saturated? We thanked Ryan for calling and told him we'd get back to him by the end of the year.

Another call came in from Wireless, a gift cataloger, and we agreed to get them MouseDrivers to feature alongside tabletop telescopes, steak branding irons, and nautical orientation T-shirts with fore, aft, port, and starboard printed on the front, back, left sleeve, and right sleeve, respectively. (A good move, as Wireless purchased 4,000 MouseDrivers over the course of the year.)

We also got a random phone order that we normally would have put in the UDS system, but got a big kick out of filling ourselves. It was someone in the defense crisis department at the Pentagon, and he wanted two MouseDrivers. MouseDriver in the Pentagon. Cool!

And a huge corporate promotions sale came through, months after we'd turned our focus away from the corporate promotions market. We'd been courting American Skandia, a big financial services company, since 1999, and now they sent payment for 1,000 logoed MouseDrivers. This would be the last logoed MouseDriver sale that we would fulfill ourselves. We would have turned it over to Burkhouse or Techpad, but neither of them had purchased product to have on hand yet, so it would take them longer to fill the order. Plus, since we'd gotten the sale set up before we signed the co-exclusive contracts, we felt like it was ours. Besides, how would we have chosen between the two?

It was all adding up: On top of payment from OCL, almost all of the checks from the PGA show sales were finally in, and now the hefty payment from American Skandia. It was the most money we'd had in our account since right before we'd placed our massive inventory order in September.

Feeling flush and encouraged, we decided that it was time to reassess our sales goals once again, incorporating the information from our most recent activities. After much number crunching and rigorous evaluation of our existing sales channels, we came up with the conservative estimate of moving

29,000 MouseDrivers by the end of 2000. That seemed definitely doable. A far cry from last year's early forecast of 400,000, but we'd been through a ton of changes since we came up with that figure. It was all part of the roller coaster, and we had to just enjoy the ride.

The universe must have seen fit to reward us for adopting such a Taoist outlook, as that very day's mail brought the envelope we had expected for so long. It was from NAGCE, and it was a check. We couldn't believe it. A check from NAGCE, a mere half-year or more after Brian had made the sale.

Revise sales goals, check. Get NAGCE check, uh, check. The next item on the to-do list was to sort through all of the applications we'd been receiving from potential affiliates, online companies like surprise.com that wanted to put MouseDriver on their sites to expand their offerings, but would send click-throughs directly to our own www.mousedriver.com ordering page. There were literally hundreds, and it looked like most of them sucked. Our problem: We had no way of knowing without reviewing their applications and looking at their sites. By the time we'd reduced the number of pending affiliates to zero, we had manually approved or disapproved more than 1,000 applications over six eye-crossing hours. Completely mind-numbing work.

And that was it. I was putting together the beginnings of a viral marketing campaign and Kyle was working on the preliminary designs for our improved MouseDriver, but with UDS, Burkhouse and Techpad, and the Bookpeddler and CJP on board, most of our day-to-day operations were covered. Just about everything was in place for Father's Day, so we had a few weeks ahead of us of just waiting to see what happened.

Kyle pulled out the Sony PlayStation we'd bought months ago (after a long e-mail debate with our friends about the merits of Sony versus Sega) and set it up. He put in Ready to Rumble Boxing and tossed me one of the handheld controllers. "Let's go," he said. "See if you can find someone who can challenge the mighty Salua Tua."

I sat down and chose Big Willy Johnson. He was seeing stars in no time flat, thanks to a big belly bounce from Salua Tua. "What, how'd you do that?" I turned and asked. Bad move. The second I looked away, Kyle put Salua Tua into a super-steroid rage and knocked poor Big Willy Johnson cold. "Damn," I said. "Reset. Let's try this again. Where'd that come from? What the hell does this button do?"

Kyle just cackled. "Here, I'll be Serlene Strike," he said. "Maybe Big Willy will do better against a girl."

Serlene Strike kicked Big Willy's ass. Several times. Kyle, apparently, had taken a look at the instructions and knew how to play the game, while I was going on pure survival instincts. "What else have we got?" I asked. "Let's try that Turbo Racing game."

More than fighting each other, even if only through animated boxers, we were fighting boredom. We'd been working side by side in our cramped kitchen for nearly ten months, and now that we seemed to have things basically under control, we were sick of it. We knew every one of each other's annoying habits and verbal tics—I ignored Kyle's mumbling; he tolerated my neck-popping and knuckle-cracking. But our enthusiasm was wearing thin, and we were struggling to stay motivated in such a lackluster environment. We needed an escape, and we found one right under our noses.

Golf.

For so long, we'd been completely focused on everything golf, but neither one of us had played enough of it to understand the deep love that all true golfers hold for the game. But honestly, golf saved us.

We started going out to the nearby Presidio golf course first thing in the morning, taking our warm-up swings at the driving range just as most people were heading off to work. After Brian and Rick's painful assessment of our golfing abilities down in Monterey (Brian couldn't believe that Kyle was the guy who had invented MouseDriver—in his mind, no one who was that bad at golf could have come up with such a beautiful golf product), we had signed up for lessons. We plunked down $240 each to turn ourselves over to Brian's friend Jobe Ross, the pro at the Mariner's Point course in Foster City, on the belief that he could turn us into presentable golfers in just five sessions.

But our lessons felt a lot more like work than golf. In fact, they were often a combination. The Mariner's Point pro shop sold MouseDriver, so we always stopped in there to see how the product was moving and if they needed any more. We'd load MouseDrivers in my trunk right along with our golf bags and shoot down the Peninsula for our appointment with Jobe, worrying about our progress since the last lesson, wondering what Brian had told Jobe about our letting him go, and trying not to notice all of the dot-com billboards lining Highway 101. Mariner's Point was right at the northern tip of Silicon Valley, within sight of Oracle's towers, and it was one of those quickie par-three courses that attracted lots of tech and dot-com types taking a long lunch. Even though we were mostly confined to the driving range, we still felt uncomfortably like outsiders.

The Presidio, in contrast, was idyllic. It was a five-minute drive from our apartment, in the middle of the old army base that was now a huge, tree-filled chunk of the Golden Gate National Recreational Area. It looked like all of the pictures in golf magazines. Most of the golfers were retirees (the old kind, not the dot-com cash-outs), who epitomized all of the game's legendary charm and etiquette.

And we were getting better. We could concentrate at the Presidio, get in the moment and lose ourselves in the quest of getting the ball in the cup. All the pressures we felt most of the rest of the time—to move more MouseDrivers, to get out of the apartment, to succeed—subsided. Almost all of my drives were going straight now, even getting some distance, and Kyle had become quite handy with the sand wedge.

But even if we played 36 holes of golf a day, we were still going to have to return to the apartment. We had work to do, and we had to check and return e-mails. The second we sat down in the office/kitchen, though, we got antsy.

Kyle looked at our QuickBooks projections and made some tentative inquiries with commercial realtors. The San Francisco commercial rental market was as bad as the apartment rental market. VC-funded dot-coms had driven prices up to an outrageous $80 per square foot. "I think we can afford an office," Kyle reported. "Maybe at the very top of the Transamerica building, with a view of the Golden Gate Bridge and Alcatraz. Yeah, that's about the right size—at least ten, maybe twenty square feet."

So it was back to Starbucks and the other cafés in the neighborhood. To free ourselves of the e-mail tether, we checked out all sorts of wireless options. For the price of just a few square feet of office space, we got not only two WAP (wireless application protocol)-enabled cell phones that could double as wireless modems, but also an endless stream of grande caffé lattes.

It was a pleasant, low-key existence. Some golf, an afternoon spent at the café. It could have been worse.

Then one morning in mid-April, we came back to the apartment from an especially good round at the Presidio (I had parred a hole, and Kyle was nearly out of the triple digits), to the news that the market was tanking.

Kyle flipped from CNN to MSNBC to the local news at noon. It was the same story everywhere. And the same story again the next day.

"Raw numbers put Friday, April 14, right up there with 1987's Black Monday and 1929's Terrible Tuesday as one of the scariest days in stock market history."

"Investors' weeklong skittishness turned to outright panic yesterday as inflation fears sparked the biggest one-day point losses ever for the Dow Jones industrial average and the NAS-DAQ composite index."

The analysts were all over the story, too:

"The bubble has popped."

"The gravy train has reached an end."

"People are clearly tired of seeing companies that don't have a foreseeable future."

"Investors want to see profits, not just revenue growth."

"The dot-coms and B-to-whatevers will fall 80% or 90% off their highs and never return."

"A lot of money has gone to money heaven, and it won't be coming back."

"This is good. People were unbelievably cocky and didn't understand risk."

Amazon.com shares dropped 11%. Microsoft neared its 52-week low. NASDAQ companies lost $1.6 trillion in market capitalization in just four weeks. EToys, which had hit a high of $86 a share after its recent IPO, had tumbled to $4.75. E-stamp, Fogdog, Pets.com, Quokka Sports, Salon.com, Webvan, and Women.com were all well below their IPO highs.

Despite the fact that both Kyle and I were invested in the market and were looking at drops in our portfolios, we were deliriously happy. It wasn't that we wanted to see all of the dot-coms tank and all of the dot-commers lose their jobs—we didn't. We were just so tired of everything being about them. We were tired of fighting to be taken seriously and getting shut out of office space and not being able to make same-day restaurant reservations. We wanted people to recognize the legitimacy of our little business, ours and all of the other non-VC-funded entrepreneurial ventures out there. And, of course, more than anything, we were so relieved that we could finally put to rest our low-point fears and nagging doubts that we'd screwed up by choosing MouseDriver over dot-coms.

That Sunday, April 16, was Kyle's thirty-first birthday. He couldn't have dreamed of a better present. But the Tao of start-ups wasn't going to let him off that easy. Poor guy spent most of his birthday on the phone long-distance to Philly, in the process of going from having a girlfriend to having an ex-girlfriend. Welcome to thirty-one.

To show my sympathy, I gave him grief. "Kyle," I mused. "So many questions. Will the Dow rebound? Will you?" Also, "Kyle, my man. Think about it. The market tanked. So did your relationship. You took a big drop in heavy trading, my friend. Your stock got dumped."

"Oh, yeah, and you're Mr. Relationship," Kyle snarled.

He had me there. My own relationship was rocky at best. They always say that entrepreneurship is tough on a family. How about on a single guy? How are you supposed to meet and date someone when your whole life is always changing from one day to the next?

Ultimately, it was up to Kyle to cheer himself up. He went out and bought a new stereo system that would have set him back the price of an engagement ring. He put on a CD of an old Phil Woods recording, cranked the volume, and pulled out his saxophone to play along. He was actually quite good (Phil Woods, I mean), but I had to leave. I had a tee time.

WE GET PAID

I walked in the door and played the voice mail back on speaker-phone.

"Kyle, hey, it's Scott Rubinstein from Brookstone. Sorry it took so long to get back to you, it's just been crazy busy here."

That's just great. He remembered Kyle's name, and not mine. Fine. Fine.

". . . yeah, the word you need to know on MouseDriver is: outstanding. Phenomenal item. Stores love it. We love it. We're buying more. You should feel very confident to ship and load your warehouse with stock so that we have ample reserve to take care of us for the holiday."

Outstanding. That was the word I needed to know. Suddenly I was feeling very confident. Because we must load our ware-house. Because we, Platinum Concepts, had to take care of Brookstone for the holiday.

I'd gotten over the name thing. This message was growing on me.

"I don't know if you've met Brad Rutt yet or if you've spoken to him on the phone. He's our merchandise planner. He's responsible for all of the allocation and how much gets purchased. I recommend you get in touch with him if you haven't. He's at 603-867-5309. And, you know, develop a rapport with him, he can probably give you a spreadsheet to let you know what the thing is worth annually so that you get a comfort level of what to throw in the warehouse."

Translation: Somewhere in the New Hampshire woods, in Brookstone's subterranean, top-secret research labs, some guy named Brad Rutt was barking orders to a hundred or so top-flight inventory analysts, who were desperately cranking out spreadsheet after spreadsheet, just so Kyle and I could reach a comfort level. To help us figure out how many zillion MouseDrivers to throw in our warehouse. How absolutely cool.

"But the item's great. It's extremely giftable. What we've noticed is that Father's Day was a huge spike. Now we're in a little bit of a lull period here, there's sort of a drop-off. So we have to be very careful to buy it right for Christmas because the spike is enormous and then it will probably drop off again in the early spring."

Huge Spike. Without a doubt, the most beautiful two-word phrase in the English language. Extremely Giftable was running a close second.

". . . very successful item and we're very happy with it. Congratulations to your company and mine."

Your company *and* mine? Now that came out weird. It sounded a little too . . . possessive. I had visions of Brookstone soldiers surrounding our warehouse and taking Platinum Concepts by force.

"FYI, if you have other items in the pipe, other things that you're getting ready to preview to other people, it behooves you to send me some digital photos or color renderings or mock-up samples, anything else you may be working on related to computer accessories, related to golf, related to anything, as we should be taking a look at items from a company that gives the kind of quality and design that yours does."

That was it. As far as I was concerned, Scott Rubinstein had left the best phone message ever. Brookstone loved us. There are times when flattery will get you everywhere with an entrepreneur. Already, I was completely over the whole Brookstone army scenario.

"So if I don't speak to you today, Friday, I hope you have a very nice weekend, and please get in touch with Brad Rutt, R-U-T-T, merchandise planner. He can help you understand what the upside is. Thanks."

No, thank you, Scott. I didn't need Brad Rutt to help me understand the upside. I was already whooping and pacing our apartment/office like a madman. Kyle walked through the door, and I replayed the message. Five times. Kyle whooped too, louder than me. And replayed the message another five times.

In Brookstone's eyes, we'd been a Father's Day hit. We'd sold well over 5,000 units, and might have done even more business if Brookstone hadn't been its customarily cautious self in dealing with newcomers like Platinum Concepts. It was great news. We hadn't exactly broken retail wide open with record-setting sales, but we'd positioned ourselves beautifully with Brookstone for the next big holiday, the Christmas/Hanukkah/Kwanzaa rush. Father's Day hadn't established Platinum Concepts as Brookstone's Most Valuable Player, but from what Scott Rubinstein had said, we were most definitely in the running for Rookie of the Year.

We'd been told by people other than Scott Rubinstein that once Father's Day was over and done with, the summer months were generally slow in retail. We hadn't experienced the sales slump in our first summer—we'd been too busy graduating, sweating through our MouseDriver education in Texas, and moving to San Francisco. And we'd yet to experience it in the early days of our second summer. Including Brookstone, MouseDriver was in nearly 500 stores. A great improvement from just a year before, when we'd been in approximately zero stores.

From April 1 until the day before Father's Day, we'd sold $90,000 worth of merchandise. From Father's Day on, we were on course to beat that figure easily in a comparable time frame. In June, we saw a steady stream of orders from the Bookpeddler and Techpad, as well as retailers like Edwin Watts and Golf Town. Maybe the lull would wait until July.

We especially marveled at how the Bookpeddler, with its squadron of sales reps, could get on the phone and make sales to the more exclusive retailers who otherwise wouldn't give Platinum Concepts the time of day. We knew because we'd tried. There was even one time when a retail buyer had abruptly hung up on me when she'd learned that Platinum Concepts wasn't an established brand name. She'd liked MouseDriver and listened to what I had to say with some interest. Then she asked who we were, and that was that. I got a dial tone and no good-bye. Unlike us, distributors didn't have to fight their way in the door—typically they had ongoing relationships with buyers, or at least they offered the prospect of repeat business, if not with the product they were pushing that day, then with something else. The bottom line: The Bookpeddlers of the world had leverage with buyers at the more exclusive stores. We didn't.

Our retail and distribution chain strategy was coming to fruition. Brookstone dug our scene, the Bookpeddler was all-powerful, and our Web site was starting to drive sales. We'd enhanced the purchase page with zip code search functionality, giving Web visitors the ability to locate nearby retailers, so they could examine and purchase MouseDriver in person, if they wanted to. The zip code search turned into an immediate hit—customers appreciated it, and just as important, our distributors and retailers were pleased with our willingness to pass sales on from our Web site to bricks and mortar. Win-win, again.

Even our evangelist network was buzzing. The network had grown by word of mouth, and we'd brought on secondary parties, friends of friends. While it wasn't exactly out of control, the network seemed to be taking on a life of its own. In Louisiana, an *Insider* subscriber named Doug Carlson had appointed himself salesman and started hitting up golf retailers in his area, thereby stepping on the toes of a few retail relationships we'd already put in place. An honest mistake, but still a problem we had to clear up.

Our favorite evangelist mix-up of the season came courtesy of Randy Chase, an entrepreneur in Illinois who wanted to rep MouseDrivers. He ran his own business, Celo Polka Cola, selling bottled soft drinks at polka events in the Midwest. As in polka parties, polka competitions, and anything going on in any polka dance hall in his territory. Randy Chase (who we liked to call the Celo Polka Coca-Cola Guy) was trucking MouseDriver everywhere in his polka travels, which was great. But he also walked into a local Sharper Image and tried to sell them on our product. A big no-no, as far as Brookstone was concerned. We had to fire off a few calls to Randy Chase and try to curb his enthusiasm. Which, with someone who's dominating the polka beverage market, wasn't easy to do.

Amid all our early summer sales commotion, we still found time to daydream about some opportunities we'd passed on. Like conquering Asia.

Out of the blue, sometime in mid-May, a Chinese golf ball manufacturer had sent in an order for 10,000 units. For us, it seemed like a fantastic total—five times what Brookstone was first talking for Father's Day, and too good to be true. It wasn't hard to fall into the trap that so many entrepreneurs before us had fallen into—of speculating about the potential of the Chinese market. Ten thousand units. A lot for us, but it could be just the tip of the iceberg in China, with its one billion or so Chinese. Never mind that the percentage of PC-owning Chinese households was very small, or that the purchasing power of the average Chinese citizen was about a thirtieth of the average American. There were *one billion* people in China. It was like the old A. Whitney Brown joke from *Saturday Night Live.*

"China has one billion people. Think about it. There are so many people in China, that if someone says you're one in a million, and you're Chinese, that means there are a thousand other guys just like you."

The daydream went like this: MouseDriver in China . . . we rename it Mao's Driver, sell a few million units in three or four weeks, and move Platinum Concepts Worldwide from our Cow Hollow apartment to five floors of an office building overlooking the harbor in Shanghai . . . we keep in touch with our friends in Texas when we fly our private jet back to Dallas a few times each autumn, to catch the football team we just bought, the Dallas Cowboys.

Or we could do what we did, which was take a pass on the 10,000-unit order. We'd never heard of the company, and we remained paranoid about international knockoffs, particularly from Asia, which had somewhat of a reputation for replicating products. Other than Kenny and East Asia Action Express, we didn't have any way of figuring out what was going on in Asia. We couldn't fly off and build relationships halfway around the world; for all our hard-earned ties and contacts, we remained a two-person company.

Besides, when the mysterious Chinese offer had come our way, we were intently focused on the immediate task at hand—preparing for Father's Day at Brookstone, the summer's key event.

After beginning with that almost-out-of-cell-range January call from Scott Rubinstein as we drove to Tahoe, we'd received our first order from Brookstone in April, for 2,016 units. It didn't seem like all that much, considering Scott was putting MouseDriver into 210 Brookstone stores; it worked out to fewer than ten units per store. Still, we were excited, because even though the initial order seemed small, it all depended on how we looked at the situation. The lowdown was this: Brookstone was going to base their forecast for MouseDriver on Father's Day results. Brookstone was essentially test-marketing MouseDriver themselves. So Father's Day amounted to market research for Platinum Concepts, conducted in a live market-place by a top-notch retailer. We would be the beneficiaries of the research, and we were getting paid for it. Not bad.

Not that it was a carefree process for us. We had to scramble to make our MouseDriver units Brookstone-ready in time for Father's Day. Though the Brookstone version, technically speaking, was the same old MouseDriver, there were a few differences.

Brookstone brands everything in their own packaging. We had to come up with "The MouseDriver Set," featuring MouseDriver and a golf-themed mousepad in Brookstone packaging. We were allowed to have our patent number on the box, but not our name. Brookstone gave us the appropriate graphics and films, which we forwarded to Hong Kong for Kenny to produce.

As a matter of fact, we were pleased with Brookstone having their own packaging, for the same reasons we liked the Golf World Ultimate Gift packaging and standard packaging. It added another level of credibility to the illusion that there were multiple versions of MouseDriver in the marketplace. When they saw that multiple versions of our brave little mouse already existed, assorted knockoff artists such as Chinese golf ball manufacturers and camera- and tripod-wielding Korean conventioneers would, we hoped, look for some other product to pick on.

We set up Brookstone with their initial order and stocked a few thousand Brookstone-ready units as a reserve in our warehouse (Brookstone requested the spares within a few weeks). MouseDriver hit Brookstone shelves about a month before Father's Day. That's when, in anticipation of our big day, we kind of lost it.

Kyle and I got into the habit of driving across the Golden Gate Bridge once a week or so, to visit the Brookstone store in Corte Madera. We'd mill around, ask the manager or the sales staff about this great new product MouseDriver, not letting on who we were. We'd talk a little too loudly within earshot of other customers, saying things like "Wow, you guys must be selling a ton of these things." I could spin it to say we were enthusiastic, but the truth was, we'd snapped. Maybe the PGA show had blown all the shyness we'd had about hawking our own wares completely out of our systems. Maybe we were just burning off nervous energy with the drive and a little play-acting in Marin. Whatever. We'd become MouseDriver groupies.

At least our enthusiasm/weirdness had a happy ending; we'd been a Father's Day hit, and we had the pleasure of working on Christmas forecasting with Brookstone to help us through the slow summer days to come.

In addition to our good fortune with Brookstone, there was another event that would help us ease our way through July and August.

In the middle of June, Kyle and I paid ourselves for the first time.

Paying ourselves with money we'd earned from the cash flows of a company we'd created stirred in us every clichéd response you might imagine. It was a joy, a thrill, a quietly satisfying moment, a validation, a relief, and a triumph, all rolled into one. It was also a milestone—how many entrepreneurs had started businesses and never even gotten this far? Not much more than a year before, Platinum Concepts had been a subpar presentation in a marketing class. Now it was paying us. After planning and manufacturing and shipping and selling, this was the last step toward becoming a full-fledged, for-profit business. A few calculations on a spreadsheet, some data entry into our accounting program, thirty seconds of handwriting, and we'd cleared the final hurdle. We'd finally gotten some money out of this thing.

We paid ourselves $7,500 each. And while we expected to pay ourselves again soon, we didn't build a regular payroll into our financial plan. But cutting ourselves paychecks was huge for us, both as a symbol and as what it was—money, which both Kyle and I needed, badly. I'd been financing my social life (what I had of one, anyway) with credit cards, and Kyle had dipped rather painfully into his IRA, incurring all sorts of penalties for early withdrawal, just to cover personal expenses.

Everybody who'd ever talked to us about being an entrepreneur talked about the feeling of living with risk. Or about what it felt like to fill your time with the hard work, your mind with the burden of uncertainty, your personal life with work conflicts. Or about the exhilaration of hitting it big and rolling in cash. But as Kyle and I walked out to our bank, we talked about how we'd never heard anyone speak about how great it was to get paid for the first time as an entrepreneur. About how the jump from nothing to something, mathematically and financially speaking, was infinite. We talked about all the great moments of the past year—Len Lodish cutting a check and launching the dream, the arrival of the first MouseDrivers, our first sale, Scott Rubinstein's first telephone call. This was right up there with them. At the moment, it was even better.

I AM FORCED
TO WEAR A SUIT

Given that I was the VP of marketing, I had been thinking a lot about big, powerful marketing and its henchmen, advertising and PR. We needed to exploit all three to build critical momentum for MouseDriver.

Fresh out of school, Kyle and I had had initially put together a grandiose marketing plan. We knew our primary target market (gift-buying women) and figured we just needed to reach and educate them on the merits of MouseDriver. Most of our plan was dedicated to communicating as directly as possible with the good women of our target market. We knew the quickest way to tell them to "Go buy MouseDrivers" was through advertising, so the plan was simple: We'd buy ads in different golf and women's magazines, and then down the line, maybe look into some endorsement deals, maybe not with Tiger Woods or Michael Jordan, but some celebrity the public associated with golf.

We knew it would work, but we hit a small snag. Ads in major magazines cost about the same as a brand-new BMW, and we certainly couldn't afford even a single one of those, let alone one every few months. And the price tag on low-level celebrity endorsements was even worse. So our straightforward, surefire plan was, quite simply, not happening.

It was a common mistake made by newly minted MBAs, putting together creative (and perhaps effective) but prohibitively expensive marketing plans and expecting the world to understand. While our grand marketing design crashed immediately, there were companies out there with enough cash to execute pricey plans. And more often than not, they were the worse off for it.

A VC-funded dot-com company, for example, might blow through millions of dollars pushing all its marketing strategies through the pipeline at the same time, before realizing that its best returns were coming from a simple $3,000 direct-mail campaign, or some chance contact the VP of marketing made with a journalist that turned into a business magazine cover story. If budget constraints had forced the company to evaluate all of its strategies before executing them, it might have prioritized better, opting for the quick, the cheap, and the immediately effective over the grand, the glamorous, and the longer-term payoffs.

Kyle and I had seen a lot of companies fall into this category during our time in San Francisco. Of course, it was a moot point for Platinum Concepts—not only did we not have that kind of money, we didn't even have access to that kind of money. VCs didn't like companies with our profile—single-product start-ups with a small-niche retail focus. In their eyes, we represented too little payoff for too much risk, of the unattractive putting-all-of-your-eggs-in-one-basket variety.

Not that we minded. In a way, our lack of funds saved us from ourselves. It kept us out of the bloated-marketing-initiative trap. Our budget forced us to focus and scrap for everything we could get, an approach that brought us resources like Rick, who took the time to teach us about golf marketing and PR and golf itself. With a big budget, we probably would have wound up with a global marketing-communications-PR agency that just sent us lots of reports, and we might have missed out on Rick altogether.

Rick's efforts had brought us a lot of product PR within the golf industry. He'd done fantastic work, utilizing his wide network of contacts to hit almost all of our golf media targets. Unfortunately, he'd done so much good work that he'd achieved his way out of his job. Rick had launched MouseDriver within the golf world, and now we needed to look further.

For Life Beyond Rick, we thought we would go the tried-and-true entrepreneurial route, looking for marketing options that could either be done on a shoestring or for free. That meant guerrilla and viral marketing and whatever PR we could do ourselves.

I had read Jay Conrad Levinson's *The Guerrilla Marketing Handbook* cover to cover, dragging my yellow highlighter across any ideas I thought might work for MouseDriver. There were quite a few, but I found myself wondering if Kyle and I were really guerrilla-marketing kind of guys. I couldn't see myself renting a golf cart and a mouse costume to wheel around shopping mall parking lots yelling, "Look, it's MouseDriver!" any more than I could imagine Kyle standing among voter registration people in front of grocery stores wearing a sandwich board and passing out flyers with the MouseDriver patent picture and our Web address. It all seemed a little too hyperactive for us.

Then there was the growing consensus on the new frontier of guerrilla marketing: Exploiting the Web with spam e-mails and site links to assault users with the message, backed up by the occasional street-level tactics like "live" billboards, sidewalk stenciling, and plain old flyers on car windshields.

That wasn't our style either. We felt certain that our buyers would respond to a targeted, subtle message, not one where they were clearly just one more tiny fish caught in an enormous net of promotion.

In the end, the guerrilla-ish marketing plan we fashioned for ourselves was a bit less aggressive—more like a real marketing plan, minus the budget. The basic approach:

(1) Send lots of personalized e-mails (no spam) to publications and organizations that might take interest in MouseDriver.
(2) Work on developing a viral marketing plan with the *Insider* at the center.
(3) Look into other options like direct mail, cold-calling, and evangelizing the product.

We also came up with a couple of hands-on, guerrilla-style stunts, both for our own amusement and to give our campaign enough street credibility to warrant the guerrilla name.

The most obvious wasn't much of a stunt at all, just something Kyle and I were doing naturally: Bombarding our friends with MouseDriver paraphernalia. Anytime someone visited San Francisco or we traveled anywhere, no one escaped without something MouseDriver-related. Now that we had ins with our two big ASI suppliers, we had a direct line to all the MouseDriver T-shirts, baseball caps, golf shirts, pens, divot fixers, and golf tees we could ever want, along with thousands of other products we never would.

At one wedding I attended in Napa in July, there was a golf scramble at the Silverado the morning before the rehearsal dinner. I outfitted all the participants with MouseDriver T-shirts and caps, which a number of people wore the entire weekend. When they all returned home to their own states and towns and neighborhoods, MouseDriver awareness was penetrating new markets.

We also gave MouseDrivers to relevant charities that requested them—which we thought was more like a grass-roots effort than a totally self-promoting guerrilla stunt. We donated to more than a dozen charity golf events, including the Brookridge Women's Golf Club Women in Golf Day in Brooklyn, New York, and the Fourth Annual Oakland Raiders Boy Scouts of America Invitational Golf Tournament, or the F.A.O.R.B.S.A.I.G.T., for short. They all received free MouseDrivers to use for auctions, prizes, and giveaways. We generated minor exposure and goodwill, along with a certain sense of . . . oh, I don't know, it just felt like a good thing to do.

As far as pure guerrilla marketing tactics went, we did pull one great stunt. Almost, anyway. We crashed Microsoft's first annual Tails of the City charity mouse exhibition and auction at the new Sony Metreon complex. The deal was that artists, business moguls, and celebrities decorated ordinary Microsoft computer mice to transform them into more interesting things, like a MouseTank or an Ikebana Mouse or a Venus Mousetrap or a Chia Mouse. The cast of the Simpsons, Kate Spade, Bill Gates, and the guy who designed album covers for the Grateful Dead (whose name was suspiciously listed on the program as Stanley Mouse) all made custom mice. The results were on display at the Metreon and on the Web for about a month before the event, so that people could start the bidding early (though the final auction was, of course, at the party itself).

Clearly, MouseDriver belonged in the mix. Unfortunately, we hadn't even heard of Tails until a friend of ours whose boyfriend had made a mouse for the event finally tipped us off. Once we found out, we were a bit hurt that MouseDriver had not been invited. Especially when we discovered that Nia Peeples was performing.

So we selected our prettiest, most perfect MouseDriver (one of the Callaway arrow ones we couldn't sell), caught a cab, and hit the XYZ bar, part of the swank, art deco W hotel near the Metreon, to go over our game plan. Fortified with a few Sapphire and tonics (Kyle) and Tanqueray and tonics (me), we strolled across Yerba Buena Gardens to the Metreon.

At the door waiting to get in, we read about how all of the proceeds from the event went to a nonprofit that gave dream trips to people with life-threatening illnesses. Instant guilt. We abandoned the crashing idea and shelled out the $150 for our tickets/donation. It seemed we'd been outguerrilla'd at the door.

Once in, I hunted for Bill Gates's mouse, curious to see how the founder of Microsoft would defile a Microsoft mouse. Meanwhile Kyle stuck to our guerrilla agenda, to help MouseDriver gain its rightful place among all the other clever mice. He found an inviting space between Microsquashed (a pulverized mouse) and Royal Mouse (a brocade, tasseled mouse on a velvet cushion, for which someone had bid an eye-popping $325). He slipped MouseDriver into the display and stepped back to make space for people to admire it.

Apparently, security at mouse-related charity events was nothing short of phenomenal. Within seconds a guard descended out of nowhere and confiscated MouseDriver before anyone had a chance to make a single bid. When I failed to find Bill Gates's creation, I rejoined Kyle as he tried to talk the guy into letting MouseDriver remain.

". . . but it's just another mouse. We're just providing healthy all-American competition. It's the foundation of our country."

"Sir, that's an unauthorized mouse."

"An unauthorized mouse? It's for charity. What're you going to do, throw us in charity mouse jail?"

"No, but how does regular jail sound?"

Miraculously, we were allowed to stay. MouseDriver, sadly, wasn't. The guard confiscated it.

We wandered around a bit, checking out mice and some of the cute mousemakers, until Kyle pulled a second MouseDriver out of his pocket and made the move to plant it alongside some salt and pepper shaker mice.

Daring, brave, sneaky Kyle.

Foolish Kyle, also. MouseDriver #2 never reached the display. The security guard had followed us, caught us in the act, and threw us out. And I never got a look at Bill Gates's mouse.

After Tails, the early returns were in on guerrilla marketing. Was it fun? Yes, except for the part where we got kicked out. Was it effective? Thus far, not really. Maybe stunts weren't our style, no matter how we did them.

We weren't worried about the spotty results of our first guerrilla efforts. We still had plenty of other plans, especially with viral marketing and PR. Besides, the MBAs in us couldn't quite let go of the idea that we had to try everything, to test different marketing mixes and see what worked. Failure wasn't bad; not trying was bad.

In this spirit, we resurrected our advertising component and started looking into developing at least one (low-cost, sensible) ad. Forget television (only cable access lay within our means, a poor fit for our upscale MouseDriver image). Forget radio too (MouseDriver had to be seen), and billboards (much as we wanted to plaster a MouseDriver ad over J.T.'s PayMyBills.com behemoth, we didn't have the cash). And Internet banner ads were just too annoying. No, we were looking at something much more basic. Probably a small print ad for placement in an affordable local publication in a golf-oriented community. Maybe Orange County.

It's funny how the outside world sometimes seems to wrap around your inner thoughts. I'd been turning Platinum Concepts' ad plans over in my head as I took in a baseball game at the San Francisco Giants' new Pac Bell Park. It was a great game, an extra-innings pitchers' duel. And the park itself was spectacular, with great views of the bay, clear sightlines to the field, warm breezes, and comfortable seats.

Yet all I could focus on was the billboard over right field. I even ignored the garlic fries.

It was just a simple sponsor's billboard, one among dozens lining the park—no tag lines, no slogans, just the company name.

Homewarehouse.com.

I couldn't get over it. Not even when Lou Seal (the mascot) nearly nailed me with his hot dog gun. I had advertising on the brain, and I couldn't stop thinking about a one-word billboard.

Homewarehouse.com.

What were they thinking? They were trying to become the online retailer for the do-it-yourself home improvement market, but why? Did they really want to compete with Home Depot and Orchard Supply and Ace Hardware? Did they think they could do it online? Don't do-it-yourselfers want to get it and fix it in the same day? Would any of them wait for deliveries? Would any of them buy tiles and light fixtures online, virtually sight unseen?

Everything about the billboard seemed cracked to me—the business, the strategy, the ad itself. Just the name, sitting in Pac Bell Park all season long, with a price tag running in the neighborhood of $2 million.

Classic marketing emphasized repetition, ensuring that your target audience viewed a consistent message more than once, making it memorable. But this Homewarehouse.com ad—what chance was there that its target audience was at the Giants game, a pricey evening-and-weekend event, primetime work hours for do-it-yourselfers? Giants season ticket holders were corporations and fat cats for the most part, not devotees of fixer-uppers.

Then again, maybe Homewarehouse.com had another agenda. Maybe they were trying to reach investors—the VCs and investment bankers with whom Giants tickets were very popular. Or maybe Homewarehouse.com knew that the corporations that bought season tickets often gave the seats to employees, many of whom might very well be do-it-yourselfers. So was the billboard idiotically wasteful, or truly inspired?

Who knew? How could Homewarehouse.com tell if its $2 million ad investment was working?

The answer was it couldn't; there was no way to measure the sales that came from it. That was the problem with most advertising. It was our problem too, just with a different twist. Unlike our dot-com billboard friends, we didn't have the funds for repetitive advertising, maybe just a one- or two-shot deal. We might get a kick up in sales and be able to point to our soon-to-be ad, but then it was anybody's guess when we'd have enough revenues to run another.

A couple of weeks after the game, I came across a notice in the *Industry Standard.* Homewarehouse.com had been leveled and annexed by Wal-Mart, cheap. Had ineffective advertising sunk them? Or had strong advertising kept them afloat longer than expected?

Who knew?

Our own ad budget was a decidedly un-billboard-like $1,200, which we spent for a quarter-page in *Golf Extra* magazine, a new publication throughout Southern California. For $250, a friend who was a big-time industry pro slashed her regular rates and developed an edgy, notice-me ad with the title "The Perfect Gift for Good Ol' What's-His-Name."

Seeing the ad in print felt great, a lot like gawking at MouseDriver when it first hit the stores or getting our first PR hits. There was something about having our efforts showcased to the public that gave us a real thrill. The only problem was we still had no idea of what worked.

We simply lacked the funds to track the effectiveness of our ad. No special product code, no separate toll-free number, nothing to truly measure response. Our marketing professors would have had our hides, and we couldn't have faulted them for it. Still, we imagined retired women in La Habra clipping the ad and bringing it to the next Women of the Republican Party meeting to show their friends this great gift idea for their middle-aged, golf-obsessed lawyer and businessman sons, and—measurements, schmeasurements—the ad just felt great.

Viral marketing (a dot-com jargon version of what was once known as word of mouth) was something we had better luck measuring, mostly because our biggest viral marketing tool was the *Insider*, and we knew when people signed up to receive it. Sometimes we could even trace the jumps. One time, for example, our friend Adam moved to London, and a few weeks later we started picking up ".uk" subscribers.

Viral marketing involved a lot of direct communication, giving its practitioners the distinct advantage of implied endorsement from a trusted source, usually a friend or acquaintance. Basically, you were a lot more likely to buy into a particular wine if your friend mentioned it when you were out to dinner than if you heard it advertised over the radio while you were driving home from work. Theoretically, this happened in ever-

increasing, often overlapping circles, word-of-mouth endorsements proliferating like rabbits, working on the same principles
as the six-degrees-of-separation concept.

A hypothetical example: We give a MouseDriver to our
friend Jaime from business school, who now works in investment banking in New York. Jaime is merrily MouseDriving
when his colleague Rob stops by his cubicle to pick up documents for a meeting Rob is going to in Los Angeles. Rob notices Jaime's cool mouse. On the plane, Rob is seated next to, of
all people, Chi Chi Rodriguez and starts to tell Chi Chi about
MouseDriver. But Chi Chi doesn't want to hear it. "My guys already turned down a deal involving that brilliant product," he
says. "It pains my heart."

Once Rob checks into his hotel in LA, he learns that his
meeting is canceled because the executive got stuck in traffic
coming back from lunch in Santa Monica. Inspired by his
chance meeting with Chi Chi, Rob has the concierge set up
some time for him at the driving range with a local golf pro. As
the pro, Chris, is correcting Rob's swing, Rob tells Chris about
MouseDriver (and Chi Chi).

Chris's next client after Rob is Burton, a low-level producer's
assistant at Universal Studios who can barely hit the ball. Desperate to fill the allotted hour lesson, Chris tells Burton about
this clever thing called MouseDriver. Burton is trying to climb
the Universal ladder by kissing up to his producer boss Tyler,
who's a golf fiend, so as soon as he gets back to work Burton
does a quick Internet search, finds www.mousedriver.com, and
buys a MouseDriver for Tyler. "Thanks, Barton," says Tyler.

Tyler is working on new movie development, considering a se-
quel to the big '80s hit *Footloose.* He talks to the right agent and
gets a meeting with Kevin Bacon to float the idea by him. So,
there's Kevin in Tyler's office, talking about how dancing could

save another small, uptight town, when he notices Tyler's computer mouse. "That is the coolest thing ever!" shouts Kevin. "It looks just like a golf driver!" Tyler gives Kevin his prized MouseDriver to seal the deal. Unfortunately, Kevin's dance moves aren't what they used to be and *Footloose, Too* flops, but not before Kevin orders MouseDrivers for the entire cast and crew for the wrap party, setting the whole cycle in motion again.

Hey, it could happen.

But rather than relying on Kevin Bacon, we expected our viral marketing to hinge on the *Insider*. Our distribution list kept growing, and people were reading current and back issues online since we'd posted it on our Web site a couple of months earlier. As long as we kept writing the *Insider* and people kept forwarding it to each other, it looked like our viral marketing plan would work.

After we'd gotten the ball rolling with advertising and guerrilla and viral marketing, we had to turn our attention to PR. I'd dabbled with PR, taking a learn-as-you-go approach, trying to build upon what Rick had done with the golf community by reaching out to the business press. I had contacted quite a few journalists with my pitch ("Your article was interesting, and it made me think you might like to hear about Platinum Concepts and MouseDriver") and gotten a few responses, including an acknowledgment from Mike Hofman, the *Inc.* reporter I'd complimented on his head-shaving razor article. He liked our *Insiders*.

PR had thrived during the dot-com boom. Our dot-com friends had taken their windfall VC funding checks straight to the PR agencies. PR retainers started at $15,000 per month and climbed north of $50,000. Some VCs had even set up direct affiliations with PR agencies, holding joint meetings that offered one-stop shopping.

A few months and tens of thousands of dollars later, the dot-coms got their shock. No matter how much they spent, PR didn't happen overnight. Journalists didn't want to write about strong management teams or revolutionary business models, and people didn't want to read about them, either. Not only did it take time to build PR, it was also largely dependent upon having a product or service that could capture the interest of the media.

PR was like advertising—unless you knew what you wanted to get out of it, the whole thing was a waste of time and money. Done well, it could boost sales, establish an image, set up an IPO. Kyle and I knew what we wanted from PR: Sales, sales, and more sales.

Our in-house PR campaign would drive sales through three key components—product PR, business PR, and guest lecturing.

Product PR would get MouseDriver in the gift guides of newspapers and golf, consumer and airline magazines, as well as maybe on some radio and TV shows if we did a good job.

Business PR meant telling the Platinum Concepts story to business magazines, building our fledgling brand through positive associations with the product, and hoping the exposure would eventually translate to sales.

Guest lecturing at business schools was in effect a combination of product and business PR brought to a very specific audience. Not only were business school students in our target consumer market, many of them were on their way to our target corporate market. Besides, some of our old professors were already using the *Insider* as a teaching tool in their entrepreneurship and marketing courses, so we were in a good position to capitalize on some early awareness.

I spent a lot of time looking for the right people to help us with each component of our plan, blowing hours doing Google searches and drilling through Internet sites (there had to be a database somewhere for this kind of stuff). Once I got the right person, I'd send the appropriate e-mail pitch—I had general newspaper, business publication, and university professor pitches that I would just tailor a bit, adding the individual's name, for instance (you'd be surprised by how many people overlooked that step).

The response was far from overwhelming. I counted any response, even "Thanks for the info," or "thx," as encouraging, but it wasn't long before I knew I wasn't going about things the right way.

We couldn't do it on our own. We needed an expert in business PR.

I floated the idea by Kyle. I talked about why PR was so important, how its credibility was higher and its costs were lower than advertising's, and how a PR professional with good contacts could get us results way, way quicker than I could. Kyle had only one question. "In time for Christmas?" When I said yes, he was sold.

So I had my next major task, finding a PR agency or consultant on our strict budget of $3,000 per month. No small task.

We mentioned the hunt for PR in the *Insider* and it was back to viral marketing land, with acquaintances of colleagues of friends e-mailing us with referrals. I put together a huge spreadsheet of all of the potential PR contacts.

The more research I did, the more relieved I was that we were getting a professional. There were tons of tricks of the trade and strategies I'd never heard of, opportunities I would have overlooked or bungled had I kept going all by myself. Besides the basic idea of obtaining press coverage from pitching the product, there were tiers of publications, editorial calendars, speaking opportunities, analyst briefings, press tours, by-lined articles, and all sorts of other activities I knew nothing about.

Within a couple of weeks, I had narrowed the list to three possibilities. One consultant in Los Angeles, and one consultant and one agency in New York City. I booked a red-eye to La Guardia to check out the latter two options. On the flight, I felt very official, headed toward the capital of world commerce for whirlwind meetings with top-notch PR people with big-name backgrounds who were willing to represent our little company. I'd even had to pack a suit.

The suit was for meeting with one of our candidates, George DeFelice, at the Union League Club, a stately, historic building on East 37th Street just off Park Avenue, of which he was a member. Founded by bigwigs to support Lincoln's policies during the Civil War, the Union League Club was the kind of place that hosted an assortment of presidents, heads of state, industrialists, entertainers, and dignitaries from all over the world. George and his business partner were the kind of guys who smoked cigars as they spent their days working their Rolodexes, taking care of business, mogul-style.

I felt damn important, sitting in one of the Union League Club dining room's overstuffed leather chairs, admiring my suit in the mahogany-framed mirror across the room, looking at George DeFelice through a cloud of cigar smoke. But George was saying that all of his PR efforts were business-focused, meaning no product PR or guest lecturing work. I would have to handle those parts myself. Hmmm . . . I told them I would get back to them, said good-bye, and got out of there without spilling my coffee on my tie.

A quick change back to khakis and an oxford, and I was on the A train to Soho to meet with the Farber Group, headed by Jason Farber, an alumnus of the global agency Porter Novelli.

Jason and his small staff were young, ambitious, and full of creative ideas. They had worked with lots of other unique products and knew the industry inside out.

Jason wanted to put us on a fast track, getting us to $1 million in sales as quickly as possible so that we could claim "success" and use that as an angle. A million sounded good to me, but I wasn't getting the kind of service vibe I was looking for. They were all the way across the country, and they were an agency, albeit a small one. If we went with them, we'd have no way of knowing who was doing the work on our account. I had the feeling it would be the more junior people, especially since we would be one of their smaller clients.

I was done by noon. I planted myself at a coffee shop in Soho and typed up a summary of the meeting on my laptop, then sent it to Kyle and downloaded e-mail using my cool WAP phone. The top e-mail of the day: Mike Hofman of *Inc.* magazine had replied to my latest message. I'd been trading e-mails with Mike for a while now, talking about the *Insider* and how Platinum Concepts and MouseDriver were doing. I'd told him I was going to be on the East Coast and asked if he would have time to get together for lunch. This message confirmed our meeting the next day, in Boston.

When I did meet Mike, I didn't barrage him with MouseDriver materials and information. We just talked casually about business, dot-coms, whatever. I thanked him for taking the time to get together and said I'd talk to him soon. No pressure, no questions about whether he might someday write a line or two about us. *Inc.* was one of the top business magazines in the country, and Mike seemed interested in our story. That was enough for me.

When I got back to San Francisco, I was down to our final PR candidate. I took the quick flight to LA and met with Rebecca

Hutchinson, another ex–Porter Novellian who had struck out on her own. Rebecca was a new entrepreneur, a new mom, and full of energy. She showed me a detailed strategy and timeline she had developed for us, starting with product PR, building into business PR, then using that momentum to extend to guest lectures.

On the flight back, I quickly listed the advantages of working with Rebecca: (1) proximity and shared time zone, (2) same gender as our primary target market, and (3) working with Rebecca, who, like Rick, knew a lot and was willing to teach.

So that was it. George DeFelice and Jason Farber had been open to talking to us not because of what we could pay, but because Platinum Concepts seemed like a good bet to them. I suspected they would lose interest in us if we didn't take off as they'd anticipated. On the other hand, Rebecca genuinely wanted our business just as we were, to do a good job and build her references. Kyle and I were both on board with that. I called Rebecca and told her to go ahead and get started on her six-month plan.

Right after I hung up with a very happy Rebecca, the phone rang. It was Mike Hofman, of *Inc.* He wanted to come to San Francisco to visit us for a couple of days. "Visit us? For a couple of days?" Kyle and I couldn't believe it. We were ecstatic. A business magazine writer wanted to fly all the way across the country to visit us.

It looked like we had just scooped our new PR consultant.

MASSAGE PARLORS, SIZZLING EXPOSÉS, LAWYERS, ONE-DAY SHOOTS, AND GAMBLING DEBTS

It was quiet. Too quiet.

And freezing. It was yet another classic San Francisco August, one of a string of strangely cold months in the city, more like mid-November in Philly than, say, any self-respecting summer month in any other town in America. It wasn't chilly and gray all over the Bay Area—driving for thirty minutes into the East, North, and South Bays bought blue skies, sun, and an extra 20 to 30 degrees. But in San Francisco, our second August had us throwing on sweaters every morning and trekking to Starbucks to stay warm, an exercise that left us, well, cold.

Back to the quiet. Our business was in a seasonal lull, a few weeks shy of the Christmas rush. It's not like we were suffering deeply or anything, but there was no getting around it: A combination of cabin fever and steadily increasing boredom was taking hold of us. We'd grown tired of slouching back from Starbucks each morning, plodding up the same flight of stairs, making the same cheap mental switch from home mode to office mode as we opened the door, setting down our coffees on the desk/kitchen table, and starting our cold, slow, claustrophobic working day.

We couldn't take a real vacation—the long, adventurous kind, where you can forget who you are and what you do—because there was just enough work to do that we couldn't take off for more than a couple of days. And we couldn't jump-start the action in retail on our own. There's a reason there are no self-serving shopping holidays in August. Half the world was barbecuing or yelling at children not to run around the swimming pool. Even if we'd invented a new gimmick, like National Buy Your Spouse A Mouse Week, the real fun wouldn't have kicked in until the next year at the earliest, not nearly soon enough to solve our problem. So we took action with the only short-term solution at our disposal.

We started whining to our friends.

The focal point of our complaining was our live/work situation. Specifically, we didn't want to have a live/work situation any more—we wanted a real office. Not an easy problem to solve for low-budget Platinum Concepts in high-rent San Francisco. Our friends were sympathetic but not all that helpful, until we went online with our cry. We made it plain in the *Insider* that we were on the hunt for office space, and wonder of wonders, the technology of the New Economy finally paid off.

We got a call from our friend Alison Smith, who had recently moved from Dallas to San Francisco to take a job at Carlson and Company, a recruiting firm for PR and marketing professionals. She caught our plea for help on the office front in the latest installment of the *Insider*. There was some relatively cheap extra space in Carlson and Company's offices on Union Street, two blocks away from our apartment. Were we interested in taking a look?

I beat Kyle out the door, but only by a foot or so. We tried not to run down Union.

Our first take on the office: It wasn't the nicest space in the world, but we loved it anyway. Alison had called it an office on the phone, but in truth it was a converted shed, one that had what the real estate business calls "character," which meant it needed a lot of work. Pre-move-in musts included a massive cleanup, some carpeting, a new coat of paint, and furniture (everything, basically). At least it didn't have what the real estate business calls "a rustic quality," which would have meant absolutely nothing worked. It may have been a shed, but this shed had a network connection, phone lines, and lights that turned on and off like they were supposed to when we flicked the switch.

The shed also had two windows that looked out on a tiny courtyard and the passageway from the street, and it had a separate entrance from Carlson and Company, a feature we found both appealing and just a bit crazy, considering the space. The office was a single 180-square-foot room, thirty feet long (which was great) by six feet wide (which was ridiculous). These were cartoon dimensions—at six-feet-plus, I could lie flat on the floor and squish between the walls, touching one with my heels and the other with my head. Not that I wanted to, but I could.

We were still coming to grips with the whacked-out measurements when Alison told us she'd heard that the space had once housed a massage parlor years before. Yes, she said, *that* kind of massage parlor, the kind still going strong in the Tenderloin, the most defiantly seedy neighborhood in San Francisco.

A six-by-thirty-foot massage parlor. How had those huge massage tables fit in the space? The masseuses must have been really skinny. The clients must have been really skinny too. What must the police raids have been like? San Francisco's finest, busting down the door, yelling, "Everybody freeze! Okay, hold on a second . . . let me just . . . get by this thing here, and . . . okay, sir, if you could just wait . . . okay, right, everybody freeze again! You're under arrest!"

We were hooked. The shed office's lurid history only added to its charm. It was tiny but affordable, more than good enough for a two-man operation such as our own, and it was only two blocks from our apartment down Union, one of the nicest streets in town, just past our former boardroom at Starbucks. We'd have the world's most enviable commute, an effortless stroll that would end almost as soon as it began. And we thought the dimensions, while hilarious, were still manageable, especially since we had no plans to install bulky massage tables.

Within days, we'd closed the deal to move Platinum Concepts, Inc. into our new ragged glory of a shed office. Starting Labor Day weekend, it was all ours.

Needless to say, we were thrilled. Just the promise of a definite escape from the confines of our kitchen lifted our spirits in the last days of August. Kyle was even more excited than I was, which I'd thought was impossible, until Labor Day weekend arrived and I found out just how motivated my partner in crime truly was about our new shed.

In the middle of our bout with off-season boredom/claustrophobia, I'd made plans for a quick getaway over Labor Day to suck down too many beers on a houseboat on Lake Shasta. Kyle stayed in town, and set himself to the task of overhauling our new office space. First Kyle flew into a cleaning frenzy. Then he painted the walls. Then he covered the floor in green carpet.

He even laid sod in the microscopic strip of earth that lined the entrance to the shed. Mildly hungover and sunburned, I surveyed the shed when I returned. "Impressive," I said.

"I was one with Home Depot," Kyle replied.

We moved Platinum Concepts the next day. It didn't take that long—it was just a few boxes, a couple phones, two desks, and three file cabinets. But before, during, and after the move that day, we were absolutely flying. Yes, moving into the office might have felt like another milestone in our business, but in truth, our minds weren't working on that level at all. To us, the move meant we were moving. That was all and that was enough. To finally pull our work life out of our kitchen, even into a tiny space only a couple of blocks from the very same dreaded kitchen, well, it was beyond words.

Plus, it wasn't lost on Kyle and me that our shed was attached to Carlson and Company, which housed a good friend of ours and a handful of her (attractive) work colleagues. Our days of pressing our faces to the window of our apartment, whether to signal UPS or to gawk at the wide, unlonely world outside, were over.

Or as Kyle put it, "Having an office doesn't suck."

The office arrived just in time, so to speak. Platinum Concepts was just over 48 hours into being fully operational in the Union Street shed when Mike Hofman, intrepid *Inc.* reporter, knocked on our door on September 7.

When Mike had called to set up our meeting, the obvious had jumped to mind, making us both excited and nervous. *Inc.* wanted an up-close glimpse at our vaunted operation, which meant Mike Hofman would be looking at everything we did for a couple of days, reporter's notebook in hand. It was by far our biggest media opportunity to date—advertising in *Inc.* would have set us back a small fortune, and here we were, on the brink of a lot of free coverage.

The flip side was that Mike had arrived in the heart of the slow season. What would he see? A few calls trickling in? Kyle and I showing him MouseDriver in action for about two minutes, and then what? If he'd have visited during the PGA show or the Christmas rush, we'd have wiped him out with entrepreneurial activity. But now in early September, when retailers weren't ready to replenish their MouseDriver inventories, the prospect of Mike firing question after question our way for hours on end seemed very likely. It was enough to make us pray for a patented disaster call from Kenny in Hong Kong.

Plus, we knew that Mike would be looking for a story angle; that was what good journalists did. Given that business magazines tend to focus on rise-and-fall stories (Steve Jobs saves Apple, Microsoft flounders in court, etc.), it wasn't hard to guess what the angle would be: With grandiose dot-coms bellyflopping all over San Francisco, it might be refreshing to dig up a little-retail-product-company-that-could in the very same city, one that was trying to chug uphill to entrepreneurial success the old-fashioned way, with a modest budget and a lot of hustle. Not a bad angle, except in September there wasn't a lot of chugging uphill to observe, so we had another possible angle to worry about: An exposé on the aftermath of the New Economy collapse, where not even non-dot-com companies could do anything right.

We had a chance to be the flavor of the month in *Inc.,* or a cautionary tale, all based on a couple days of observation by one reporter. So we were nervous. Not terrified, but nervous.

Mike Hofman was a real professional; he'd expected us to be nervous, and quickly tried to set us at ease. He was our age, and immediately took the formality right out of the process. We kicked off his visit by taking him to our apartment and just telling stories about customer service and the times we'd had to do everything on our own, and how we'd grown sick of our office/kitchen (and sometimes each other) in the process. He scribbled in his notepad the whole time, asking questions easily in the flow of conversation. Double-checking our backgrounds, examining what finally made us jump into business, asking what we hated and enjoyed and feared and looked forward to in our everyday lives as small business owners. We answered almost everything—the few questions we didn't were along the lines of manufacturing costs, equity structure, and capital investment details.

Then he started asking about the *Insider*—why we'd decided to write it, who was reading it, who was benefiting from it, etc. It wasn't hard to tell that Mike was trying to determine whether it was just a pure marketing ploy (the cynical, untrue view) or something legitimate (our take on it). We did our best to convince him of our view, but we had no way of knowing what he thought. He just smiled and laughed as we talked, and kept writing notes.

After we'd run through our stories and he'd exhausted his supply of questions, Mike kind of hung out with us in the office, watching us answer phone calls and respond to e-mails—all boring office stuff, which he'd interrupt with an occasional question. We knew we weren't thrilling to watch, but honestly, we were just glad enough was going on that we looked busy, and that Mike had succeeded in putting us at ease.

When Mike returned the next day, the office was dead. Almost no calls came in, and there wasn't too much that needed our immediate attention. Before his visit, Kyle and I had discussed what we'd do during such a lull. There were some long-term items we needed to discuss at some point, like budgeting for 2001 and building out our corporate promotions strategy for the new year—things we could work on during a dead stretch.

But when the work lull arrived, that strategy seemed fake. Besides, we were having fun with Mike; we couldn't be sure, but at least on the surface, he seemed to be getting a real kick out of our story. So we gave up any pretense and asked Mike if he wanted to play golf at the Presidio or drive across the Golden Gate Bridge to Sam's, a restaurant in Tiburon with a big sunny deck. Mike said no to all that. He just wanted to hang out, observe, and ask questions as they came to him.

Finally, in the late afternoon, we stole a few beers from the Carlson and Company refrigerator and just relaxed with Mike, whom we were genuinely starting to like. He left a short while later, saying he couldn't make any promises, but expected the article to run sometime early in the new year.

It had been fun, but the questions remained. We'd posed for a few photographs inside and outside our shed. Would they be printed with a negative article and a giant title, "Young Jackasses of the Post–New Economy?" Or would the article catapult our business to a new level, with the colossal title "Visionary Start-Up Studs Lead the Way Out of Dot-Com Nightmare"? And if so, what were the next steps? Securing new funding to advertise nonstop? Trying to become the warm-up act for Alan Greenspan on the business speakers' circuit? Asking *People* magazine for Jennifer Lopez's telephone number?

"... J-Lo, hi, it's J-Lu and K-Ha from Platinum Concepts ... yes, we're down with the new Hip-Hop MouseDriver ... "

There was no way to tell how Mike's writing would depict us before the article ran. We'd just have to be patient. At least the two-day interview had helped us ditch the doldrums of late summer.

And the funny thing was, things started to pick up just after Mike left us. Not so much in the sales department—the Christmas season moved for no one—but in the story department. A couple days after the Mike episode, we received a letter from a patent attorney in Dallas, the one who had filed the patent paperwork for MouseDriver years before. He'd seen MouseDriver featured in Southwest Airlines' *Spirit* magazine, and wanted to let us know how psyched he was to see one of his patents make it into the marketplace. Apparently, patent lawyers rarely see their paperwork turn into real products. It felt great hearing from him.

A couple of days after that, we crossed paths with airline media once more.

Our friend Caskie Collet struck again. He'd lined up our first real MouseDriver sale, through Bank of America, and now he'd set Kyle up with an appearance on "CEO Spots," a video production to air on Delta and British Airways that was produced by Caskie's company, Chalk.com. Chalk.com had a deal with the airlines to produce five-minute segments featuring CEOs, to air during flights. Kyle was to be included with a segment featuring the CEOs from Applied Materials and a couple of marketing and PR firms.

Kyle Harrison, the brave young president and cofounder of Platinum Concepts, Inc., was now officially a rising star in the business world.

Kyle's one-day shoot (okay, one afternoon) took place across from Palomino restaurant on the Embarcadero, with the Bay Bridge serving admirably as the background scenery. He had to wait while another CEO shot his segment. That guy talked forever. By the time he'd finished, it was almost dark—there were only about twenty minutes left of usable natural light. Kyle fielded the rapid-fire questions with ease—where the idea for

MouseDriver came from, what were our biggest mistakes and most exciting moments, pretty straightforward stuff. He worked in a plug to help out other entrepreneurs, if only they would contact us at Platinum Concepts.

Kyle even tried to sneak a MouseDriver into his shots, holding it in his hand during the entire interview, lifting it into the camera frame several times. But the interviewer wouldn't go for it. Each time Kyle tried, it was "Hey, move your hand away from your face. I can't see you." So MouseDriver stayed out of the picture.

In the end, Kyle's smooth patter was reduced to thirty seconds in a five-minute video that was loaded with quick cuts, lots of interviewer questions and commentary, and four other CEOs. Fortunately, they kept what Kyle thought were some of his best comments, including what he'd said about entrepreneurs having to believe deeply in what they were doing just to keep afloat. Nothing too deep, but not bad sound bite material either.

Kyle had fun shooting the video, and a couple of months later, we got unexpected feedback on his performance, when Tracy Yuen, a Wharton friend of ours, caught his in-flight act while traveling to Europe during the Christmas holidays. She called us shortly after she'd landed, saying she'd nearly fallen out of her seat when she saw Kyle, her "little in-flight movie star." Ha!

*   *   *

We closed out September with a trip to another convention, the PGA International Golf Show in Las Vegas. Before the summer doldrums struck, we hadn't wanted to go. We didn't have a booth at the show, and we'd heard that the Vegas convention paled in comparison to the Orlando PGA show we'd hit in February. Even the word "International" in the Vegas show's title appeared to be a bit of a misnomer, as most of the overseas vendors in the golf industry attended the Orlando show in lieu of spending time in the Nevada desert.

Still, we were on board for Vegas, in part because we wanted to close out the last few weeks before the Christmas rush with any kind of fun we could drum up, and in part because it made good business sense to stay in touch with our network of contacts in the industry. It was like the old saying—sometimes you go to trade conventions to show everybody you're not dead. Besides, we were starving for some guaranteed sun.

There we were on a cheap Southwest flight to Vegas, with absolutely no intentions of gambling. We didn't have any money to lose. Our new office, while inexpensive, cut into our operating budget, and our big sales volume for the year remained very much in front of us.

Despite all that, Vegas turned out to be a good call. Most people visit the city seeking sensory overload—how else can you explain Wayne Newton? But taking in a convention without any real responsibilities turned out to be a relaxing, rejuvenating experience for Kyle and me. We checked into the Hotel Paris and cabbed it over to the Las Vegas Convention Center. We touched base with Ryan Howard of Golf World and a few people from the Bookpeddler, attended the *Golf Retailer* magazine party and caught up with our friend Pete McQuaid, and generally just took in the whole scene.

As advertised, the PGA Vegas show was much smaller and more relaxed than Orlando. But it wasn't without some minor drama for us. On the first day of the show, the first person we saw was Brian, sitting on a golf cart in the booth of some company, cheerfully chatting up some customers.

The sight of Brian turned us into instant undercover commandos. We snuck in and out of people's booths, trying to get around him. Skulking away struck us as funny and absolutely necessary at the same time—we were still uncomfortable with how everything had turned out with Brian. We didn't think he saw us.

At night, we finally succumbed to Vegas and decided to splurge a little, courtesy of Platinum Concepts, Inc. Accounting is accounting, and our expenditures eventually worked their way to our bottom line, but we figured what the hell, we were on the verge of our year's busiest stretch, and we'd never really splurged after we'd started our company. We were due. Or at least we were good at talking ourselves into thinking we were due.

The chief temptation driving our rationalization wasn't a casino. It was a steakhouse. Del Frisco's, our favorite from Dallas, had just opened in Vegas. We just couldn't pass it up. We ate steaks and lobster and drank good wine, all for the price of about a month's supply of San Francisco burritos and Starbucks grande caffé lattes. Then we retired to Del Frisco's cigar and scotch bar, to smoke cigars and drink scotch, completely overlooking the fact that neither of us knew a thing about cigars, nor did we drink scotch. It all just seemed to fit after gorging on pricey surf and turf. We felt like bloated, hard-drinking, hardliving ugly American titans of industry. Which, for one evening in Vegas, was all kinds of fun.

Somehow we found ourselves capping off the evening at the blackjack tables, a great follow-up to the cigar bar, because we knew even less about blackjack than we knew about single malts and fine Havanas. Even though I had little interest in gambling, and Kyle even less, Vegas got the better of us. I couldn't believe what I was hearing.

"John, we're in Vegas. Look at all of these people throwing money away. It's our duty as Americans to lose money in a casino."

A cute joke, except when Kyle lost money ($100, a substantial loss, considering he'd only committed to gamble $50). Losing put Kyle in a mildly bad mood. Watching me win $150 off of my own $50 stake put him in a lousy mood. When I quit playing at 1 A.M., reasoning it was best to get out when I was still ahead, he hit the roof. After taking beating after beating from Kyle on the video game front, I had fun watching him lose it over my beginner's-luck gambling. Touché.

The next evening, we were back in San Francisco, in our apartment that was now only our apartment, two blocks from our office, a few weeks from the Christmas rush, and possibly a couple months from the publication of Mike Hofman's *Inc.* article. The dull September we'd feared in the slow days of late August had never materialized. We'd made minor strides, had a lot of fun, and we were ready for a big year-end. I turned off the lights in my room and listened to Kyle in the kitchen/former office, grumbling over the phone to his brother Kevin about his gambling loss.

FULL CIRCLE

We closed out 2000 with the most important of our three critical events of the year. We survived early jitters and late-night drinking in our four days at the PGA show in Orlando, fared even better than we'd hoped during the Brookstone retail rush of Father's Day, and now we'd arrived at the party we'd missed altogether in 1999—the retail version of Christmas.

Retail Christmas was a six-week sprint that began in mid-October, an explosion of activity out of the doldrums of late summer. Everything rocketed upward—sales, phone calls, customer service inquiries, PR, and Web site sessions. When it ended at the beginning of December, in time for the shopping onslaught, retail Christmas had netted approximately 40% of our sales for the year. With December 25 and all of Hanukkah still weeks away, all that really remained for Platinum Concepts was to transfer last-minute inventory to resellers and retailers, and for Kyle and me to take stock of what had happened during the year.

We'd opened our first holiday rush inauspiciously, at the tail end of our slow September, with an e-mail from Kenny.

From: Kenny
To: Kyle
Subject: MouseDriver
I get a very bad news from the factory that they were running into
financial difficulties. The owner were too heavily invested in the
IT industry. It will be wind up in the near future.
I will relocate yr product to other factory. I will have everything set
up by next week. There will be some delay in yr upcoming order, I
feel very sorry for this.
The one box of display including the end Sept delivery will be de-
layed. I will have a serious meeting with the maker and will get
back with you with a firm date.
Rgds,
* Kenny*

We couldn't believe what we were reading, not after all we'd
done to prepare for the season. We'd ordered 25,000 additional
units via Kenny and East Asia Action Express well ahead of
schedule, so that they could be manufactured and inexpensively
shipped (rather than air-mailed) to reach the United States in
time for the holiday rush. We'd planned out everything right this
time, and executed perfectly. Our reward? The worst e-mail
Kenny had ever sent our way, a symphony of smashed sen-
tences, offbeat abbreviations, and bad news throughout.

It will be wind up in the near future. Translation: The manufacturer Kenny had us contracted with had gone belly-up, without finishing our run of MouseDrivers.

There will be some delay in yr upcoming order. Translation:
Wr dead. Platinum Concepts only had 2,000 MouseDrivers remaining in inventory. Without the shipment of 25,000, there
would be no retail Christmas for us, and Platinum Concepts
will be wind up in the near future.

It was nice to hear that Kenny planned on having a serious meeting with the maker. If the shipment came too late for Christmas, Kyle and I also expected to meet the maker—we planned to die of embarrassment.

Fortunately, Kenny Taketh Away, but Kenny Also Giveth. Sure enough, as promised, he'd succeeded in lining up another manufacturer for us, who matched the quality of our previous (and now defunct) manufacturer and shipped our badly needed units on time. We admired how Kenny took everything in stride—it was a true entrepreneurial trait, one we'd tried to emulate during our run with Platinum Concepts. He'd sent us Moon Cakes again in September, right on time. Then he'd learned the bad news about our original manufacturer, calmly relayed the news as soon as he'd gotten it, and quickly turned our all-out disaster into a brief scare. He made everything seem like business as usual, and we loved him for it.

Just after the Hong Kong panic vanished, the Christmas rush kicked in, with lots of orders and calls and e-mails back and forth with our distribution chain, with the biggest Platinum Concepts customers for the season turning out to be Brookstone, Wireless, and the Bookpeddler. We would have worked the phones day and night through the season, if we hadn't decided (rather eagerly) to honor a couple of commitments we'd made during the summer that took us out of the holiday madness in our Cow Hollow shed and carried us east for a few days, back to Wharton.

In mid-October, we flew into Philadelphia, returning to Wharton to guest-lecture in Len Lodish's entrepreneurial marketing class, and then hopped on a plane for Ithaca, New York, to plow through another lecture, this time for Pankaj Kumar, a Cornell business school professor whom we'd gotten to know through the *Insider* and a series of e-mails. Pankaj had taken to using the *Insider* in his class, so it was an odd but fun experience to appear before students who had been reading all about us already. It wasn't any different than Kyle and my meeting Pankaj face to face for the first time, after corresponding for months.

It was also a strange but great feeling to speak in front of Len, in a class we'd attended ourselves eighteen months before. It was flattering that Len had called us, wanting us to present our early entrepreneurial experiences to his class. But it was also hard to sum up all we'd done and how we felt about Platinum Concepts, Inc. in under an hour, so we didn't try. We stuck to the basics instead, talking about how we'd set up our company and what we were trying to accomplish, running through a slide presentation with a series of bullet points, the kind we'd grown all too familiar with at our old consulting jobs and at Wharton.

It wasn't until we took questions at the end that our feelings came out, but even then it was hard to tell whether we were getting through to everyone. We were battling the dot-com legacy. One student heard our whole presentation and asked how we were going to make money if we weren't putting banner ads on our Web site. In disbelief, I asked him to repeat the question. "I just don't understand your revenue model," he said.

"Um, the plan is to sell MouseDrivers," I explained.

I suspect the students who were truly interested in forging out into the marketplace with a product of their own got what we were saying; the rest may have been just coasting toward a grade, listening politely, but with their minds still on the traditional job market. Either way, Kyle and I (and Pankaj and Len) thought it was a good experience all the way around, our standing up in front of a class of students who were our age with a report from the field. After all the case studies we'd waded through, by speaking in front of the two classes, we'd informally become a case study in our own right.

After Pankaj's class, we flew back to Philadelphia for one more day, to attend the Wharton Campaign for Sustained Leadership Gala, an event for which we'd donated MouseDrivers as gifts for the attendees. It was our first charity event as representatives of Platinum Concepts, Inc. (not including getting thrown out at Tails of the City) and our first in black tie. And because we were listed in the program as two of seven Wharton alums who had donated to the event, we felt our odds of getting the boot from security this time were quite low.

Our seats for the gala at the naval shipyard landed us right in the middle of business school celebritydom. To our right, Len Lodish and Ian MacMillan, two of the most respected entrepreneurship professors at Wharton. To our left, two Wharton grads in their mid-fifties, now the heads of major investment banks. And one row behind, who else but Maria Bartiromo, a.k.a. the CNBC Money Honey, the voice and face of the tumultuous New Economy stock market, sitting next to her husband, whose family name graced one of Wharton's main buildings. And there we were, proud representatives of MouseDriver and recent Wharton grads everywhere, smack in the middle. Go figure. We tried to take it all in stride as Tony Bennett took the stage and started crooning.

We had killer seats for Tony Bennett, and sometime that night the CNBC Money Honey was taking home MouseDriver. What did it all mean?

It was hard to make heads or tails of that one. Perhaps a better question was, now that we'd been in business a while, how would we have done on Maria Bartiromo's cable show? She was absolutely great at blowing past all the spin doctoring thrown her way by company officials and analysts, always going for the nitty-gritty instead. She blasted through whole industry sectors in minutes without missing a beat. She'd have wrapped up Platinum Concepts, Inc. in thirty seconds flat.

"Okay, we're live with John Lusk and Kyle Harrison of Platinum Concepts. John and Kyle, tell us about what you do."

We make computer mice that look like golf club heads, Maria.

"Golf mice. Cute. What kind of revenues are you looking at for 2000?"

Just under $600,000, Maria. That's including Christmas. By the time the year's over, we'll have sold around 50,000 MouseDrivers.

"Is that good?"

Well, it's not what we'd planned, but it's not bad, Maria.

"Any profits?"

Some, Maria. Enough to pay ourselves modest salaries, but nothing to jump up and down about.

"So the bottom line is not bad for 2000. That's all from Platinum Concepts. We'll be back with Jack Welch of GE after these messages."

That was our year in a nutshell, after we'd flown back from Philly and worked our way through the Christmas rush. Over half a million in sales, not three million, and 50,000 units sold, not 300,000. More than 80% off the predictions we'd made in our first pro formas, but still selling units, still booking revenues, still afloat.

We'd gone into the business with certain hopes and expectations and come out the other end with our view of the company entirely changed. We looked back on our initial plans to see what had happened.

After eighteen months in business, here's what we knew.

We had a product. MouseDriver, a clever mouse that both looked good and worked, that everyone understood and liked once they saw it. Mike Hofman of *Inc.* saw its appeal, as did Len Lodish and even Ken Hakuta. Our media reviews had been uniformly favorable. (There was one notable exception—an article in the *Los Angeles Times* listing holiday "turkeys," including MouseDriver, which the author dubbed "a chunky, clunky mouse." Ouch.) In general, we had a likable, generally appealing product offering.

So why hadn't we sold more?

In some respects, we hadn't done enough with MouseDriver. Maybe if we'd have gotten through a couple of cycles of manufacturing, promoting, selling, clearing inventory, and reaping profits, we'd have gotten into some other interesting entrepreneurial areas, like expanding the product line from our single modest model. If we'd done so, we might have faced a number of issues earlier that might have helped us sell better.

For the golf market, we might have offered different styles of club heads, like old-fashioned woods, and nostalgic club head brands that no longer existed. We might have contracted with big companies like Callaway and Ping to produce MouseDrivers with their logos or developed deals to offer autographed MouseDrivers from Phil Mickelson or legends of yesteryear like Ben Hogan. We could have made agreements with specific PGA Tour events to offer commemorative MouseDrivers (for example, the official 2000 Kemper Open MouseDriver). These types of product extensions might have broadened our market not only for first-time Platinum Concepts customers, but also for repeat buyers—more models and different commemorative features might have turned MouseDriver into a collectible. In fact, MouseDriver-as-collectible wasn't such a far-fetched notion—people collect anything they're interested in and can afford (provided it features a certain element of variety), running the gamut from abstract art to butter dishes to Pez dispensers. MouseDrivers didn't seem out of line with the lower end of that spectrum.

Or for the broader PC market, the obvious move was to have come up with other clever themes for computer mice—a mouse that looked like something other than a golf club head. An egg. A turtle in a shell. A bar of soap. A hunk of cheese. A Chinese dictator (the Mao's Driver we'd joked about while dreaming of Shanghai). Anything whimsical, anything that brought life to a computer in a cubicle.

If we'd have pushed our way through a couple of sales cycles, and had the chance to have done any of these, we would have remembered something we'd misplaced along the way—the sense of fun that our product generated.

As we talked, it struck Kyle and me that while we were still enthusiastic about our business, in the rigors of it all we'd lost some of our enthusiasm for the product itself, the kind we had felt when we showed the big gray prototype to our classmates at Wharton. MouseDriver had been a vehicle for our entrepreneurialism, but somewhere amid the cycles of stress and elation brought on by phone calls with Kenny, the tacky horrors of the PPAI show, and the deadening effects of cold-calling and getting shut out right and left, we'd forgotten how likable our product was.

If we would have remembered this while slugging our way through all the obstacles we'd encountered, it might have changed almost everything. We might have looked at entirely different candidates for mentoring, for example. Ken Hakuta had attracted us because of his ties to Len Lodish and because of his experience with the Wacky Wall Walker, a novelty item that came out of nowhere, with no practical application. If we'd remembered the source of the fun of MouseDriver—how it was a play on an ordinary item everyone already owned—we might have looked at an entirely different kind of entrepreneur as our model. Like Nicholas Graham, the creator of San Francisco's own Joe Boxer, who took plain old boxer shorts (an item people already owned and didn't care about) and turned them into a minor design empire.

If we'd have worked with Graham or someone like him, we might have focused a little less on the golf market (which had brought us good, but not spectacular, returns) and a little more on the broader market for whimsical impulse and gift purchases (which, beyond Brookstone, we'd largely failed to tap). We were in the clever gadget market every bit as much as we were in the golf game. In getting Platinum Concepts up and running, we'd somehow forgotten this.

We had a business plan. Looking back on our original business plan, we'd been right about two things: East Asia Action Express and our gross margins.

Carmine, Kenny, and EAAE had provided us with a steady source of aggravation and a few scares along the way, but in the end everything had turned out for the best when it came to manufacturing. Our MouseDrivers were what we'd expected them to be, both in terms of price and performance. Our latest concern over our manufacturer floundering was troubling, but the incident had served to reassure us that we had the right agent taking care of things in Asia.

It was good that we trusted Carmine and Kenny, because the fact remained that we'd still had little choice in the matter. If we'd wanted to switch manufacturing agents, we would have had to do it cold, without a referral (we hadn't found out about anyone else in our eighteen months in business). And even if

we'd switched, we would have been saddled with the same limitations inherent to the East Asia Action Express arrangement—we would still be thousands of miles away from our
manufacturing and dependent on our agent to navigate the
complex web of manufacturers in China, Taiwan, Vietnam,
Hong Kong, Korea, and the rest of the region. We remained a
two-man operation, and while we probably needed to schedule
a trip to Hong Kong to look at what we'd contracted for, taking
on more manufacturing responsibility (or switching partners)
wasn't worth the hassle.

Financially speaking, wherever else we'd been wrong about
MouseDriver, we'd been dead right about one critical item:
Our gross margins held up as we'd anticipated they would. It
was a critical insight we'd made while conjuring up our pro formas, one that carried us through a lot of missteps in other areas.
Creating and defending solid gross margins was no small feat
for a business of any size; you could chart the rise, fall, and res-
urrection of Apple, a company whose revenues were over a
thousand times our own, on the basis of gross margins alone.

Every business has to have a lever in its business plan, one
strength that drives the business forward—it could be high asset
turnover (the ability to sell a lot of units quickly), financial leverage (the ability to borrow money and make returns that exceed
the interest payments), or return on sales, the forte of Platinum
Concepts. Even with our relatively low sales volume and our
modest financing, we were able to make respectable returns on
every sale, and it helped us overcome a lot of weaknesses.

Speaking of weaknesses in our business plan, overly aggressive sales forecasting definitely topped the list. We'd begun
Platinum Concepts thinking MouseDriver was appealing
enough to nearly sell itself, and then been rapidly disabused of
that notion. There are lots of appealing products that struggle
or fail because they never get in front of the consumer the right

way. We'd gotten out of the blocks slowly—something we might have predicted, but didn't—and never built the sales momentum we'd anticipated, either in late 1999 or early 2000.

But what had really gone wrong? Had we missed a series of realistic targets, or had we misestimated in the first place? We'd expected to move 150,000 units through our corporate marketing efforts in 2000; we'd sold around 3,000 as we mostly geared up for corporate sales through Burkhouse and Techpad in 2001. Although we were well short of our retail targets for 2001 as well, perhaps we'd overestimated the size of the golf novelty market and underestimated the size of the PC novelty market, which we'd all but neglected during the year.

The bottom line: Kyle and I wouldn't be anything close to millionaires by 2001. But perhaps the Rule of Four applied—everything from our understanding of the marketplace to setting up distribution had taken much longer than we'd anticipated. In truth, our actual 2000 more closely resembled our pro forma 1999 than our pro forma 2000. Maybe we were right about our estimates, but we were wrong about the timing. Maybe 2000 was our real education in the marketplace, and the first few months out of the gate in 1999 had been all about taking entrance tests and buying school supplies. Maybe 2001, not 2000, was to be our breakout sales year.

We had a marketing plan. There was no way to sugarcoat it: We'd been repeatedly whipsawed by our own marketing plans. At first, we'd imagined hitting high-end corporate and retail at the same time. Then we'd dropped retail and gone after corporate. Then we'd jumped back into retail when doors to corporate failed to open wide for us. We'd hemmed and hawed about following the tried-and-true promotional product life cycle of generating buzz in retail before even attempting corporate. We'd taken far too long to figure out our distribution, taking too many sales-rep-inspired missteps along the way.

In retrospect, we might have ramped up faster if we'd been less particular about how perfectly deals fit into our grand strategy (which changed all too often, a fact we'd failed to admit to ourselves). Maybe we would still have passed on John Baron and Chi Chi Rodriguez and company, but we also might have wasted less time wrangling with our ASI problems (which looked increasingly trivial as time went on) and gotten on board with suppliers and distributors much, much faster.

Nowhere were our arrogance and overconfidence in our backgrounds more exposed than in decisions like these. The truth was, with the exception of a few bright spots like Caskie Collet, our corporate contacts failed to carry us into the promotional markets—we had to get in line like everyone else in ASI. And we'd fallen in love with product design and high-minded strategy, when we would have been better served by just resolving to sell to an obvious market—like gift-buying golf widows—and chucking everything else out the window until we'd made that work.

We'd forgotten that although business may be difficult, it's seldom complex. Instead, we'd gotten tied up in knots, probably because of a mildly toxic mix of our industry ignorance, our own egos, and our MBA training. However we'd done it, we'd somehow gotten it precisely backward—we'd wanted the business of Platinum Concepts, Inc. to be a complex problem that, once solved, yielded revenues effortlessly. So instead of trusting in the power of the simple elements we'd gotten right (like a good, straightforward, likable product and strong gross margins), we'd gotten wrapped up in chasing down mentors and deciphering the nuances of market positioning and the implications of alliances, all of which slowed down our progress. There's a delicate balance every entrepreneur fights to maintain, between honing a strategy and executing it. We'd lost that balance. We were busy thinking, when we should have been busy selling.

Encouragingly, there was good news to be found in our mistakes. MouseDriver's simple strengths remained, and the modest results of 2000 woke us up to what we'd been doing wrong. Every sin we'd committed could be redeemed, if we changed our ways in 2001.

We had financing. All things being equal, we'd done well here—we may have made a handful of mistakes, but none were deal-killers, and we'd essentially stayed on plan, starting with a small base, borrowing off credit cards for inventory investments, and paying them off by working down our accounts receivable.

We had yet to pay off investors, but it was still early in the game, and, unlike our dot-com brethren, we didn't have a life-threatening burn rate (dot-com jargon for spending money); within our first eighteen months, we'd gotten to the point where we were financing our operation out of good, old-fashioned return on sales. With each investor having committed only relatively small sums to the venture, no one was grumbling for an immediate return on their investment.

The only lesson we wished we'd learned earlier was to apply for credit precisely when we didn't need it. We had a small line of credit with our bank (around $25,000) and we should have expanded it when we had the time and the balance sheet to do so. Each time we hit a liquidity crunch, we were always swamped, and the banks don't cater to businesses in time-sensitive binds—that's more the territory of the Mafia or credit cards. We chose the latter of these two.

We had the same goals. Kyle and I started out with the same goals—to have a full entrepreneurial experience, to make a real business from a product we'd created.

We'd also had a time horizon of two years.

Entrepreneurs often like to get in and get out. At the end of 2000, we couldn't sell out—we had revenues, but no story of ongoing profits to roll out to someone else; at this point, Platinum Concepts, Inc. was a work in progress. One with a lot of potential in the next 12 to 18 months, but a work in progress just the same.

If we wanted the company to continue, we were stuck running it.

I viewed this as a blessing. To me, the venture Kyle and I had started wasn't just a business, and it wasn't just a fun ride. It was an experience that exposed our strengths and weaknesses faster than any traditional jobs we might have taken. We'd learned we weren't naturals at selling. We'd found out the price of our arrogance when it compounded our ignorance as we worked our way up the learning curve of our industry. We'd also learned how resilient and resourceful we could be in the face of adversity, and where our strengths lay in anticipating business problems and piecing together solutions as they arose. We'd learned that we enjoyed taking risks even more than we expected, and we'd developed a taste for the victories, both small and large, that only running our own business could bring.

But having absorbed all those invaluable self-discoveries, where were we now?

In a nutshell, I wanted to keep on, and Kyle wanted to move on. I thought we'd worked out the kinks in distribution; we knew what we were doing, finally, and there was so much left on the horizon. New markets, new product extensions, new contacts, maybe even a new mentor. We'd done all the hard work, and there seemed to be so much still left on the table, both in terms of revenues and entrepreneurial experiences.

Kyle agreed on most fronts, but he was ready to move beyond MouseDriver to something bigger. He wanted to put

MouseDriver on autopilot, hire some part-time help to handle the day-to-day activities, and reduce his commitment to ten to fifteen hours a week.

I blurted out my case.

"Kyle, you can't go. You've got to wait until Brookstone tells us what they think about MouseDriver for next year. Wait for the *Inc.* article to come out. Who knows what'll happen when that thing hits? Rebecca's just started with us, our PR's just kicking in. We've only just begun selling MouseDriver. We've already had our mistakes smack us in the face, we know what to do now. We're not hemorrhaging money, we're making it. We're on the verge, I know it. We're going to be huge. Techpad and Burkhouse will be beating down our door. Think how we're going to absolutely kill at the PGA show, now that we know how much drinking's involved. Besides, we have to teach Kenny more conversational English, and there's all kinds of cool product ideas to pursue. We've got a shed in Cow Hollow and we golf at the Presidio. We have more fun than you'll ever have in an office. We're just a few months away from being brutally ripped by Maria Bartiromo on cable TV, and you're telling me you want to leave all this for . . . a job?"

Kyle didn't say anything for a minute. He just kept staring me in the eye.

"You really think Maria Bartiromo's going to rip us?"

I didn't flinch. "Definitely. I'm telling you, our PR's going to pay off. There's no way we won't be on Maria's show, getting totally destroyed, a few months from now. That's the plan."

"That's the plan?"

"That's the plan, Kyle."

It took a few more minutes, but I talked him into another year. I am, after all, the vice president of marketing.

EPILOGUE

That's our story so far. Though not necessarily the way I would have told it—I'm more of a to-the-point guy myself. It's a good thing I didn't write this book, otherwise you would have bought a book that read something like:

Part One
- Saw J.T.'s PayMyBills.com billboard. Ouch.
- Joined a gym. As partners.
- Finalized MouseDriver design and worked out production issues.
- Typhoon York hit Hong Kong and an earthquake hit Taiwan.
- Got Moon Cakes from Kenny.

Part Two
- Went to the PGA show.
- Established limited distribution in golf and gift stores.
- Achieved profitability.

You get the idea. Oh, and yes, I would have been a lot clearer about how frequently I walloped John in Ready to Rumble Boxing.

I'm Kyle Harrison, president and cofounder of Platinum Concepts, Inc. I worry about product design and manufacturing, operations and margins. John handles all of the relationships business—getting the product and story to the media, working on marketing and promotions with suppliers/distributors/retailers, and strengthening our evangelist network.

We balance each other perfectly, which makes for excellent strategy sessions. Between the two of us, we've got most bases covered.

One place John and I come together is our shared interest in helping other aspiring or first-time entrepreneurs. Since we began this venture, we've learned so much about bringing a new product to market, about running a business on next-to-no budget, and about keeping an even keel through it all.

We know how it is to work in an environment where every dollar you spend has to have a return. And we like nothing better than putting this information to use to help other entrepreneurs build better businesses—cutting their mistakes, timelines, and expenditures by half or more. If you've got an idea, consider this an open invitation to run it by us. Send us an e-mail at info@mousedriver.com.

You'll get advice from the perspective of what it's like to launch a real start-up, completely different from that of a company working with $30 million or even a quarter million in funding. Speaking of which, J.T.'s PayMyBills.com got bought by a similar company, PayTrust, as part of an all-equity deal at the end of 2000. Team Mouse, the Dallas company with the PGA logo rights, got bought as well. And *Inc.* magazine did run our story. John and I appeared on the cover of the February 27, 2001, issue, under a two-inch-type headline—"An American Start-Up."

Different entrepreneurs, different experiences. But that's the essence of entrepreneurship. No matter how much funding, which relationships, or what luck you have, you never know what will happen. It's an adventure.

Ever the marketing guy, John even took the four Ps of marketing concept and turned it into the four Ps of entrepreneurship: Passion, persistence, patience, and purpose (as in your company having one). Not bad.

I especially agree with the passion part. You've got to spend your life doing what makes you happy. Success is not measured in money. We went into this adventure with the idea that we would make millions, but we've come out with something worth even more—the knowledge of how to turn ideas into reality. Along the way, we've learned that we really enjoy implementing our own strategies, making our own decisions, and facing our own outcomes. In the end, it's impossible to assign a value to the experience of seeing people lined up at a cash register, ready to spend their hard-earned dollars on a product that didn't exist before it became an idea in your own head.

Looking back over the past two years, we now realize that our investment in MouseDriver was an investment in ourselves. All that time we weren't drawing paychecks, we were adding to our personal balance sheets, in the category of long-term assets.

Who knows how far MouseDriver will ultimately take us? Right now, we're looking beyond MouseDriver. Our biggest asset is no longer our inventory, but our business knowledge and skills and the relationships we've developed for every stage of the product life cycle. Our challenge is now to leverage those assets to take Platinum Concepts to the next level. That means sourcing and developing new products that people just love to buy. We've got a few in the pipeline. Stay tuned.

While you're here, I'd also like to take this opportunity to set a few things straight.

First, the only reason I failed my MouseDriver marketing presentation was that my numbers in one column of a 46-column spreadsheet didn't add up to the set minimum. That did it. Fix those, and MouseDriver was a clear pass.

Also, I carried far more boxes than John when we moved the mice into our apartment.

And by the way, I never danced to Hootie. That was definitely John.

One last thing: In retail, in the end, it's all about markets. Never forget what market you're trying to reach. Don't deviate. Don't let personal biases get in the way. Case in point—we manufactured MouseDriver to hit the largest mouse-using market. Right-handed PC users who like golf. We never worried about who that market left out. Including me, the inventor. I'm left-handed.

We hope that our story has fueled your excitement to embark on your own entrepreneurial experience. Good luck, and let us know how it goes.